The Return of Cultural Artefacts

Alper Taşdelen

The Return of Cultural Artefacts

Hard and Soft Law Approaches

Springer

Alper Taşdelen
Hannover, Germany

ISBN 978-3-319-44059-0 ISBN 978-3-319-44060-6 (eBook)
DOI 10.1007/978-3-319-44060-6

Library of Congress Control Number: 2016953674

Printed on acid-free paper

This Springer imprint is published by Springer Nature
The registered company is Springer International Publishing AG Switzerland

To my beloved parents

Preface

The legal regulation regarding the return of cultural artefacts transferred in times of peace is a relatively new phenomenon and far from being concluded. It is still an ongoing process involving various stakeholders, ranging from states to individuals, with different and often contradicting interests. Moreover, the actors involved often dispute about objects that have been transferred in a colonial context or at a time not covered by any existing and enforceable legal regime. Hence, from a legal point, the return of cultural artefacts is an area presenting many challenges. At the same time, this lack of enforceable rules with regard to a great number of disputes is the very reason why this field is strongly affected by moral claims, personal persuasion and ethics in general.

This intermingling of law and ethics as well as the cultural dimension of the subject matter is the reason why it is so fascinating to me. It allows me, as someone with a background not only in legal studies but also in cultural sciences, to combine the skill sets of both disciplines.

Luckily for me, with the Interdisciplinary DFG Research Unit on the Constitution of Cultural Property at the University of Göttingen, Germany, I found the perfect place to pursue this interest of mine and realise this PhD project, in the realisation of which many persons have played their part.

First and foremost, I wish to thank my doctoral supervisor, Prof. Dr. Peter-Tobias Stoll, for his superb supervision and for giving me the leeway to pursue my own path. I would furthermore like to take the opportunity to thank him not only for supporting this thesis and all the other projects I had over the years, such as studying abroad, but also for the 6 years I had the pleasure of working for him, ever since I started as a student assistant at the Institute for International Law and European Law of the University of Göttingen, Germany. With his fatherly, unformal and humorous yet professional nature he has always created and maintained a pleasant work climate and been an inspiring example. I have learned many things from him on both a professional and personal level.

Special thanks are also due to Prof. Dr. Regina Bendix, Spokesperson of the Interdisciplinary DFG Research Unit, and Prof. Dr. Brigitta Hauser-Schäublin,

Co-Project Director of my sub-project, for their support and the fruitful discussions we had. Their (socio- and) cultural-anthropological perspective and input has expanded my horizon, especially furthered my understanding of the role of the actors involved, and contributed to this work at hand. I want to thank Prof. Dr. Brigitta Hauser-Schäublin in particular for the opportunity to participate in the field studies conducted in Thailand and Cambodia in February 2013. It is not everyday that a lawyer has the opportunity to be in the field and experience the issue he is engaged with and its challenges firsthand. This trip was quite some experience and I will keep it in good memory, not least because of the amicable and productive atmosphere.

I also owe many thanks to all the colleagues and fellow PhD candidates of both the Interdisciplinary DFG Research Unit and the Institute for International Law and European Law. The fruitful discussions I had with them and their ability to keep me motivated were well appreciated. I wish to thank the fellow PhD candidates of the Interdisciplinary DFG Research Unit, in particular, for contributing to my comprehensive understanding of the subject matter by opening my eyes to the working methods and approaches of their respective disciplines.

Further thanks are due to the E.W. Kuhlmann Foundation, the German Research Foundation (Deutsche Forschungsgemeinschaft; DFG) and Springer for making the publication of this book possible.

Last but not least, I am most thankful to my family; my sisters Esra and Rima, and my dearest parents Gülbahar and Yüksel Taşdelen. Throughout the course of my education, be it this thesis, the LL.M. programme I have completed or the admission to the New York State Bar, they have always supported me without any reservations and with an unfailing patience. I know that it has not always been easy for them and I am deeply grateful for having them.

Washington, DC, USA Alper Taşdelen
4th July 2016

Contents

Abbreviations

EC	European Community
EFTA	European Free Trade Association
EU	European Union
GR	Genetic Resources
ICJ	International Court of Justice
ICOM	International Council of Museums
ICPRCP	Intergovernmental Committee for Promoting the Return of Cultural Property to its Countries of Origin or its Restitution in case of Illicit Appropriation
ILA	International Law Association
INTERPOL	International Criminal Police Organization
IP	Intellectual Property
LUAB	Uniform Law on the Acquisition in Good Faith of Corporeal Movables
OIM	Office International des Musées
Roerich Pact	Treaty on the Protection of the Artistic and Scientific Institutions and Historic Monuments
TCE	Traditional Cultural Expression
TK	Traditional Knowledge
UN	United Nations
UNESCO	United Nations Educational, Scientific and Cultural Organization
UNIDROIT	International Institute for the Unification of Private Law/Institut International pour L'Unification Du Droit
Washington Treaty	Treaty on the Protection of Movable Property of Historic Value
WIPO	World Intellectual Property Organization

Chapter 1
Introduction: Cultural Property vs. Cultural Heritage

Abstract Throughout history cultural objects have attracted the attention of mankind for numerous reasons: In times of war, they have been looted as trophies, to pay troops, or to further humiliate the enemy. In times of peace, they have been not only subject to clandestine excavations but also served as gifts for foreign dignitaries and were objects of trade. In recent centuries, they also became objects of scientific interest. While some of these activities have long been illegal, such as clandestine excavations, others have only become illegal with the passing of time, such as the looting of an enemy's cultural treasure. Some continue to be legal, for instance, the legal trade in cultural property, whereas others, even though they still may be considered legal in a strict sense, raise moral issues, such as the transfer of artefacts from colonies to the colonial powers in former times. The example of cultural objects transferred in colonial times has brought about many claims for the return of these cultural artefacts and these claims have given rise to disputes. This book analyses how the international community tries to resolve the issue concerning the return of cultural objects transferred in times of peace by employing different instruments. The Introduction lays the foundation for an understanding of the general problems the international community is confronted with in its endeavour by highlighting the various positions of the major actors, the ideological concepts they employ and how these are reflected even in the use of terminology.

Cultural objects have been significant to mankind throughout history, and remain so today. Cultural artefacts are unique manifestations of intellectual creativity imbued with, among other attributes, aesthetic and/or spiritual value.[1] Because of this, they have attracted the attention of men for many reasons.

Looting and even the destruction of the cultural property of one's enemy were common, and until recent centuries, accepted practices.[2] Pillaging served many purposes; taking spoils of war as trophies, paying troops, and further humiliating an enemy catered to both practical and political needs.[3] However, appropriating

[1]Cf. Stumpf (2003), p. 41.

[2]Ehlert (2014), p. 15; Thorn (2005), p. 23; Zimmerman (2015), p. 15; cf. also Isakhan (2016), p. 268.

[3]Cf. Hartung (2005), pp. 11–12.

A. Taşdelen, *The Return of Cultural Artefacts*, DOI 10.1007/978-3-319-44060-6_1

artefacts of the enemy also served to obtain his (spiritual) power, which was believed to be embodied in certain objects.[4] But, cultural objects not only changed hands in the context of war. Valued for their aesthetic beauty, such items served also as gifts for foreign dignitaries, were objects of trade,[5] and naturally, subject to clandestine excavations.[6] In more recent times, cultural heritage has furthermore become the object of scientific interest.[7] As can be seen, there have been many reasons—both legal and illegal—why cultural objects have been relocated throughout the centuries.

While some of these causes remain illegal, such as clandestine excavations, others have become illegal with the passing of time, including the looting of an enemy's cultural treasure.[8] Some practices continue to be legal, for instance, the legal trade in cultural property, whereas others, even though they still may be considered legal in a strict sense, raise moral issues.[9] This is particularly true for cultural objects transferred from the territory of colonies by their former colonial powers during their dominion. Though no binding legal obligation exists for the former colonial powers to return these objects, few today would deny that colonial occupation was wrong. However, this admission subjects the transfer of cultural property by the colonial powers from their territories to moral doubts.[10]

The transfer of cultural objects in colonial times has brought about many claims for the return of cultural property and these claims have given rise to disputes. However, such disputes not only involve cultural heritage relocated in former times. With the increasing demand for cultural artefacts on the international art market,[11] particularly in the United States of America, the United Kingdom, Japan, France, Sweden, and Switzerland,[12] clandestine excavations, theft, and illegal exports of cultural property remain a serious, if not greater problem than ever before. Today, the worldwide illicit trafficking of cultural objects is at a comparable level to the illicit trade in weapons and drugs.[13] A fact that should not be completely surprising given that all three are heavily intertwined and the illicit trafficking of

[4]Dagens (1995), pp. 20–21.

[5]Cf. http://www.festival.si.edu/past-festivals/2002/silk_road/istanbul_treasure.aspx.

[6]Cf. Veres (2013–2014), pp. 94f.

[7]Cf. Davis (2011), p. 168.

[8]Cf. Stumpf (2003), pp. 39ff.

[9]Cf. Roodt (2015), p. 69.

[10]A related area in this context is the issue of Nazi-looted cultural objects. Even though claims for restitution are barred by time limitations, there is a strong moral imperative to return the objects. Cf. on this issue for instance Woodhead (2014), pp. 113–142.

[11]Wessel (2015b), p. 16; cf. Gerstenblith (2013), p. 9; cf. also Zimmerman (2015), p. 15.

[12]Cf. Forrest (2010), pp. 136f.

[13]Nafziger and Paterson (2014), p. 13; cf. also http://www.unesco.org/new/en/brussels/areas-of-action/culture/illicit-traffic-of-cultural-properties/.

cultural objects plays a significant role in financing terrorism[14] and in organised crime.[15]

The international community has become increasingly aware of the disputes over the return of cultural objects and, for some time now, has undertaken efforts to address the problem. However, there are two opposing camps making the process of finding a solution to this issue complicated; on the one hand, there are those countries, including former colonies, which suffer from the illegal exploitation of their cultural objects. On the other hand, there are those states, generally including former colonial powers, which have amassed major collections of foreign cultural heritage with somewhat dubious provenance themselves or which host museums and private collectors with such collections.[16] These states also generally have a lucrative market in the trade of cultural property.[17] The former colonial territories, as one would expect, advocate a comprehensive duty to return cultural objects, including items transferred in the past.[18] The latter states almost universally consider such demands as excessive and not only a threat to their national collections and those of museums as well as private collectors located within their borders,[19] but also a danger to the principle of free trade in cultural property and for their art markets.[20] In addition, they are concerned by the fact that such obligations would affect their legal system,[21] since these would render their legislation concerning time limitations and the protection of bona fide purchasers inoperative or at least impair it.[22]

Furthermore, both parties employ ideological concepts to support their opposing viewpoints. The source states refer to the theory of cultural nationalism, which argues that cultural objects are primarily national heritage, since they are part of the national identity and community.[23] In addition, this point of view reasons that having the items in their place of origin allows understanding them within their social, historical, and cultural context, which is of more value than looking at them isolated in a glass box within a museum.[24] The market states, on the other hand, invoke the concept of common heritage or cultural internationalism, which argues that cultural objects are the common heritage of mankind and do not primarily belong to one single nation. Making them accessible to as large an audience as possible as well as protecting and preserving them for future generations is of

---

[14] Wessel (2015b), p. 16; cf. also Amineddoleh (2014), p. 732. See further on the linkage of illicit trafficking of cultural property and financing terrorism Tribble (2014).

[15] For the connection of illicit trafficking of cultural objects and drugs see Yates (2014), pp. 23ff.

[16] Cf. Polk (2013), pp. 111f.

[17] Cf. Slattery (2012), p. 842.

[18] Cf. Roussin (2008–2009), p. 570.

[19] Cf. Nafziger and Paterson (2014), p. 16.

[20] Cf. Forrest (2010), pp. 136f.

[21] Cf. O'Keefe (2007), p. 9.

[22] Cf. Veres (2013–2014), pp. 104ff.

[23] Cf. Roehrenbeck (2010), p. 190.

[24] Cf. Woodhead (2011), p. 54; cf. also Gerstenblith (2012), p. 625.

central importance to this view.[25] Furthermore, supporters of this theory argue that bringing them to 'foreign' museums has saved them from destruction,[26] that these museums are better suited to preserve these objects[27] and—themselves contradicting the idea of common heritage[28]—that these cultural objects have also become part of the heritage of the countries whose museums have cared for them[29] or even assumed world heritage status.[30] In addition, this view emphasises the importance of cultural exchange, since it benefits the cultural life of all mankind and promotes mutual respect and appreciation.[31] This plays into the hands of market states as they advocate the free trade of cultural objects.[32]

This dichotomy in positions is also reflected in the terminology: firstly, with regard to the subject matter itself and, secondly, when it comes to claiming back cultural objects. While different terms are actually in use to refer to the subject matter itself, such as (cultural) artefacts, (cultural) patrimony, and cultural objects, two terms are predominant in both the literature and practice: cultural property and cultural heritage. Though all terms are, in general, used interchangeably, the latter two are not as neutral as the former ones and have particular connotations. Cultural heritage emphasises the linkage and emotional bond between certain items and their source nation,[33] whereas cultural property stresses the aspect of ownership and the fact that cultural objects are material goods which can be traded as any other goods.[34] By doing so it prioritises the interests of right holders over those of society.[35,36] However, even though the United Nations Educational, Scientific and Cultural Organization (UNESCO) remains faithful to its philosophy and consistently employs the term cultural property to refer to cultural objects and in other cases both terms are basically used synonymously, today the term cultural heritage has become widely predominant—at least in the literature.[37]

In reference to the claims, a similar picture has emerged. Both in practice and literature, a variety of terms is used interchangeably: repatriation, restitution, return, recovery, and so forth. Here again, there is a small difference in connotation.

---

[25]Cf. Roehrenbeck (2010), p. 190.

[26]Cf. Wessel (2015a), p. 103; Cf. Gerstenblith (2012), p. 624.

[27]Slattery (2012), p. 836; cf. also Shyllon (2013), p. 136.

[28]Same Shyllon (2013), pp. 138f.

[29]Stamatoudi (2011), p. 23.

[30]Cf. Mugabowagahunde (2016), p. 156.

[31]An idea also found in Paragraph 2 of the Preamble of the 1970 UNESCO Convention.

[32]Cf. Forrest (2010), p. 166; cf. also Nafziger et al. (2014), p. 406. See further on the controversy how to address matters of cultural heritage in context of the World Trade Organization Schnelle (2016), pp. 101ff.

[33]Cf. Roussin (2008–2009), p. 570; cf. also Shyllon (2016), p. 55.

[34]Cf. Woodhead (2011), p. 56. On the financial significance of cultural property cf. further Graham (2014), pp. 319–338.

[35]Vadi and Schneider (2014), p. 6.

[36]For further elaboration on the distinction and interaction of property and heritage see Fincham (2010–2011), pp. 641–683.

[37]Cf. Nafziger and Paterson (2014), p. 12.

While repatriation, recovery, and return are neutral terms, with return maybe being the most neutral, restitution is linked with wrongfulness. Its use emphasises that some wrong has occurred that has to be corrected. However this having been said, it has to be highlighted that there is still no uniform use of terminology at this point in time.[38]

Nevertheless, despite this polarisation and inconsistency in the use of terminology, the international community has managed to adopt a set of rules applicable to disputes concerning the return of cultural objects and to create certain instruments to address them. The present research analyses how the international community tries to resolve the issue concerning the return of cultural objects by employing different instruments. For this purpose it examines in particular the instruments adopted, including their genesis, and how they interact. However, the research is limited to the controversial issue of cultural objects transferred in times of peace and leaves out the topic of objects transferred in times of war for which a comprehensive legal framework of general acceptance is already in place.[39]

References

Amineddoleh L (2014) Protecting cultural heritage by strictly scrutinizing museum acquisitions. Fordham Intellect Prop Media Entertain Law J 24:729–781

Chamberlain K (2013) War and cultural heritage: a commentary on the Hague Convention 1954 and its two protocols, 2nd edn. Institute of Art and Law, Leicester

Cunliffe E, Muhesen N, Lostal M (2016) The destruction of cultural property in the Syrian conflict: legal implications and obligations. Int J Cult Prop 23:1–31

Dagens B (1995) Angkor: heart of an Asian empire. Thames & Hudson, London

Davis T (2011) Supply and demand: exposing the illicit trade in Cambodian antiquities through a study of Sotheby's auction house. Crime Law Soc Change 56:155–174

[38]Cf. Stamatoudi (2011), pp. 14–19.

[39]The key legal instruments with regard to the transfer of cultural artefacts in times of war are the IV. Hague Convention respecting the Laws and Customs of War on Land of 1899 and 1907 and the 1954 Hague Convention for the Protection of Cultural Property in the Event of Armed Conflicts with its two protocols of 1954 and 1999. The IV. Hague Convention of 1899 and 1907 was the first multilateral treaty on a global level that contained with Article 3 of its Annex a legal basis to reclaim cultural objects transferred in wartimes in violation of the convention. Its regulations have already become international customary law. The 1954 Hague Convention, on the other hand, was the first international treaty that was solely devoted to the protection of cultural property in times of war. However, regulations relevant for the protection of cultural objects during war and for their return afterwards can also be found in other international conventions. Article 33 (2) of the IV. Geneva Convention relative to the Protection of Civilian Persons in Time of War, for instance, constitutes a prohibition to pillage.

For a general overview on the law concerning the return of cultural artefacts transferred in times of war cf. Hartung (2005). For further information on the 1954 Hague Convention see O'Keefe (2011) and Chamberlain (2013).

For a contemporary example of the ongoing destruction of cultural heritage in times of war see Cunliffe et al. (2016), pp. 1ff.

Ehlert C (2014) Prosecuting the destruction of cultural property in international criminal law: with a case study on the Khmer Rouge's destruction of Cambodian heritage. Martinus Nijhoff Publishers, Leiden
Fincham D (2010-2011) The distinctiveness of property and heritage. Penn State Law Rev 115:641-683
Forrest C (2010) International law and the protection of cultural heritage. Routledge, London
Gerstenblith P (2012) Art, cultural heritage, and the law: cases and materials, 3rd edn. Carolina Academic Press, Durham
Gerstenblith P (2013) Models of implementation of the 1970 UNESCO Convention: can their effectiveness be determined? In: Prott LV, Redmond-Cooper R, Urice S (eds) Realising cultural heritage law: festschrift for Patrick Joseph O'Keefe. Institute of Art and Law, Builth Wells, pp 9–25
Graham J-L (2014) Art exchange? How the international art market lacks a clear regulatory framework. In: Vadi V, Schneider HEGS (eds) Art, cultural heritage and the market: ethical and legal issues. Springer, Heidelberg, pp 319–338
Hartung H (2005) Kunstraub in Krieg und Verfolgung: Die Restitution von Beute- und Raubkunst im Kollisions- und Völkerrecht. De Gruyter, Berlin
Isakhan B (2016) Heritage under fire: lessons from Iraq for cultural property protection. In: Logan W, Craith MN, Kockel U (eds) A companion to heritage studies. Wiley Blackwell, Chichester, pp 268–279
Mugabowagahunde M (2016) African indigenous heritage in colonial and postcolonial museums: the case of the Batwa of Africa's Great Lakes Region. In: Logan W, Craith MN, Kockel U (eds) A companion to heritage studies. Wiley Blackwell, Chichester, pp 146–159
Nafziger JAR, Paterson RK (2014) Introduction. In: Nafziger JAR, Paterson RK (eds) Handbook on the law of cultural heritage and international trade. Edward Elgar, Cheltenham, pp 1–18
Nafziger JAR, Paterson RK, Renteln AD (2014) Cultural law: international, comparative, and indigenous. Cambridge University Press, Cambridge
O'Keefe PJ (2007) Commentary on the 1970 UNESCO Convention, 2nd edn. Institute of Art and Law, Leicester
O'Keefe R (2011) The protection of cultural property in armed conflict. Cambridge University Press, Cambridge
Polk K (2013) The trade in antiquities: is it time for additional approaches to reducing destruction and theft? In: Prott LV, Redmond-Cooper R, Urice S (eds) Realising cultural heritage law: festschrift for Patrick Joseph O'Keefe. Institute of Art and Law, Builth Wells, pp 111–120
Roehrenbeck CA (2010) Repatriation of cultural property – who owns the past? An introduction to approaches and to selected statutory instruments. Int J Leg Inf 38:185–200
Roodt C (2015) Private international law, art and cultural heritage. Edward Elgar, Cheltenham
Roussin LA (2008-2009) The trade in antiquities: heritage for sale? ILSA J Int Comp Law 15:569-572
Schnelle MA (2016) Der Abwanderungsschutz von Kulturgütern im Lichte der Freihandelsordnungen von AEUV und GATT. Nomos, Baden-Baden
Shyllon F (2013) Museums and universal heritage: right of return and right of access for Africans. In: Prott LV, Redmond-Cooper R, Urice S (eds) Realising cultural heritage law: festschrift for Patrick Joseph O'Keefe. Institute of Art and Law, Builth Wells, pp 133–144
Shyllon F (2016) Cultural heritage and intellectual property: convergence, divergence, and interface. In: Logan W, Craith MN, Kockel U (eds) A companion to heritage studies. Wiley Blackwell, Chichester, pp 55–68
Slattery AJ (2012) To catch an art thief: using international and domestic laws to paint fraudulent art dealers into a corner. Villanova Sports Entertain Law J 19:827–871
Stamatoudi IA (2011) Cultural property law and restitution: a commentary to international conventions and European Union law. Edward Elgar, Cheltenham
Stumpf E (2003) Kulturgüterschutz im internationalen Recht unter besonderer Berücksichtigung der deutsch-russischen Beziehungen. Peter Lang, Frankfurt am Main

Thorn B (2005) Internationaler Kulturgüterschutz nach der UNIDROIT Konvention. De Gruyter, Berlin

Tribble J (2014) Antiquities trafficking and terrorism: where cultural wealth, political violence, and criminal networks intersect. In: Monterey terrorism research and education program. www.miis.edu/media/view/37908/original/illicit_antiquities_networks_final_1.pdf. Accessed 25 April 2016

Vadi V, Schneider HEGS (2014) Art, cultural heritage and the market: legal and ethical issues. In: Vadi V, Schneider HEGS (eds) Art, cultural heritage and the market: ethical and legal issues. Springer, Heidelberg, pp 1–25

Veres Z (2013-2014) The fight against illicit trafficking of cultural property: the 1970 UNESCO Convention and the 1995 UNIDROIT Convention. Santa Clara J Int Law 12:91-114

Wessel G (2015a) Das schmutzige Geschäft mit der Antike: Der globale Handel mit illegalen Kulturgütern. Ch. Links Verlag, Berlin

Wessel G (2015b) Nachschub für einen gigantischen Markt: Raubgrabungen zerstören das kulturelle Erbe der Menschheit. Politik und Kultur 16

Woodhead C (2011) Cultural heritage principles and interference with property rights. Cambrian Law Rev 42:52–68

Woodhead C (2014) Redressing historic wrongs, returning objects to their rightful owners or laundering tainted objects? 21st-century UK remedies for Nazi-era injustices. Int J Cult Prop 21:113–142

Yates D (2014) Displacement, deforestation, and drugs: antiquities trafficking and the narcotics support economies of Guatemala. In: Kila JD, Balcells M (eds) Cultural property crime: an overview and analysis of contemporary perspectives and trends. Brill, Leiden, pp 23–36

Zimmerman O (2015) Die Zerstörung, der Raub und der illegal Handel mit Kulturgut: Besitz von Raubkunst muss gesellschaftlich und rechtlich geächtet werden. Politik und Kultur 15

Chapter 2
The Classical Approach: International Treaties—Part I

Abstract International treaties are not only a source of international law; they are also a classical means to regulate matters of concern to the international community. Hence, it is not surprising that the international community's first approach to resolve the issue concerning the return of cultural objects was to rely on an international treaty. This approach was further encouraged by the fact that issues surrounding cultural artefacts were generally perceived as national or state affairs. This chapter focuses on the 1970 UNESCO Convention on the Means of Prohibiting and Preventing the Illicit Import, Export and Transfer of Ownership of Cultural Property, the first international agreement for times of peace on an international scale exclusively devoted to the regulation of the return of cultural objects. After an overview of the first endeavours of the international community to enact such an agreement and the historical developments leading to the adoption of the treaty along with the challenges that had to be overcome in the course of the negotiation, the convention is analysed in depth. Its purpose, scope and regulations are broken down in the light of the convention's genesis and the different actors' positions with an emphasis on the rules concerning the return of cultural objects. Finally, the relevance as well as the strengths and weaknesses of the treaty are more closely scrutinised.

2.1 First Steps

Faced with the issue of cultural objects transferred from their countries of origin and respective disputes, the international community first tried to solve the matter in a classical manner by adopting international treaties. In fact, the first international treaty which provided a legal basis that could be employed to reclaim cultural property dates back to the beginning of the twentieth century, namely the 1907 Hague Convention IV with respect to the Laws and Customs of War on Land, a revised version of the 1899 Hague Convention II. Article 3[1] of this treaty allows states to claim back cultural objects removed from their territories. However, the

[1]Article 3 of the 1907 Hague Convention IV with respect to the Laws and Customs of War on Land: "A belligerent party which violates the provisions of the said Regulations shall, if the case

A. Taşdelen, *The Return of Cultural Artefacts*, DOI 10.1007/978-3-319-44060-6_2

treaty regulates warfare and hence its provisions are only applicable to cultural objects that have been transferred in the course of war.[2]

It was not until 1970, almost three quarters of a century later, with the adoption of the UNESCO Convention on the Means of Prohibiting and Preventing the Illicit Import, Export and Transfer of Ownership of Cultural Property that an international treaty providing a legal basis for reclaiming cultural property illicitly trafficked in periods of peace came into effect. This seemingly late adoption, however, cannot be blamed on a lack of efforts to regulate the matter. Not only had several states enacted laws protecting their cultural patrimony in the late nineteenth century,[3] but the matter was also approached, due to the international character of the illicit trafficking of cultural property,[4] on an international level. In 1932 the General Assembly of the League of Nations decided to address the issue and delegated the Office International des Musées (OIM) to prepare a draft convention on the return of either lost or stolen cultural artefacts.[5]

In 1933 the OIM presented its first draft,[6] which could not be adopted due to the reluctance of, in particular, the Netherlands, the United Kingdom, and the United States of America.[7] The United States of America, for instance, criticised the draft as it would require domestic courts to enforce the laws of foreign countries.[8] In order to make the draft more acceptable for these states and increase its likelihood of being adopted, in 1936[9] and 1939[10] the OIM prepared two further drafts,[11] each with a narrower scope. The three drafts not only varied with regard to the cultural property covered, but also differed in the state parties' obligations regarding the return of such cultural artefacts.

While the first draft encompassed all tangible objects of artistic, historical, and scientific character, the second draft restricted the scope to tangible objects of a specific paleontological, archaeological, historical or artistic nature. The third draft narrowed the scope still further to only those tangible objects of specific paleontological, archaeological, historical or artistic nature that are the property of or in the possession of either the state or a public entity and, in addition, are inventoried as part of a national collection.[12]

demands, be liable to pay compensation. It shall be responsible for all acts committed by persons forming part of its armed forces.".

[2]Cf. Baufeld (2005), p. 87.

[3]Stamatoudi (2011), p. 31; Siehr (2011), p. 94.

[4]Vogel (2010), p. 1149.

[5]Raschèr (2000), p. 50.

[6]OIM (1939a), pp. 51f.

[7]O'Keefe (2007), p. 3.

[8]Vrdoljak (2008), pp. 112f.

[9]OIM (1939b), pp. 69ff.

[10]OIM (1939c), pp. 78ff.

[11]Cf. Vrdoljak (2008), p. 115.

[12]Cf. Weidner (2001), p. 230; Odendahl (2005), pp. 173f.

The drafts show a similar increasingly restrictive tendency in regard to the obligations of state parties concerning return. According to the first draft, any transfer of property from the originating state was void if the stated objects had reached the territory of the receiving party by breaching national export regulations of the state of origin. This regulation was abandoned in the second draft.[13] The third draft narrowed the state parties' obligations further by acknowledging claims for return only for cases in which the objects had been transferred to the territory of the receiving party by breaching regulations of the state of origin which are enforced by penalty.[14]

In addition, the third draft re-regulated the role of the bona fide purchaser. While according to the first draft the bona fide purchaser had a claim for compensation only in case the state of origin had not informed the OIM of the loss and the OIM had not made it public,[15] the third draft permitted the respondent state to make the return conditional on compensation for the bona fide purchaser.[16] Unfortunately, with the outbreak of World War II the negotiations came to an abrupt end and none of the drafts were ever adopted.[17]

The 1930s are, however, not only of great relevance for the emergence of a global regime of return for periods of peace due to the drafts of the OIM, but also because of the Treaty on the Protection of Movable Property of Historic Value (Washington Treaty)[18] that was adopted on 15 April 1935 and entered into force on 17 July 1936.[19]

Even though the Washington Treaty is only a regional treaty of the Pan-American Union,[20] its significance lies in the fact that it is the first multilateral treaty explicitly devoted to cultural property removed during peacetime.[21,22] Unlike the Pan-American Union's Treaty on the Protection of the Artistic and Scientific Institutions and Historic Monuments (Roerich Pact)[23] of the same day, which due to is limitation on immovable cultural property could only regulate the protection of cultural heritage,[24] the

---

[13] Cf. Odendahl (2005), p. 174.

[14] Cf. Schaffrath (2007), p. 11.

[15] Cf. Weidner (2001), p. 229.

[16] Cf. Odendahl (2005), p. 174.

[17] Cf. UNESCO Doc CUA/115, 14.04.1962, p. 3.

[18] Printed in Hudson (1941), pp. 51ff.

[19] von Schorlemer (1992), p. 270.

[20] The Pan-American Union is the predecessor form of the Organization of American States, a regional organisation that can be traced back to 1889. For further details on the Organization of American States and its history see http://www.oas.org/en/about/our_history.asp.

[21] Cf. Pabst (2008), p. 60; Hönes (2006), p. 166.

[22] Nonetheless, Article 8 of the Treaty also contains a war-related regulation prohibiting the treatment of cultural property as spoils of war.

[23] Printed in Hudson (1941), pp. 56ff.

[24] Cf. von Schorlemer (1992), p. 270.

Washington Treaty includes a rule concerning the return of illicitly exported objects.[25]

However, besides being a regional agreement with only a limited number of state parties, which in addition shared similar interests, the signatories only agreed to a legally binding obligation to return illicitly exported cultural objects back to the state of origin because the scope of the Washington Treaty is restricted in several ways.

First, the treaty seems to have an extremely broad nature as it regards the problem of the fragmentation of immovable cultural property in its definition of covered objects.[26] It in fact includes natural movable wealth, zoological specimens of beautiful and rare species threatened with extermination or natural extinction and whose preservation may be necessary to the study of fauna.[27] Moreover, it does not even narrow its scope in principle on cultural objects of particular value.[28] However, this does not supersede the enumerative nature of the cultural objects to which the regulations of the treaty are applicable. Furthermore, an obligation to return a certain cultural object only exists in those cases in which the particular object has been transferred without the required export licence.[29] This licence, however, can only be granted if other identical or similar objects are located within the territory of the respective member state of origin.[30] Last but not least, by excluding the question of compensation for the bona fide purchaser[31] the state parties avoided another highly contentious point. This ultimately enabled them to adopt the Washington Treaty.

However, though the scope of the treaty is limited and the treaty did not have significant relevance in practice,[32] the value of the Washington Treaty as the first multilateral treaty, albeit regional in nature, explicitly containing a norm on return for times of peace, was its role as a precursor for future international agreements.

It was, however, not until after World War II negotiations for an international convention concerning the return of cultural objects illicitly transferred in times of peace could be recommenced on a global level. This eventually led to the adoption of the 1970 UNESCO Convention on the Means of Prohibiting and Preventing the Illicit Import, Export and Transfer of Ownership of Cultural Property and the 1995 Convention on Stolen or Illegally Exported Cultural Objects of the International Institute for the Unification of Private Law (Institut International pour L'Unification Du Droit: UNIDROIT).

---

[25]Cf. Odendahl (2005), p. 174.

[26]Cf. Article 1 lit. a) of the Washington Treaty.

[27]Article 1 lit. d) 2) of the Washington Treaty.

[28]Article 1 of the Washington Treaty only requires books (lit. b) and species (lit. d) 2)) to be rare and collections of manuscripts to have a high historic significance in order to be subject to the treaty. For all other listed objects there is no further requirement of particular value.

[29]Articles 2, 5 of the Washington Treaty.

[30]Article 3 of the Washington Treaty.

[31]Cf. Odendahl (2005), p. 175.

[32]Cf. Weidner (2001), p. 232.

2.2 The 1970 UNESCO Convention on the Means of Prohibiting and Preventing the Illicit Import, Export and Transfer of Ownership of Cultural Property

2.2.1 *Overview*

The 1970 UNESCO Convention on the Means of Prohibiting and Preventing the Illicit Import, Export and Transfer of Ownership of Cultural Property can rightfully be considered as the most important multilateral treaty regarding the return of cultural property. It is the first convention for times of peace on an international scale with, even though not self-executing,[33] rules establishing a set of fundamental principles concerning the return of cultural objects, comprising a definition for cultural property,[34] and promoting international cooperation in this field. Moreover, it allows state parties to exceed the minimum level set by the convention by adopting higher standards. The agreement is the result of long-lasting negotiations dating back to the League of Nations. These negotiations which have somewhat watered down the treaty obligations allowed a consensus which is now supported by a cross-interest based coalition comprising both major art market states as well as states prone to illicit trafficking of their cultural property. And last but not least, being negotiated and adopted in the context of UNESCO, the agency of the United Nations (UN) specialised on cultural matters, bestows an additional legitimacy on the convention. These facts constitute the pillars upon which the convention's significance is built.

2.2.2 *The Historical Developments Leading to the Adoption of the 1970 UNESCO Convention*

The negotiations on an international scale regarding a convention regulating the return of cultural property relocated in times of peace could only be resumed and intensified after World War II.[35] However, with the establishment in 1945 of the United Nations Educational, Scientific and Cultural Organization, a specialised agency of the United Nations, a new platform for these kinds of negotiations became available.[36] Nevertheless, almost ten years elapsed until a first document relevant for matters of the return of cultural objects was adopted within the scope of UNESCO.

[33]Weidner (2001), pp. 234f; Boos (2006), p. 48; Hönes (2010), p. 86.

[34]Odendahl (2005), p. 134.

[35]Cf. Ochoa Jiménez (2011), p. 40.

[36]Hüfner (2005), p. 32.

It was at its 9th session on 5 December 1956 that the General Conference of UNESCO adopted the Recommendation on International Principles Applicable to Archaeological Excavations.[37] This aims to induce member states to consider the adoption of regulations to govern the trade in antiquities so as to ensure that this trade does not encourage smuggling of archaeological material or affect adversely the protection of sites and the collecting of material for public exhibit.[38] In this regard, it advises member states to take all necessary measures to, inter alia, prevent the export of objects obtained by clandestine excavations and damage to monuments.[39] Furthermore, it recommends to member states to ensure that museums offered archaeological objects not only ascertain their provenance, but also bring any suspicious offer to the attention of the services concerned.[40] Regarding the return of such objects, the recommendation calls upon both the member states as well as excavation services and museums to take the necessary measures and cooperate in order to ensure and facilitate the recovery of these objects.[41]

Even though the recommendation is due to its nature not legally binding,[42] it cannot be dismissed as a solely symbolic act. The UNESCO Constitution imposes a duty on member states to bring recommendations to the attention of their competent authorities within a period of one year from their adoption.[43] Hence, member states arguably have an obligation to take them into consideration in their law-making process.[44]

Although the 1956 Recommendation proved to be quite successful in terms of setting standards for national legislation,[45] it was insufficient to significantly inhibit the illicit trade of cultural objects. For this reason at the 11th General Conference of UNESCO in 1960, Mexico and Peru, two member states heavily affected by the illicit trade in their cultural objects, put the matter on the agenda and urged for an effective international tool to prevent the illicit trade of cultural objects in times of peace.[46] The 12th General Conference of UNESCO in 1962 then agreed upon an international convention being the most effective instrument to achieve the desired goal. However, a preliminary survey conducted together with the International Council of Museums (ICOM) and UNIDROIT on the measures necessary in

---

[37] Printed in Yusuf (2007), pp. 345ff.

[38] Article 27 of the Recommendation on International Principles Applicable to Archaeological Excavations.

[39] Cf. Article 29 of the Recommendation on International Principles Applicable to Archaeological Excavations.

[40] Cf. Article 30 (1) and (2) of the Recommendation on International Principles Applicable to Archaeological Excavations.

[41] Cf. Article 31 (1) and (2) of the Recommendation on International Principles Applicable to Archaeological Excavations.

[42] See Ochoa Jiménez (2011), p. 41.

[43] Article IV (4) (3) of the UNESCO Constitution.

[44] Cf. Schaffrath (2007), p. 12.

[45] O'Keefe (2007), p. 5.

[46] Cf. Thorn (2005), p. 58; Streinz (1998), p. 82.

order to work out a respective draft,[47] led the 12th General Conference of UNESCO to regard the preparation of such a convention as impossible before the 13th General Conference. Therefore, it concluded with the decision to prepare a recommendation first.[48]

Based on this development, on 19 November 1964 at the 13th General Conference of UNESCO, the Recommendation on the Means of Prohibiting and Preventing the Illicit Export, Import and Transfer of Ownership of Cultural Property was adopted.[49] This was developed by experts drawn from 30 member states.[50] It took, however, another four years until the General Conference of UNESCO mandated a committee of experts to draft the actual convention, whereupon the Director General appointed a principal and four consulting experts from different regions for the committee.[51]

The compiled Preliminary Draft Convention on the Means of Prohibiting and Preventing the Illicit Import, Export and Transfer of Ownership of Cultural Property[52] was circulated by the secretariat on 12 August 1969 for the member states to comment on.[53] Within the determined deadline, which was extended from 27 February 1970 to 15 March 1970,[54] a number of member states, in particular the major art market states, raised a number of strong objections.

Germany, for example, deemed the obligations imposed by the draft regarding import and export controls as well as the control of internal transfers, in particular the export licence, as too burdensome and not realisable from an administrative point of view. Furthermore, it criticised the draft as far too intrusive into the national legal order of proprietorship and thus sovereignty.[55]

The United States of America, which had not participated in the whole process for a long time and only entered into the negotiations at a very late stage,[56] also considered the obligations imposed by the draft as both too burdensome[57] and expensive. In addition, they concurred with Germany's concerns regarding the draft's effects on the national legal order of proprietorship.[58] Moreover, both member states were very reluctant to include the idea of designation. They objected

---

[47]Cf. Raschèr (2000), p. 51.

[48]UNESCO GC 12 C/Resolution 4.413, 28.06.1963; cf. also O'Keefe (2007), p. 5.

[49]Printed in Yusuf (2007), pp. 377ff.

[50]Schaffrath (2007), pp. 12f.

[51]O'Keefe (2007), p. 7.

[52]UNESCO Doc SHC/MD/3 Annex, 08.08.1969.

[53]UNESCO Doc SHC/MD/5, 27.02.1970, p. 2.

[54]Schaffrath (2007), p. 13.

[55]UNESCO Doc SHC/MD/5 Add. 1, 10.04.1970, pp. 3ff; an argument still encountered in context of the eventual 1970 UNESCO Convention: cf. Boos (2006), pp. 50f; Weidner (2001), p. 238.

[56]O'Keefe (2007), p. 7.

[57]Steinbrück (2012), p. 58; von Schorlemer (1992), p. 429.

[58]UNESCO Doc SHC/MD/5 Annex I, 27.02.1970, p. 21.

that by being forced to accept foreign states' registers, they were subject to foreign states' laws without having influence in the process of legislation.[59]

Since a convention not ratified by the major market states was considered to be ineffective,[60] the draft circulated by the secretariat was revised[61] by a special commission of governmental experts in the light of the objections raised. This, however, led to an ambiguity of the draft's substance.[62]

This final draft was adopted as the Convention on the Means of Prohibiting and Preventing the Illicit Import, Export and Transfer of Ownership of Cultural Property by the 16th General Conference of UNESCO on 14 November 1970[63] and entered into force on 24 April 1972 in accordance with its Article 21.[64] Hitherto, 131 states, including the major art market states, have become parties to the convention.[65]

2.2.3 The Purpose of the 1970 UNESCO Convention

According to Article 31 (2) of the Vienna Convention on the Law of the Treaties, a preamble is part of the text of a treaty and therefore part of its context for the purpose of its interpretation. Thus it is, in general, one of the central sections of an international convention to trace its objectives and serve as a guideline setting general interpretational principles.[66] The Preamble of the 1970 UNESCO Convention contains both national and international goals.[67]

According to Paragraph 4 and 8 of the Preamble, the 1970 UNESCO Convention was adopted considering that cultural property constitutes one of the basic elements of civilisation and national culture and that its true value can be appreciated only in relation to the fullest possible information regarding its origin, history, and traditional setting and furthermore that the illicit import, export, and transfer of ownership of cultural property is an obstacle to the understanding between nations. To this end, the convention postulates a set of fundamental principles regarding the

---

59 Thorn (2005), p. 59.

60 Vrdoljak (2008), p. 242.

61 Cf. for the Revised Draft Convention on the Means of Prohibiting and Preventing the Illicit Import, Export and Transfer of Ownership of Cultural Property UNESCO Doc SHC/MD/5 Annex III, 27.02.1970.

62 Cf. Ochoa Jiménez (2011), p. 43; cf. also Rietschel (2009), p. 22.

63 Raschèr (2000), p. 51.

64 http://portal.unesco.org/en/ev.php-URL_ID=13039&URL_DO=DO_TOPIC&URL_SECTION=201.html.

65 http://www.unesco.org/eri/la/convention.asp?KO=13039&language=E.

66 Similar O'Keefe (2007), p. 32. However, Bator (1982), p. 377 seems to have another opinion on the legal value in particular of this Preamble.

67 Gordon (1971), p. 541.

protection and return of cultural property as well as promoting international cooperation in this field.[68]

However, the treaty does not condemn all forms of transfer of cultural property. In fact, according to Paragraph 3 of the Preamble, state parties acknowledge that the interchange of cultural property among nations for scientific, cultural, and educational purposes increases the knowledge of the civilisation of man, enriches the cultural life of all peoples, and inspires mutual respect and appreciation among nations. Thus, the convention only aims at preventing and annulling illicit transfers of cultural property, including illicit loans.[69] This can be attributed to the agreement being a compromise between the interests of the source and major art market states,[70] with the latter advocating a free trade of cultural property.[71]

This understanding of the aims of the treaty is, however, also reflected in the articles of the convention. In Article 2 (1) of the 1970 UNESCO Convention the state parties reconfirm the consideration made in Paragraph 9 of the Preamble by recognising that the illicit import, export, and transfer of ownership of cultural property is one of the main causes of the impoverishment of the cultural heritage of the countries of origin of such property and that international cooperation constitutes one of the most efficient means of protecting each country's cultural property against all the dangers resulting therefrom. Furthermore, in accordance with Article 2 (2), to this end, the states parties undertake to oppose such practices with the means at their disposal, and particularly by removing their causes, putting a stop to current practices, and by helping to make the necessary reparations.

Article 3 of the Convention, finally, provides clarity for the term illicit defining it as any import, export or transfer of ownership of cultural property effected contrary to the provisions adopted under the treaty by the states parties thereto. While Article 2 of the Convention is predominantly accepted as imposing at least some sort of obligation to adopt a policy minimising the illicit import, export or transfer of ownership of cultural property,[72] the legal content of Article 3 of the Convention remains highly controversial.[73] While Bator dismisses the provision simply as a "mysterious provision that will not be operative in the United States,"[74] O'Keefe[75] represents the contrary perspective by interpreting Article 3 as requiring state parties to render in their national law transactions as illicit which breach the

[68]Cf. Schaffrath (2007), p. 16; cf. also Stamatoudi (2011), p. 33.

[69]Boos (2006), p. 55.

[70]For an elaborated distinction between source and market states and their interests involved when it comes to cultural property see Slattery (2012), pp. 835ff; see also Herzog (2001), p. 145; cf. also Nafziger et al. (2014), p. 290.

[71]Cf. Forrest (2010), p. 166; Steinbrück (2012), p. 79; cf. also Abramson and Huttler (1973), p. 949.

[72]Bator (1982), p. 377 and Hönes (2010), p. 89 seem to have another view. However, see O'Keefe (2007), pp. 39f with further references.

[73]Cf. Steinbrück (2012), pp. 67f.

[74]Bator (1982), p. 377.

[75]Stamatoudi (2011), pp. 34f seems to share this understanding.

national law of another state party whose law is in accordance with the treaty.[76] There are two further views on the legal relevance of Article 3 of the Convention which fall between these two extremes. According to Sandrock, this provision requires state parties to hold void any contract between a party in the country of origin and a party in another state party, but only if the object is still in the country of origin and its export would imply a breach of an export regulation.[77] Fraoua,[78] on the other hand, has taken another approach. He links the issue of illicitness to particular provisions of the convention, in particular Articles 6 (b), 7 (b), and 13 (a). Thus, state parties have to consider as illicit those transfers that were made unlawful by national laws adopted in compliance with these provisions, since those acts become unlawful under international law.[79]

The controversy on the legal relevance of Article 3 of the Convention can only be resolved by having a close look at the wording of the rule and consulting the regular means of interpretation. The wording of the provision does not furnish any indication that restricts the application of the term illicit to cases in which the object has not been transferred from the country of origin.[80] Considering Article 31 (1) of the Vienna Convention on the Law of the Treaties, which demands that a treaty shall be interpreted in good faith in accordance with the ordinary meaning to be given to the terms of the treaty in their context and in the light of its object and purpose, restricting the scope of Article 3 of the 1970 UNESCO Convention in such a manner would clearly interfere with the treaty's objective mentioned above, to prevent and annul unlawful transfers. Thus, such an interpretation of Article 3 of the 1970 UNESCO Convention cannot be considered to have been done in good faith and is therefore not to be favoured in light of Article 31 (1) of the Vienna Convention on the Law of the Treaties.

As the wording of Article 3 of the 1970 UNESCO Convention does not make reference to any particular provisions, for the same reason just provided, an interpretation of the article restricting it to particular norms of the treaty by recognising that only transfers made unlawful by national laws adopted in compliance with these provisions become unlawful under international law and hence have to be considered by state parties, is not acceptable.

Therefore, O'Keefe's view on the legal content of Article 3 of the 1970 UNESCO Convention seems to be preferable. However, he also restricts the

[76] O'Keefe (2007), p. 41.

[77] Standrock (1985), pp. 460, 464 and 478.

[78] Raschèr (2000), p. 50 seems to share this view. However, he uses the term "particularly" regarding the provisions specified by Fraoua, which could be interpreted as him agreeing in general with the idea of tying "illicit" to particular provisions of the convention, but not with regard to the list of norms specified by Fraoua.

[79] O'Keefe (2007), p. 41; Stamatoudi (2011), p. 35.

[80] Stamatoudi (2011), pp. 34f also rejects this view, but with a different reasoning. She particularly argues that in "both circumstances, whether the object is outside its country of origin or is due to leave its country of origin, an illicit export will either have taken place or will be about to take place. The underlying reasons for considering such an act as illicit are in both cases the same".

provision unnecessarily to national laws. It is correct that by referring to provisions adopted under this convention, Article 3 references norms outside of the treaty. These, however, need not be solely national laws. Provisions of international treaties or supranational regulations adopted by the state parties for the purpose of specification or implementation of the 1970 UNESCO Convention also meet this requirement.

Thus, Article 3 of the Convention has to be interpreted as requiring state parties to classify as illicit in their national law transfers which breach the national law of another state party or an international / supranational norm which is in accordance with the convention.

Furthermore, inspired by the 1943 London Inter-Allied Declaration against Acts of Dispossession committed in Territories under Enemy Occupation and Control,[81] Article 11 of the 1970 UNESCO Convention extends illicitness to cases of export and transfer of ownership of cultural property under compulsion arising directly or indirectly from the occupation of a country by a foreign power. While compulsion arising directly from occupation apparently covers cases in which the occupying power demands the transfer of cultural property or its ownership, it is not so obvious what is meant by cases of compulsion arising indirectly from occupation. However, this alternative would require member states to also annul the effects of exports and transfers of ownership of cultural property in cases in which the occupation triggers an attributable series of events which forces an owner to part with his cultural property.[82,83]

This provision does not impose further obligations on those state parties to the 1970 UNESCO Convention which are also party to the 1954 Hague Convention for the Protection of Cultural Property in the Event of Armed Conflict and its two Protocols of 1954 and 1999, because the latter contain a much more detailed regime for the protection of cultural property in armed conflicts. However,[84] it establishes a basic regime for the protection of cultural property in armed conflicts for the other state parties to the 1970 UNESCO Convention.[85]

That having been said, the convention does extend its protection to occupied territories and also to dependent territories. According to Article 12, the state parties shall respect the cultural heritage within the territories for the international relations of which they are responsible and shall take all appropriate measures to prohibit and prevent the illicit import, export, and transfer of ownership of cultural property in such territories. It is important at this point to realise in this context that

[81]Vrdoljak (2008), p. 208.

[82]Similar O'Keefe (2007), p. 78. He brings up the sale price. While an under value sale price can be seen as a strong indicator for forced selling, the contrary cannot be automatically assumed for a sale at value. A person who has to flee the occupied territory might not be able to take his belongings, but might be lucky enough to find someone who pays him the appropriate value. However, this does not mean that the seller parted willingly.

[83]For the various views on the explicit legal meaning of the provision see O'Keefe (2007), p. 78. Cf. also O'Keefe (2013), pp. 454f on the issue.

[84]On the matter of occupation see, for instance, Article 5 of the 1954 Hague Convention.

[85]O'Keefe (2007), p. 78.

illicit is only what is contrary to the provisions adopted under the convention by the state parties. Since the colonial powers had effective influence on the dependent territories and were able to prevent corresponding legislation, this provision, in practice, was not qualified to regulate the transfer of cultural property between colonies and colonial powers, i.e. to protect the cultural heritage of the colonies from the motherland.[86]

2.2.4 *The 1970 UNESCO Convention's Scope of Application*

2.2.4.1 Definition of "Cultural Property" (and "Cultural Heritage")

The 1970 UNESCO Convention is a treaty adopted to prohibit and prevent the illicit import, export, and transfer of cultural property. As a consequence, the definition of cultural property is essential for the scope of the treaty. Accordingly, the definition of cultural property is contained in the very first article of the convention.

Following this, for the purposes of the convention, the term cultural property means property which, on religious or secular grounds, is specifically designated by each state as being of importance for archaeology, prehistory, history, literature, art or science and which belongs to one of the categories[87] listed in Article 1 of the Convention.[88]

[86]Consequently, the provision does not address several important issues. It does not deal with the transfer of cultural property to the "motherland", nor does it deal with the question of what has to be done with such objects once the dependent territories become independent or incorporated into the motherland. See for these and further issues O'Keefe (2007), pp. 80f.

[87]For more detailed information on the particular categories see Ochoa Jiménez (2011), pp. 86–90; Hönes (2006), pp. 167f.

[88]Article 1 of the Convention: "the following categories:

(a) Rare collections and specimens of fauna, flora, minerals and anatomy, and objects of palaeontological interest;
(b) property relating to history, including the history of science and technology and military and social history, to the life of national leaders, thinkers, scientists and artist and to events of national importance;
(c) products of archaeological excavations (including regular and clandestine) or of archaeological discoveries;
(d) elements of artistic or historical monuments or archaeological sites which have been dismembered;
(e) antiquities more than one hundred years old, such as inscriptions, coins and engraved seals;
(f) objects of ethnological interest;
(g) property of artistic interest, such as:

 (i) pictures, paintings and drawings produced entirely by hand on any support and in any material (excluding industrial designs and manufactured articles decorated by hand);
 (ii) original works of statuary art and sculpture in any material;
 (iii) original engravings, prints and lithographs ;
 (iv) original artistic assemblages and montages in any material;

Thus, in order to fall within the scope of the treaty, an object must fulfil the two complementary requirements of falling under the abstract definition and also under one of the categories of Article 1 of the Convention.[89] This approach can be attributed to a compromise.[90] Former colonial powers and major art market states were especially reluctant to accept a purely general definition, because they feared that such a definition would broaden the scope of the treaty. Therefore, they favoured an enumerative definition. Whereas the countries of origin, on the other hand, advocated the inclusion of a general definition. In the end, both were incorporated.[91] However, what seems to be a compromise at first glance proves to be a triumph for the importing countries, since the definition now is even more restrictive than the pure enumerative one,[92] as the object now has to satisfy the general definition in addition to falling under one of the enumerated categories.[93] Another sign of the victory of the former colonial powers and major art market states is the exhaustive character of the list provided for in Article 1 of the Convention. The catalogue is not of exemplary nature[94] which is why some argue that certain (important) objects are excluded.[95]

There are still two further matters with regard to the general definition that warrant consideration. The first is the religious and secular grounds on which the property has to be specifically designated. This phrasing has to be seen as a clarification to avoid later controversies of whether property can only be designated on religious or secular grounds or on both grounds.[96]

The second issue is the matter of designation.[97] According to the wording, property has not only to be of importance for archaeology, prehistory, history, literature, art or science, but has also to be specially designated. There is some controversy on how specifically this has to be done.[98] While some argue that every piece has to be individually listed with its specifications to fall under the protection

(h) rare manuscripts and incunabula, old books, documents and publications of special interest (historical, artistic, scientific, literary, etc.) singly or in collections;
(i) postage, revenue and similar stamps, singly or in collections;
(j) archives, including sound, photographic and cinematographic archives;
(k) articles of furniture more than one hundred years old and old musical instruments."

[89]Stamatoudi (2011), p. 36; Pallas (2004), p. 53.

[90]Cf. Schnelle (2016), p. 47.

[91]Cf. O'Keefe (2007), p. 35; cf. also Stamatoudi (2011), pp. 37f.

[92]Stamatoudi (2011), pp. 37f.

[93]However, in practice it seems unlikely that an object falling under one of the categories of Article 1 of the Convention does not satisfy the general definition.

[94]Hönes (2010), pp. 87f; Steinbrück (2012), p. 60.

[95]Cf. Kurpiers (2005), p. 155.

[96]Stamatoudi (2011), p. 37 assigns the wording a excluding character. According to her interpretation the wording could be understood "to exclude objects which cannot be considered cultural in the common sense of the word".

[97]Neither the original draft nor the revised draft required a special designation. Cf. Article 1 of the Original and Revised Draft (Chapter 2, n 49 and 61).

[98]Ochoa Jiménez (2011), p. 85.

of the treaty, others consider general categories of objects and regimes of classifications of cultural objects as sufficient.[99] Since the preparatory work does not indicate any intention to restrict the scope of the convention by using this particular wording[100] and as in practice various states have adopted different methods in order to designate their cultural property,[101] the former view has not gained much ground.

However, there is a further controversy in the context of designation; the question to what extent a state party may designate its objects. Some authors object to the idea that a state party may designate its entire cultural material,[102] whereas others see no harm in this.[103]

Three objections have to be raised against the view limiting the state parties' right to designate. First, as mentioned previously, the preparatory work does not indicate any intention of the drafters to restrict the scope of the convention by using this particular wording. Second, for some countries which, for various reasons, have lost almost their entire cultural heritage, that which remains is of essential importance.[104] Third but not least, the existence of Article 13 (d) of the Convention is a strong indication against such a limitation. According to this provision, the states parties to the convention also undertake, consistent with the laws of each state, to recognise the indefeasible right of each state party to classify and declare certain cultural property as inalienable which should therefore ipso facto not be exported and to facilitate recovery of such property by the state concerned in cases where it has been exported. Hence, state parties possess the non-forfeitable and non-transferable right[105] to provide particular cultural heritage they consider as extraordinarily valuable for their cultural identity with a higher level of protection by classifying and declaring it as inalienable. This means that such objects cannot be legally transferred and ownership of them cannot be gained by adverse possession, good faith acquisition or any other rights.[106] The state can claim these objects back at any time given and, in case the object has been exported, the other state parties are obliged to facilitate its recovery.[107]

In light of this provision, an interpretation of "specially designated" restricting the extent to which a state party may designate its cultural objects seems highly questionable. Such an understanding would lead to a practice in which state parties

---

[99]Cf. Schaffrath (2007), p. 17; cf. also Raschèr (2000), p. 54; O'Keefe (2007), p. 36; Stamatoudi (2011), p. 37; Steinbrück (2012), pp. 61f; Rietschel (2009), p. 27.

[100]Cf. O'Keefe (2007), p. 36.

[101]Cf. Raschèr (2000), p. 54; cf. also Stamatoudi (2011), p. 37.

[102]Cf. Bator (1982), p. 381.

[103]Cf. for instance O'Keefe (2007), p. 37.

[104]Cf. O'Keefe (2007), p. 37.

[105]Cf. Stamatoudi (2011), p. 40; cf. also O'Keefe (2007), p. 85.

[106]Cf. O'Keefe (2007), p. 85.

[107]For the concept of res extra commercium see Weidner (2001), p. 242. According to Forrest (2010), p. 173 Article 13 (d) of the 1970 UNESCO Convention is inspired by the civil law jurisdictions' concept of inalienability.

could only designate objects of high value, which would significantly blur the dividing line between Articles 1 and 13 of the Convention and result in an overlap of the area of application of both norms. Thus, "specially designated" in the sense of Article 1 must be interpreted as permitting state parties to designate their cultural property at their own discretion. Therefore, it only imposes the obligation on state parties to publicise the objects they want to protect in advance. But it does not require them to merely nominate objects of extraordinarily high value to their cultural identity.

Article 4 is another norm that, in addition to Article 13 (d), specifies the scope of the treaty, as established by Article 1.[108] According to Article 4 (a), state parties recognise that for the purpose of the convention, property which belongs to the following categories forms part of the cultural heritage of each state: cultural property created by the individual or collective genius of nationals of the state concerned and cultural property of importance to the state concerned created within the territory of that state by foreign nationals or stateless persons resident within such territory. All cultural property created by nationals is hence considered to be part of the cultural heritage of that state. The treaty, as noted above, acknowledges that cultural property created by non-nationals can be of value to their resident state and thus be part of that state's cultural heritage. However, cultural property has to fulfil two requirements in order to be accepted as the cultural heritage of a state when the creator is not a citizen. First, it has to be manufactured in the particular state and, secondly, it has to be of importance to the state concerned. There is some controversy on this requirement. Some argue that in order for cultural property created by non-nationals to be of importance for a particular state, there must be a close relationship between the state and the artist, requiring that the non-national has not only briefly lived in the state of concern.[109] This restriction is neither reflected in the wording of the provision which requires solely that the cultural property is of importance to the state concerned, nor does it take account of realty. Throughout history, in all countries, sovereigns have assigned foreign artists to paint tableaus of them or build monuments which later have become national emblems.[110] In many cases, these artists returned to their country of origin as soon as their work was accomplished. To strip these nations, therefore, of their right to consider these cultural objects as their own cultural heritage seems dubious. Hence, the view requiring the artist to have a closer and longer term relationship with the nation concerned has to be refuted.

Article 4 (b) of the Convention, on the other hand, declares all cultural property found within the national territory to be its cultural heritage. This is an outcome stemming from the idea of territorial sovereignty, which attributes the sovereignty of every piece of soil of a country to the respective state.[111] This idea of sovereignty

---

[108]Cf. Raschèr (2000), p. 54; Pallas (2004), p. 53 interprets the attribution according to Article 4 of the Convention as a prerequisite for the applicability of the treaty.

[109]Cf. O'Keefe (2007), p. 45.

[110]Cf. O'Keefe (2007), p. 45.

[111]Cf. Kau (2013), pp. 180f.

is so deeply rooted in minds that even cultural property found within the territory of a state that clearly belongs to a community which has moved or/and formed a state somewhere else, or even ceased to exist, is attributed to the current state.[112]

Furthermore, cultural property acquired by archaeological, ethnological or natural science missions with the consent of the competent authorities of the country of origin of such property is, according to Article 4 (c), also considered to be the cultural heritage of the state it has been transferred to. In addition, cultural property which has been the subject of a freely agreed exchange (Article 4 (d)) and cultural property received as a gift or purchased legally with the consent of the competent authorities of the country of origin of such property (Article 4 (e)) is considered the cultural heritage of the state it has been transferred to.[113]

However, an issue which can arise in the context of Article 4 of the Convention is that the very same cultural object can be based on the provision the cultural heritage of more than one country.[114] Though the 1970 UNESCO Convention does not provide rules to regulate the competing interests of states,[115] it does not leave it solely to state parties to determine which cultural property is their cultural heritage.[116] In these cases, UNESCO may, in accordance with Article 17 (5) of the Convention, at the request of at least two state parties which are engaged in a dispute over the implementation of the convention, extend its good offices to reach a settlement between them.

Regarding the scope of the treaty, it has to be additionally mentioned that even though Articles 1, 4, and 13 (d) stipulate a general notion of cultural property and thus the scope of the treaty, certain individual norms further restrict their own scope. Article 7 (b), for example, narrows its scope to cultural property stolen from a museum or a religious or secular public monument or similar institution.

2.2.4.2 Addressees and Territorial Ambit

Addressees to the 1970 UNESCO Convention are exclusively state parties.[117] This is also reflected in a number of provisions, such as Article 4 which speaks of the

---

[112]Cf. Stamatoudi (2011), p. 39.

[113]For further details, including lit. f of the Draft Convention, cf. O'Keefe (2007), pp. 45ff.

[114]Cf. also Kurpiers (2005), p. 156 who, in this context, points out that Article 4 lit. c–e might be considered to be lex specialis to Article 4 lit. a and b of the Convention.

[115]O'Keefe (2007), p. 47.

[116]Schuschke-Nehen (2008), p. 33.

[117]A remarkable exception to the fundamental concept of the convention to solely address state parties is Paragraph 7 of the Preamble: "The General Council [...] Considering that, as cultural institutions, museums, libraries and archives should ensure that their collections are built up in accordance with universally recognized moral principles [...] adopts this Convention." Even though the provision does not directly impose "legal" obligations on cultural institutions, it calls upon them and seems to impose some sort of "moral" obligation on them.

cultural heritage of each state.[118] Hence, the norms of the treaty only take effect between states.[119] Private parties do not directly obtain any rights from it.[120] The non-self-executing agreement thus needs to be implemented into national legislation in order for private parties to benefit from it.[121]

The territorial scope of the convention, however, is extended by Article 22, according to which the states parties recognise that it is applicable not only to their metropolitan territories but also to all territories for the international relations of which they are responsible. Thus, state parties have to ensure that their dependent territories do justice to the obligation arising from the convention, where necessary by undertaking to consult the governments or other competent authorities of these territories on or before ratification, acceptance or accession with a view to securing the application of the convention to those territories. On the other hand, according to Article 23 (1), they are also authorised to denounce the treaty on behalf of such territories.[122]

Article 11 of the Convention puts forward another aspect regarding the territorial scope of the agreement. According to this clause the export and transfer of ownership of cultural property under compulsion arising directly or indirectly from the occupation of a country by a foreign power shall be regarded as illicit. Thus, state parties themselves not only have to omit the transfer of cultural property from occupied territories by compulsion, but also prevent transfers resulting indirectly from occupation.[123] Hence, the convention extends some protection to occupied territories.

2.2.4.3 The Crux: Retroactivity

Whether or not the 1970 UNESCO Convention ought to have a retroactive effect was one of the most controversial matters during the negotiations.[124] Formerly colonised states which still were heavily affected by the illicit transfer of their cultural heritage had hoped to create an instrument not only giving them capacity to reclaim cultural property which would be illicitly transferred in the future, but which would also empower them to recover their cultural heritage lost in colonial times.[125] However, the major art market states feared that a retroactive effect would lead not only to an inestimable number of claims depleting the collections of their

---

[118]Fishman (2010), p. 357.

[119]Boos (2006), p. 48; Gornig (2007), p. 52; Chechi (2013), p. 182.

[120]Steinbrück (2012), p. 59.

[121]Raschèr (2000), p. 53; Stamatoudi (2011), p. 34; Thorn (2005), pp. 62f.

[122]Article 23 (1) of the Convention: "Each State Party to this Convention may denounce the Convention [...] on behalf of any territory for whose international relations it is responsible.".

[123]On compulsion arising indirectly from occupation cf. p. 23.

[124]Cf. O'Keefe (2007), p. 9.

[125]Prott (2009), p. 12; Vrdoljak (2008), p. 206; Brodie (2015), p. 318.

national museums and collectors, but also be damaging for the general principle of free trade.[126] As a result, the 1970 UNESCO Convention was adopted without any general clause[127] on the temporal applicability of the treaty.[128] Thus, in compliance with Article 28 of the Vienna Convention on the Law of the Treaties,[129] the 1970 UNESCO Convention has no retroactive effect,[130] meaning that state parties can only rely on the convention to claim back cultural property transferred illicitly from their territory after the treaty entered into force.[131] Cultural objects transferred illicitly prior to that date can only be requested back based on other rules.

However, as compensation for not bestowing a retroactive effect on the convention, Article 15 clarifies that nothing in the convention itself shall prevent state parties from concluding special agreements among themselves or from continuing to implement agreements already concluded regarding the restitution of cultural property removed, whatever the reason, from its territory of origin, before the entry into force of the convention for the states concerned. Hence, state parties are not only free to conclude further reaching arrangements on which ground they may return cultural objects illicitly transferred before the entry into force of the treaty, but may also simply return these based on national legislation.

Another issue that is not dealt with in the convention is time limitation—the time after which a legal title becomes incontestable.[132] Therefore, state parties are free to apply their own national rules on time limitation.[133] Special declarations or reservations are not required.[134]

---

[126]Gruber (2013), p. 350; Tucker (2011), pp. 631f; see also Carleton (2007), p. 26.

[127]Article 7 of the Convention is the only provision addressing the issue of the temporal applicability of the convention, but it is limited to its own scope.

[128]The late 1960s, when the convention was drafted, were a time during which former colonies intensely brought forth claims for return of cultural material transferred from their territories by their colonial powers during the colonial period. Consequently, a number of states requested in their comments on the original draft the convention to have a retroactive effect. The former colonial powers, however, objected due to the cultural objects already in their territory and prevailed. Cf. O'Keefe (2007), p. 9.

[129]Article 28 of the Vienna Convention on the Law of the Treaties: "Unless a different intention appears from the treaty or is otherwise established, its provisions do not bind a party in relation to any act or fact which took place or any situation which ceased to exist before the date of the entry into force of the treaty with respect to that party.".

[130]Cf. for example Stumpf (2003), p. 215 and Blake (2015), p. 39; cf. also Planche (2010), p. 146.

[131]A highly important issue in this regard is the timing of the export and import. Problems can arise in cases in which at the time of unlawful import both countries were party to the convention, but at the time of illicit export only the country of origin was party. Cf. O'Keefe (2007), pp. 9f.

[132]Cf. O'Keefe (2007), p. 27.

[133]Stamatoudi (2011), p. 63.

[134]The United Kingdom, however, stated in its acceptance of the convention as the only state party so far that it "interprets Article 7 (b) (ii) to the effect that it may continue to apply its existing rules on limitation to claims made under this Article for the recovery and return of cultural objects". http://portal.unesco.org/en/ev.php-URL_ID=13039&URL_DO=DO_TOPIC&URL_SECTION=201.html#RESERVES.

2.2.5 *The 1970 UNESCO Convention's Rules on Return*

The 1970 UNESCO Convention contains three specifically return related norms of which two constitute separate legal bases for the return of stolen cultural property—Articles 7 (b) (ii) and 13 (c)—and one—Article 13 (b)—obliges state parties to cooperate in the restitution of illicitly exported cultural property. While Article 13 (c), however, refers to the national level and solely secures the possibility of the rightful owner to bring respective claims to court in the state parties, Article 7 (b) (ii) constitutes an autonomous legal basis for a claim.[135]

2.2.5.1 The Heart: Article 7 (b) (ii)

Article 7 (b) (ii) of the 1970 UNESCO Convention is the central provision of the treaty concerning the return of cultural property. It provides state parties with an autonomous legal basis. The importance of the provision is also highlighted by the fact that it is one of the few provisions whose compliance, according to Article 8, has to be ensured by state parties by introducing penalties or administrative sanctions.[136]

2.2.5.1.1 The Prerequisites for Any Return

According to Article 7 (b) (ii) (1), the state parties to the convention undertake at the request of the state party of origin, to take appropriate steps to recover and return any such cultural property imported after the entry into force of the convention in both states concerned, provided, however, that the requesting state shall pay just compensation to an innocent purchaser or to a person who has valid title to that property. Beyond its length, the provision gives rise to a number of controversies; the first of which arises in the context of the rightful claimant.

It is undisputed that an importing state does not have to take measures and return a cultural object ex officio, but solely upon the request of the state party of origin. This can affect the prospect of the country of origin to reclaim an object, since it may lack the commitment, the competence, or the financial means to do so, or simply because the diplomatic relations between it and the importing country are suspended.[137]

However, the question of which state party actually has the right to reclaim such cultural property is controversial. Article 7 (b) (ii) (1) itself does not identify or supply criteria to specify the state party of origin. Thus, there are conflicting views

---

[135] Schaffrath (2007), p. 17.

[136] On the relation between Article 8 and Article 7 (b) of the Convention cf. pp. 45f.

[137] Cf. O'Keefe (2007), p. 60.

on this subject. One opinion focuses on the actual origin of the object concerned. According to this view, every country from which it has been exported illicitly is a country of origin and therefore has the right to activate Article 7 (b) (ii) (1).[138] Another view cross-references to Article 4 to determine the state party of origin. Consequently, according to this position, a state is only allowed to invoke Article 7 (b) (ii) (1) in case the cultural property in question is part of its cultural heritage.[139] Considering the purpose of the convention, to secure the cultural heritage of the state parties, the later view is preferable.[140] With this in mind, permitting a country to reclaim cultural objects based merely on actual possession could lead to the convention being used absurdly. A country which does not have any cultural ties to an object could claim it and later refuse to return it to a country which has a cultural bond with it for several reasons, such as time limitation or stricter onus regulations than itself faced when claiming it back. Thus, the state party of origin has to be interpreted in a way that a state is only allowed to activate Article 7 (b) (ii) (1) in case the cultural property in question is part of its cultural heritage.

This interpretation, however, gives rise to a knock-on effect. The controversy turns on the question of which country has the right to reclaim a cultural object when it is part of the cultural heritage of more than one state. Some argue that in this case a mere chronological criterion should be utilised. Only the state party that was the last legal possessor of the object should be allowed to reclaim it.[141] This would doubtlessly admit an unambiguous attribution of the object and thus the right to claim it. However, it is questionable if such an approach is favourable. For various reasons, the last legal possessor of the object might be unwilling or incapable of meeting the requirements to demand the object at issue back. Thus, to only allow the last legal possessor of such cultural property to reclaim the artefact, would deprive other state parties that may well have cultural ties with the object as well as the means and the will to demand its return, of their possibility to reclaim it. Hence, it is preferable to permit all states, whose cultural heritage the object is part of, to reclaim it. In cases where more than one state seeks to reclaim it, the states concerned can join their efforts. This may naturally lead to controversies between the claimants on which one has a stronger bond and thus should be prioritised. However, the question as to which particular state party the object has to be returned to and under which conditions such a return should be realised can be resolved after a court has held that the object has been imported illicitly and has to be returned. Nonetheless, this solution, which poses some follow-up issues, seems preferable to a solution which only allows the last legal possessor to reclaim an

[138]Dicke (1984), p. 25.

[139]Boos (2006), p. 212, for example, argues that in the case of cultural objects on loan, only the lender is entitled to return.

[140]Cf. Schaffrath (2007), p. 21.

[141]Cf. Schaffrath (2007), p. 22.

object, since the risk that the object remains in the illicitly imported country is mitigated and the object is more likely to return to a country that has a cultural bond with it.

A second issue in the context of Article 7 (b) (ii) (1) is the "appropriate steps" a state party has to take. The provision itself does not feature any enumerative list of measures, neither exhaustive, nor exemplary. However, the usage of the expression "appropriate" does allow the conclusion that the measures to be taken are at the state parties' discretion, as long as they do not contradict the aims of the treaty. Thus, state parties are free to seize the cultural object themselves or even prosecute the importer.[142]

Whether or not a state party is also free to content itself with informing the state party of origin and await the outcome of the civil claim brought forward by the latter at a court of the former, is controversial. Some argue that the "appropriate steps" require the state parties to supplement their existing measures by introducing new, more effective ones or by rendering current procedures more effective.[143] Not only do most states already have laws in place banning the trafficking of stolen cultural property,[144] it can also be assumed that the court systems of the major art market states, which are in general the recipients of such claims, function effectively and the option of seizure as an interim relief is a commonly available instrument for claimants. Hence, requesting states are free to ask the court for an order to seize cultural property to ensure the possibility of access in case the court grants its claim. Furthermore, the wording of the provision does not provide for any hint of the former interpretation. The provision does not say "introduce" appropriate steps, but "take". This does not exclude actions already existing within the national legal system of a state party. Therefore, the reference to a court has to be seen as adequate, as long as it is not evident that the court will deny a rightful claim. However, though there is no requirement to the magnitude of the steps a state party has to take, remaining passive clearly constitutes a breach of the obligation imposed by the provision.

A third controversial subject regarding Article 7 (b) (ii) (1) is its scope, namely the question of what "such cultural property" refers to. Some argue that it only references Article 7 (b) (i) and thus Article 7 (b) (ii) (1) can only be utilised to reclaim cultural property stolen from a museum or a religious or secular public monument or similar institution in another state party.[145] According to others, however, "such cultural property" refers to Article 7 of the Convention in its entirety. This would mean that Article 7 (b) (ii) (1) could be activated to demand back all cultural property originating in another state party which has been illegally exported after entry into force of the convention in the states concerned.[146] The

[142] O'Keefe (2007), p. 62.

[143] Cf. Stamatoudi (2011), p. 50.

[144] Gerstenblith (2013), p. 11.

[145] Schaffrath (2007), pp. 18f; cf. Thorn (2005), pp. 61f.

[146] Cf. Siehr (2005), p. 37.

latter view has to be rejected.[147] First of all, the formation of the norm has to be taken into consideration. The draft of the secretariat stipulated a comprehensive rule of return for cases of illicitly trafficked objects. However, this regulation was not incorporated into the final convention because it was severely criticised by several states.[148]

Furthermore, the structure of Article 7 of the Convention militates against this view. Article 7 (b) (ii) (1) is a sub-section of Article 7 (b). If the obligation to return was intended to cover all cultural property illicitly transferred, the provision would have been entitled as Article 7 (c) of the Convention. Being headed as Article 7 (b) (ii) (1) thus shows that the drafters only intended "such cultural property" to refer to Article 7 (b) (i).[149] Therefore, Article 7 (b) (ii) (1) can only be invoked to claim back cultural property stolen from museums and similar institutions or religious and secular public monuments.[150]

Last but not least, a final point of issue in the context of Article 7 (b) (ii) (1) is the requirement to pay just compensation to an innocent purchaser or a person who has valid title to that property. However, at the same time, this point is the most controversial one in the context of the provision. It gives rise to two issues; firstly, the criteria that have to be fulfilled in order for a compensation to be deemed "just" and, secondly, who exactly has to be compensated.

The issue of "just compensation" is closely tied to the question of which rights a purchaser of stolen cultural property can obtain with regard to the object. Generally, common law jurisdictions tend to favour the original owner, which is why the purchaser of stolen goods does not enjoy any special protection at all.[151] Whereas in most civil law countries the bona fide purchaser is not only protected but can also obtain the ownership of the stolen good by various means; in some jurisdictions he gains a title directly with the purchase, in others he can rely on acquisitive prescription.[152] Though the convention itself does not say what happens to this ownership or title, it can be assumed that it is withdrawn from the innocent purchaser or title-holder.[153] However, even accepting that the innocent purchaser or title-holder is permitted to retain ownership or the title, it becomes in effect

[147] Friehe (2013), pp. 115f; cf. also Kurpiers (2005), p. 154, n 634.

[148] Schaffrath (2007), p. 19.

[149] Similar Schaffrath (2007), p. 19.

[150] Boos (2006), p. 49 emphasises that non-stolen cultural objects and the cultural property of private collections do not fall within the scope of the provision.

[151] O'Keefe (2007), p. 61; Siehr (2011), p. 103; Renold (2009), p. 309; Fincham (2008–2009), p. 121.

[152] UNIDROIT Secretariat (2001), p. 479; see for an exemplary list of national legislations Schmeinck (1994), pp. 128ff; see further for the tension between cultural heritage protection and private ownership rights and approaches to reconcile both interests using the example of Belgium de Clippele and Lambrecht (2015), pp. 259–278.

[153] Cf. Renold (2009), pp. 309f; see also Schnabel and Tatzkow (2007), Chapter I for more specific regulations of various countries concerning this matter with a focus on cultural objects looted during World War II.

valueless as the requesting state party acquires possession of the cultural property. The fact that the return of the cultural property constitutes or corresponds to an expropriation, depending on the legal system, is the very reason that compensation is required.[154,155] Considering this also prescribes the amount of the compensation: it has to be equal to the value of the cultural property expropriated.

However, this leaves one important question unanswered: the value at which point of time?[156] Compensation could be paid according to the current value or regarding the value at the time of purchase. The original secretariat draft contained a clarification on this subject.[157] According to Article 10 (d), fair compensation corresponding to the purchase price had to be paid. However, this passage was replaced by "just compensation". Since no comment was made on this alteration,[158] the intention behind the change is not completely discernible. However, taking into account the price fluctuation, especially the increase in the value of cultural objects within the art market[159] and the idea that an innocent purchaser or title-holder should have no loss due to his purchase but by the same token not make a profit, the change in the wording cannot be understood as a general rejection of the idea that the price at purchase is the relevant figure upon which compensation has to be determined. In this way, the innocent purchaser or title-holder is on the one hand protected from possible financial loss but on the other hand it guarantees that he does not profit from his purchase. The change in phrasing, however, more likely arose from an intention to take into account the state parties' special needs which arise due to their different legal systems by allowing them to take different aspects into consideration in the determination of the compensation's amount. Compensation purely symbolic in nature, however, is precluded.[160]

In accordance with the principles regarding the innocent purchaser or title-holder, it seems furthermore appropriate that the amount of the compensation consists in principle of the purchase price, the costs related to a purchase, such as transportation costs, and any expenditure made on preservation.[161] However, the compensation has to be adjusted by two factors. First, the expenses related to the purchase and the preservation have to be necessary and reasonable. It is excessive to burden the requesting state with the requirement to compensate expenses clearly unnecessary or disproportionate to the value of the cultural object. Furthermore, it

---

[154]Cf. Schaffrath (2007), p. 20.

[155]Prowda (2014), p. 147 therefore argues questionably that the 1970 UNESCO Convention and the 1995 UNIDROIT Convention have adopted the civil law position in protecting the good faith purchaser.

[156]Cf. Abramson and Huttler (1973), p. 953.

[157]UNESCO Doc SHC/MD/3 Annex, 08.08.1969, Article 10 (d).

[158]O'Keefe (2007), p. 63.

[159]Cf. O'Keefe (2007), p. 64.

[160]Same Thorn (2005), p. 151 with regard to the 1995 UNIDROIT Convention.

[161]See O'Keefe (2007), pp. 63f for an overview of different regulations regarding the amount of compensation in different countries and the development within the various drafts.

has to be considered that the requesting state is at least as much a victim as the innocent purchaser or title-holder. Thus, it ought to be only the compensator of last resort. If the innocent purchaser or title-holder is therefore legally and practicably able to regain costs and expenses from the bad faith seller, the amount recoverable is to be deducted from the compensation to be paid by the requesting state. In some cases, the innocent purchaser or title-holder can recover all costs and hence has no further claim against the requesting state.

In the context of compensation, however, the question of who has the right to claim compensation is at least as important as the amount of the compensation. According to Article 7 (b) (ii) (1), just compensation has to be paid to an innocent purchaser or a person who has valid title to that property.

Since the word "or" is used in the convention without any indication that one of the terms of the conceptual pair constitutes a sub-group or example of the other, such as "innocent purchaser or *another* person who has valid title to that property," both phrases have to be seen as distinct and autonomous from each other. Thus, both terms have to be defined individually and their difference has to be elaborated.

The term "innocent purchaser" is foreign to both civil and common law systems.[162] It could equate to a "bona fide purchaser" which is a term of art in the civil law systems. However, the phrase "bona fide purchaser" was used in the original secretariat draft and later on replaced by the term "innocent purchaser".[163] This change in terminology has to be seen as a compromise between both legal systems,[164] likely owing to the unwillingness of the common law jurisdictions to adopt the civil law concept of a bona fide purchaser. Thus, an innocent purchaser cannot be viewed as being the precise equivalent of a bona fide purchaser under the civil law system.[165]

However, though the intentions of the drafters are not entirely obvious, considering the drafting history and the selection of the term "innocent", an innocent purchaser cannot be something completely different from a bona fide purchaser. Some sort of good faith is required.[166] Thus, the innocent purchaser must be seen as someone who is not aware of his misconduct.[167]

A person who has valid title to cultural property, on the other hand, has to be seen as different from an innocent purchaser. Some argue that the difference lies in the necessity of acquiring a title.[168] Thus, while an innocent purchaser would not necessarily need to have obtained a legal title, the title-holder only has to be compensated when he did so. The title-holder would hence be compensated for the loss of his title, whereas the innocent purchaser would be reimbursed for the

---

[162]Cf. O'Keefe (2007), p. 65; cf. also Rietschel (2009), p. 37.

[163]Cf. Article 7 (g) of the Draft (Chapter 2, n 52).

[164]Cf. O'Keefe (2007), pp. 65f.

[165]With another view Steinbrück (2012), p. 70.

[166]Stamatoudi (2011), pp. 50f.

[167]Cf. O'Keefe (2007), p. 66.

[168]Cf. Weidner (2001), pp. 239f; Schaffrath (2007), p. 20.

expenses accrued in good faith, such as transportation costs and any expenditure made on preservation. Since, however, the provision unambiguously distinguishes the innocent purchaser and the title-holder using the word "or", compensation could only be claimed on one ground, either as an innocent purchaser or the title-holder. Innocent purchasers acquiring a title could only ask for compensation for the expenses made in good faith or compensation for the loss of title. This, however, obviously leaves them in an unfavourable position.

Additionally, the aim of the convention, to facilitate the return of cultural property,[169] has to be kept in mind. In common law jurisdictions, the good faith purchaser is not entitled to compensation. The former interpretation, however, would require common law countries to introduce just this requirement for claims concerning cultural property. This would bestow a higher level of protection to a person without title than this person would originally have enjoyed under his own national law, which would in effect contradict the aim of the treaty. Thus, both, the innocent purchaser and the title holder, must have acquired title.

Hence, the difference between the two categories has to be seen in the element of good faith. While the innocent purchaser must have acquired his title unwittingly in disharmony with the law, the person who has valid title to that property must have obtained his title by other means, such as adverse possession or lapse of time, but was irrespectively aware of its unlawful grounds.[170]

This interpretation could well reduce the significance of the conceptual pair to a mere clarifying role. However, this clarification is of importance as it avoids any doubt as to whether only the person who acted in good faith is to be compensated or also the person who acted in bad faith. Furthermore, the question of whether or not the purchaser is innocent has also influence in the context of the "just compensation". What may seem as an adequate and thus "just compensation" in the case of a person who has valid title, might be seen as insufficient and therefore unjust in light of the innocence of the purchaser.

There is, however, one point in the context of Article 7 (b) (ii) (1) which is not controversial: the temporal scope of the provision. It can only be activated for cultural property imported after the entry into force of the convention in both states concerned. Hence, it is not sufficient to activate Article 7 (b) (ii) (1) if only one state concerned was at the time of export or import party to the convention.

2.2.5.1.2 The Procedure

Article 7 (b) (ii) (2) reflects the non-self-executing character of the convention as requests for recovery and return have to be made through diplomatic offices. Thus, unlike in the draft of the secretariat, which permitted the owner of the cultural property in question, his authorised agent or the state of which he is a national to

[169] Cf. Schaffrath (2007), p. 20.

[170] Cf. O'Keefe (2007), p. 66; cf. also Stamatoudi (2011), p. 50.

reclaim the respective cultural property,[171] private parties, including the owner are not permitted to invoke Article 7 (b) (ii) (1) of the Convention. The right to activate this provision is strictly reserved for state parties.[172]

2.2.5.1.3 The Obligations of the Requesting State

Though Article 7 (b) (ii) (1) serves to facilitate the return of cultural property, this does not mean that the requesting state does not have to bear any burden whatsoever. First of all, according to Article 7 (b) (ii) (3) the requesting party shall furnish the documentation and other evidence necessary to establish its claim for recovery and return. Thus, the onus to establish a case lies with the requesting state. It has to provide sufficient evidence to satisfy the requirements to invoke Article 7 (b) (ii) (1). What might be relatively easy for countries with a well established inventory system that maintain adequate records, could prove to be an obstacle for countries lacking such a system. Some countries may also not have the required documents or miss the legal or diplomatic personnel to present their case.[173] Bearing especially in mind that states which are most often victim to the illicit export of their cultural property regularly fall within the latter category highlights how much of an obstacle this provision can prove to be for the return of cultural objects to the state party of origin in practice.

Furthermore, Article 7 (b) (ii) (3) requires that the requesting state parties not only furnish the documents to establish their claims at their own expenses, but Article 7 (b) (ii) (5) also imposes the burden on them to bear all expenses incident to the return and delivery of the cultural property. Again, this could well frustrate rightful claims of state parties with limited financial means when the expenses related to the return appear to be comparatively high.

However, any other arrangement regarding the burdens of the requesting state parties would be either impractical or undesirable. Neither the state party to whose territory the cultural property has been illicitly transferred, nor the purchaser are likely to hold any documents proving that the cultural property at issue has at no time been illicitly exported from the requesting state party. Besides this, imposing the costs of the return on the state party to whose territory the cultural property has been illicitly transferred, on the grounds that it did not prevent its illicit import, would have led to an ongoing reluctance of states to become party to the 1970 UNESCO Convention. However, the costs that the requesting state has to bear for the return could be mitigated using the "just compensation" which has to be paid to the innocent purchaser or title-holder. In cases in which the title-holder is not innocent, but aware of the illicitness of the transfer from the state party of origin,

[171] UNESCO Doc SHC/MD/5 Annex III, 27.02.1970, Article 10 (c).

[172] Schaffrath (2007), p. 17.

[173] Same O'Keefe (2007), p. 60.

the costs for the return could be deducted from the compensation which has to be paid to him.

However, in a certain way the convention takes the financial interests of the requesting state party into account, since according to Article 7 (b) (ii) (4) the state party in whose territory the cultural property has been illicitly transferred shall impose no customs duties or other charges upon cultural property returned pursuant to Article 7.

2.2.5.2 Covering the National Level

Article 13 (c) of the Convention requires state parties to admit actions for recovery of lost or stolen items of cultural property brought by or on behalf of the rightful owners without specifying any criteria that national legislation has to fulfil. In fact, it leaves the determination of these criteria to the discretion of individual state parties by stating that their efforts have to be consistent with the laws of each state. This has to be understood as taking the different legal systems of state parties and thus their different needs and requirements into account and allowing them to implement the obligation in a manner consistent with their national legal system.[174]

Since all legal systems provide for some sort of action to recover stolen items, this provision does not impose any additional legal obligation on state parties.[175] This does, however, not mean that the provision is an empty phrase without any legal value. The very existence of the norm clarifies that Article 7 (b) (ii) of the Convention is not an exclusive legal basis to reclaim stolen cultural property, but that there are also other options which can be invoked in addition or as alternatives.

In this context, it is of importance to note that Article 13 (c) has a significantly different scope than Article 7 (b) (ii). Article 13 (c) is applicable to all lost or stolen items of cultural property, whereas Article 7 (b) (ii) can only be invoked for cultural property stolen from a museum or a religious or secular public monument or similar institution in another state party. Hence, the scope of Article 13 (c) is in three regards wider than the scope of Article 7 (b) (ii). Firstly, it applies to cultural artefacts not stolen from one of the above sites. Secondly, it additionally covers cultural material lost or stolen within the same state party, whereas Article 7 (b) (ii) is only utilisable for cultural property stolen in another state party.

The third regard in which the scope of Article 13 (c) is wider than the scope of Article 7 (b) (ii) is the parties having locus standi. While only states can activate

[174]Similar O'Keefe (2007), p. 82 who requires a state party to "at least use its best efforts". Bator (1982), p. 378, however, denies the provision—due to the limitation—any significance. Gordon (1971), p. 554, on the other hand, regards Article 13 of the Convention as "one of the most difficult and contradictory articles of the Convention".

[175]Steinbrück (2012), p. 77; Bator (1982), p. 378.

Article 7 (b) (ii), Article 13 (c) is open to any rightful owner or anyone acting on his behalf.[176]

Besides the wider scope, relying on Article 13 (c) instead of Article 7 (b) (ii) can be beneficial for another reason: Article 7 (b) (ii) requires a payment of just compensation to an innocent purchaser or to a person who has valid title. In jurisdictions providing for a provision which permits the claiming back of cultural property without the requirement to pay any compensation, bringing forth a claim in accordance with Article 13 (c) rather than Article 7 (b) (ii) financially unburdens the requesting state.[177]

However, as Article 13 (c) refers to the national level and since Article 7 (b) (ii) needs to be implemented on a national level due to the non-self-executing character of the 1970 UNESCO Convention,[178] it is likely that in most state parties a single provision will be issued or adjusted to do justice to the obligations arising from both articles.[179] Hence, though having different scopes and requirements in theory, the distinction between both articles seems rather diluted in practice.

2.2.5.3 The State Parties' Obligation to Facilitate the Return

While Articles 7 (b) (ii) and 13 (c) of the Convention establish legal bases for the return of stolen cultural property, Article 13 (b) requires state parties to ensure that their competent services cooperate in facilitating the earliest possible restitution of illicitly exported cultural property to its rightful owner.

Even though the term "competent services" brings the national services of Article 5 of the Convention to one's mind, they are not the only services addressed by this clause. Other services such as customs, but also public cultural institutions, often have to be induced by state parties to cooperate as well.[180]

The content of this duty to cooperate needs clarification at this point. As previously stated, the competent services have to cooperate in facilitating the earliest possible restitution of illicitly exported cultural property. Some authors are overly focused in this regard on legal actions and seem to tie the obligation too closely to court trials.[181] The context of the provision has to be more fully taken into consideration. Article 13 (c) already requires state parties to admit actions for recovery of lost or stolen items of cultural property. Thus, the obligation to cooperate in facilitating the earliest possible restitution of illicitly exported cultural

[176]On the controversies in the context of the rightful owner cf. p. 43.

[177]Cf. Schaffrath (2007), p. 24.

[178]Siehr (2011), p. 93; Walter (1988), p. 54.

[179]However, the German law implementing the 1970 UNESCO Convention only allows states party to the convention, but not individuals, to reclaim cultural material. Cf. § 7 Kulturgüterrückgabegesetz.

[180]Cf. O'Keefe (2007), p. 84.

[181]This seems to be the case in Stamatoudi (2011), p. 52.

property cannot mean to simply refer claimants to courts. In order for Article 13 (b) to have its own scope, besides activities connected to trials, such as gathering evidence for the claimant and helping him translate documents proving his case, it has to cover real, extra-legal activities, such as notifying custom services and distributing information to cultural institutions.[182] However, again the obligation is subject to the limitation "consistent with the laws of each state". Thus, state parties do not have to undertake activities which would be in violation of their national laws to help facilitate the restitution. They are, for example, not required to give the claimant personal information about the respondent, if this would violate national data protection regulations.

Furthermore, some authors appear to have concerns with the term "rightful owner".[183] The determination of the rightful owner seems to be something of an incommodity to them and may explain why they relate the term to materials which are described as inalienable in terms of Article 13 (d) of the Convention.[184] Though inalienable cultural heritage is in this regard relevant, an interpretation of the term limiting it solely to these objects is, however, too narrow.

Including the term "rightful" in the convention text serves two purposes. First, it prevents unwanted situations. If the term "rightful" had not been inserted, every owner could request back cultural property illicitly exported. Hence, in cases in which the cultural object ended up with the rightful owner after having been stolen from a "not rightful" one and after having been exported illicitly, the "not rightful" owner could reclaim the cultural property. Thus, including the term "rightful" excludes "not rightful" owners from the benefits of the provision.[185]

Furthermore, integrating this term also imposes an obligation on the owner to prove the validity or legality of his title. This relieves state parties from the burden of becoming active at every request, even unsubstantiated ones. For the determination of the validity of a title, state parties can rely on their general practice regarding the recognition of foreign documents and titles.[186]

However, one issue remains in the context of the rightful owner. What if the cultural property was illicitly exported by the rightful owner?[187] Considering the fact that his title is valid and only the actual export was illicit, the cultural object has to be returned to the rightful owner. This does, however, not mean that the rightful owner cannot be subject to sanctions imposed by the state of origin.[188] Hence, it is left to the discretion of the latter to sentence him according to its national legislation, which can include the expropriation of the object from the rightful owner.

---

[182] These actions are also seen as covered by the provision by O'Keefe (2007), p. 84.

[183] Cf., for example, Stamatoudi (2011), p. 52.

[184] Cf., for example, O'Keefe (2007), p. 83.

[185] Schaffrath (2007), p. 29 e contrario.

[186] The question of which law has to be applied to define the rightful owner is a question raised by some authors. Cf. for example Stamatoudi (2011), p. 52.

[187] Stamatoudi (2011), p. 52.

[188] Cf. O'Keefe (2007), p. 83.

2.2.6 *The 1970 UNESCO Convention's Regulations Combating Illicit Trafficking and Supporting Return*

The 1970 UNESCO Convention, furthermore, contains a number of provisions flanking the norms regulating the return of cultural property by establishing a system to prevent the illicit transfer of the cultural objects in the first place.

2.2.6.1 National Services

Articles 5 and 14 of the Convention are two tightly interrelated provisions as both are concerned with national services. While Article 5 specifies the functions to be conducted by the national services, Article 14 commits the state parties to provide these services with an adequate budget. However, both provisions take into account the different financial and administrative capacity of state parties.[189] A state party's obligation is thus limited by its capability.[190] It is only obliged to a best effort standard,[191] rather than to meet an objective standard.[192]

Furthermore, although both provisions deal with national services, they do theoretically have a slightly different scope. State parties have to set up national services and carry out the functions mentioned in Article 5 to ensure the protection of their cultural property against illicit import, export, and transfer of ownership, whereas in accordance with Article 14 they have to provide these national services with an adequate budget in order to prevent illicit exports and to meet the obligations arising from the implementation of the convention. Hence, Article 14 has a broader scope.[193] Its aim is not only limited to the protection of the cultural heritage of each respective state party, but covers also the prevention of illicit export in general, as well as the fulfilment of all obligations arising from the implementation of the convention, not only those relating to illicit trafficking.

For this purpose, Article 14 invokes state parties to provide the national services responsible for the protection of its cultural heritage with an adequate budget. This could be understood as calling upon state parties to provide these national services with sufficient budget to prevent illicit exports and to meet the obligations arising from the implementation of the convention by all necessary means. However, the

[189] Article 5 of the Convention reads: "the States Parties to this Convention undertake, as appropriate for each country, to set up within their territories one or more national services [. . .]." Article 14 of the Convention: "each State Party to the Convention should, as far as it is able, provide the national services [. . .] with an adequate budget.".

[190] The same interpretation is also favoured by O'Keefe (2007), pp. 52f and Fraoua (1986).

[191] Cf. also Stamatoudi (2011), p. 41.

[192] Abramson and Huttler (1973), p. 962, however, deny Article 5 of the Convention any legally binding effect at all and advocate the view that this wording "converted legal obligations into moral ones".

[193] Stamatoudi (2011), p. 44 seems to indicate that both provisions essentially have the same scope.

key element in this phrase is the word "adequate". Article 14 itself sets a criterion for the determination of the adequacy of a budget. A state party should only act in this regard as far as it is able to do so. Thus, the financial and administrative means of a state party have to be taken into consideration when establishing whether a budget provided by a particular state party to its national service is to be deemed adequate or not.[194] Hence, more financially robust state parties are invoked to provide their services with higher budgets than those state parties lacking such means.

Article 14, furthermore, appeals to state parties to set up a fund for this purpose, but only if necessary. The objective of such a fund is to put the national services in a financial position that ensures they are capable of fulfilling their task.[195] A consideration of the original draft of the convention provides insight into how the fund could be used to aid national services in accomplishing their tasks. It could be utilised not only to finance normal operating costs but also to increase public awareness about lost cultural property and to purchase certain cultural items of special importance for public collections. Such a fund could also be used to reward those who make archaeological discoveries or trace cultural property which has disappeared by making a payment proportional in value to that of the property discovered or traced.[196]

However, Article 14 is not the only provision concerned with providing the national services with sufficient means to fulfil their tasks. Article 5 also obliges state parties to supply their national services with a qualified staff sufficient in number for the effective carrying out of their tasks. It is important to note that there is a significant difference in the wording between Articles 5 and 14. While Article 14 only uses the phrase "should" in the context of providing an adequate budget, Article 5 speaks of "undertake to set up". Hence, the provision establishes a clearer, legally binding obligation with less discretion on the part of state parties than Article 14, even though this obligation is again limited by the financial and administrative capability of each state party, as the words "as appropriate for each country" reveal.[197] Moreover, the provision accepts that different countries may have different ways of structuring their national services, since it permits states parties, as appropriate for each country, to set up within their territories one or more national services. Allowing for even greater flexibility, the provision allows state parties to assign the tasks to already existing agencies.[198]

---

[194]See O'Keefe (2007), p. 87 for a list of possible deficiencies concerning an adequate budget.

[195]Australia, for example, established a fund to enable museums to buy cultural material that has not been granted an export permit. Cf. O'Keefe (2007), p. 87.

[196]At the international level, a similar fund has been established in the context of UNESCO's Intergovernmental Committee for Promoting the Return of Cultural Property to its Countries of Origin or its Restitution in Case of Illicit Appropriation (ICPRCP). For further information on the fund cf. pp. 140ff.

[197]Due to the phrase "as appropriate for each country" appearing in the wording of the provision, Abramson and Huttler (1973), p. 962 deny Article 5 of the Convention any legally binding effect at all.

[198]Cf. Gordon (1971), p. 547.

However, though each state party has the right to decide for itself how to structure its own system, the national services of each state party do have the same functions to carry out effectively. These are determined by Article 5 of the Convention. First of all, it is, according to Article 5 (a), their task to contribute to the formation of draft laws and regulations designed to secure the protection of the cultural heritage, and particularly prevention, of the illicit import, export, and transfer of ownership of important cultural property. Most states already have sufficient legislation on these respective matters in place and this requirement is easily met by reviewing the existing set of rules and adjusting them to current needs.[199] However, fulfilling this function can prove to be quite difficult in state parties which do not have proper legislation or none at all due to a lack of financial means or qualified personnel. These latter state parties may overcome their deficiency of knowledge and/or qualified personnel by calling on the technical assistance of UNESCO in accordance with Article 17 (1).[200]

Another duty of these national services is to establish and keep up to date a list of important public and private cultural property whose export would constitute an appreciable impoverishment of the national cultural heritage (Article 5 (b)). The relationship between this list, which has to be established on the basis of a national inventory of protected property, and the list drawn up based on the specifically designated requirement of Article 1, has been subject to discussion.[201] In this context the secretariat's comment on Article 5 has to be taken into consideration. Accordingly, the inventory in the context of Article 5 is not established for the purpose of the customs, but for scientific purposes which will encourage the study and classifying of the various items that make up the cultural heritage and determine those objects which should be preserved and subject to export prohibition and those the legal transfer of which from the country can be authorised.[202] Hence, it is clear that both lists are not completely identical. The list of Article 5 (b) aims at encouraging the general study and classification of cultural heritage, whereas the special designation requirement of Article 1 ultimately serves to determine the cultural objects which will be governed by the regime of the convention and its benefits. Thus, the inventory of Article 5 (b) is not subject to the same narrow regulations like the list based on the special designation requirement in the context of Article 1 of the Convention is.[203] The list required by Article 5 (b) does not, for example, necessarily have to be a single document. Instead, each museum, town or region can establish the sections relating to their respective cultural property.[204] Furthermore, it can contain categories of objects. Artefacts do not have to be

[199]O'Keefe (2007), p. 48; Gerstenblith (2013), p. 11.

[200]On Article 17 of the Convention cf. pp. 53ff.

[201]O'Keefe (2007), p. 48.

[202]UNESCO Doc SHC/MD/5 Annex II, 27.02.1970, p. 5.

[203]Stamatoudi (2011), p. 41.

[204]UNESCO Doc SHC/MD/5 Annex II, 27.02.1970, p. 5.

individually itemised[205]—a highly disputed issue in the context of the special designation requirement of Article 1.[206] However, even though the inventory of Article 5 (b) does have a different purpose and thus may not even contain information relevant for the customs services, it still can be of value for purposes of the return of cultural property. Furthermore, the inventory of Article 5 (b) can be used as a basis to produce a list for the purposes of the special designation requirement of Article 1. Moreover, although both provisions have different aims, this does not mean that states are not free to use the very same list to fulfil both requirements. They are free to create a list that will on the one hand encourage the study of certain cultural property and on the other hand serve as a special designation list according to Article 1.[207]

A third duty of the national services, according to Article 5 (c), is to promote the development or the establishment of scientific and technical institutions, such as museums, libraries, archives, laboratories, and workshops that are required to ensure the preservation and presentation of cultural property. The word "development" reveals that national services can fulfil this requirement, not only by establishing the mentioned bodies themselves, but also by supporting private initiatives and institutions.

Organising the supervision of archaeological excavations, ensuring the preservation in situ of certain cultural property, and protecting certain areas reserved for future archaeological research (Article 5 (d)) is the fourth function of the national services. This serves to not only implement widely accepted practices in archaeology, such as in situ preservation,[208] but also obligates state parties to undertake measures to counter clandestine excavation to protect areas reserved for future archaeological research.[209] Hence, even if state parties currently lack the financial means for conducting archaeological excavations or research, they are still obliged to preserve culturally important sites so that future archaeological excavations or research may be possible. However, preserving such sites can, in addition, be seen as an expression of the idea that cultural heritage is worth being protected for its own intrinsic value.

As a fifth function, the convention charges national services with establishing for the benefit of those concerned, such as curators, collectors, and antique dealers, rules in conformity with the ethical principles set forth in the convention and taking steps to ensure the observance of those rules (Article 5 (e) of the Convention). This provision is necessary as only state parties are addressees of the convention and, therefore, bound by its obligation.[210] However, in day to day practice, cultural

---

[205] Cf. Stamatoudi (2011), p. 41.

[206] On the dispute cf. pp. 18f.

[207] Cf. O'Keefe (2007), p. 49; cf. also Brodie et al. (2000), p. 38.

[208] Cf. Stamatoudi (2011), p. 43 for a list of international treaties recognising this principle.

[209] O'Keefe (2007), p. 51.

[210] On the addressees of the 1970 UNESCO Convention cf. p. 29; however, also see the exception to this rule provided in Chapter 2, n 117.

institutions and private collectors are those dealing with cultural property and thus the ones generally involved in its illicit traffic, hence they are also those whose assistance is needed to effectively prevent it. According to this, the provision requires state parties to remit the obligations of the treaty to cultural institutions and private collectors. However, the norm does not require state parties to adopt the convention's provisions verbatim to their national laws. Concerning the choice of legal instrument to adopt, they are free to choose as long as the spirit of the convention is upheld and the rules are effective.[211] This is in particular emphasised by the requirement to not only adopt the regulations, but also the obligation to ensure their observance.[212]

According to Article 5 (f), the national services must also undertake educational measures to stimulate and develop respect for the cultural heritage of all states, and to spread knowledge of the provisions of the agreement. One important detail in this regard is that state parties not only have to take educational measures to increase the knowledge of the convention and the respect for their own cultural heritage, but the cultural heritage of all states. This must be assumed to be an expression of the universalist approach to cultural material, which sees cultural items as the common heritage of all mankind that is comprised, inter alia, of the cultural objects of individual nations.[213] However, again the convention does not restrict the state parties to specific measures by providing an exhaustive list, but leaves it to their discretion to determine the measures employed.

Lastly, Article 5 (g) obligates national services to see that appropriate publicity is given to the disappearance of any items of cultural property. The understanding of the key term "appropriate" is in this regard essential for the determination of the obligation imposed by this provision on national services. The use of the term "appropriate" undoubtedly leaves some room for discretion by state parties. They are free to adjust the measures to be taken according to the value they assign to the particular object and their individual capability. In this context it is at the course of wisdom here to examine the commentary on the original draft, which provides some insight into what the drafters of the provision had in mind by "appropriate publicity".[214] The draft itself proposed in particular the usage of the latest mass

---

[211] According to Stamatoudi (2011), p. 42 the provision "does not necessarily provide for the establishment of laws but rather for soft laws, such as codes of ethics, best practices, guidelines, and so on".

[212] Most authors are however primarily concerned with imbalances that might occur. They emphasise that rules should be binding for all parties and not make, for example, museums subject to rules private collectors are not bound by. Cf. for example O'Keefe (2007), p. 51.

[213] The idea of cultural material being the common heritage of mankind is a general approach encountered in practically all cultural heritage related international conventions. Cf., for example, Paragraph 2 of the Preamble of the 1954 Hague Convention; cf. also O'Keefe (2007), p. 53 for a list of further international treaties embodying this idea.

[214] UNESCO Doc SHC/MD/3, 08.08.1969, p. 7 Paragraphs 53 and 54: "The disappearance of any cultural object should, at the request of the State claiming that object, be brought to the knowledge of the public by means of appropriate publicity, particularly through the latest media of mass communication. If such publicity should not lead to the immediate recovery of the cultural object,

communication media. Furthermore, the commentary explicitly introduces the idea of international campaigns. State parties should not only restrict their efforts to the national level, but should also involve international endeavours. For this purpose they can, in modern times, rely on several databases which have been established to this end. In addition to utilising the national databases of other state parties, tools such as the Art Loss Register, the International Criminal Police Organization (INTERPOL) and the ICOM databases are available.[215]

Besides the fact that publicity may lead to the immediate recovery of the cultural object, or at least make it unmarketable, with the result that the holder, to avoid serious trouble, may be induced to restore it to its rightful owner, the commentary itself raised another important aspect of publicity. Namely, widespread publicity might also have legal consequences. In a civil lawsuit it may cast doubt on the good faith on the acquirer of any such property, in such a way that he would cease to be protected, and an action for recovery would be possible even where it is held that "possession is title".

2.2.6.2 Export Certificates and Their Impact on Import

Another subject regulated in the 1970 UNESCO Convention is that of export certificates, a practice now widely accepted.[216,217] According to Article 6, state parties undertake to introduce an appropriate certificate in which the exporting state would specify that the export of the cultural property in question has been authorised. The certificate should accompany all items of cultural property exported in accordance with the regulations.[218] Furthermore, they have to prohibit the

---

it would have the merit *of* drawing the attention of the public, specialist circles in particular, to the object in question. The latter would then be unmarketable, with the result that the holder, to avoid serious trouble, might be induced to restore it to its owner.

It might further be said that such national publicity could be supplemented by an international campaign (Article 14) organised in special publications. The International Institute for the Unification of Private Law highly approves such advertising for lost cultural property, and attaches important legal consequences to it; being of the opinion that, if it were possible to organises a wide international publicity campaign every time a cultural object disappeared, it might be possible in a civil lawsuit to cast doubt on the good faith on the acquirer of any such property, in such a way that he would cease to be protected, and an action for recovery would be possible. Publicity might prove an effective means of justifying such an action, even where it is held that 'possession is title'.".

[215]Stamatoudi (2011), p. 43.

[216]Cf., for example, Stamatoudi (2011), p. 46, n 40 for an exemplary list of EU Regulations on this matter. However, cf. also Vigneron (2014), p. 128; cf. also Nafziger et al. (2014), p. 299.

[217]UNESCO has jointly with the World Customs Organization prepared a Model Export Certificate for Cultural Property. For further information on the issue and in particular the Mode Export Certificate see http://www.unesco.org/new/en/culture/themes/illicit-traffic-of-cultural-property/legal-and-practical-instruments/unesco-wco-model-export-certificate/; cf. on the matter also Roca-Hachem (2005), p. 542.

[218]For an overview of the current national systems for controlling the export of cultural material cf. ILA 2010.

exportation of cultural property from their territory unless accompanied by the above-mentioned export certificate. Lastly, state parties are obligated to publicise this prohibition by appropriate means, particularly among persons likely to export or import cultural property.

A question arising in this context is the dimension of this obligation to introduce export certificates. Though the wording covers all cultural property and some authors seem to comprehend the provision as requiring state parties to introduce export certificates and thus export controls for all items,[219] this does not seem appropriate. The 1970 UNESCO Convention is constructed on and, therefore, reflects the idea that different cultural objects have—for various reasons—different values for different nations and thus need differing levels of protection. It is left to state parties to define the value of a given piece of cultural material for their respective nation and, thus, determine the level of protection attached to the cultural object in question. In light of this consideration, requiring state parties to introduce export certificates for all cultural property would be a contradiction since it would eliminate the state parties' right to deem certain cultural objects as not worthy of particular protection. Hence, it is the right of state parties to decide for which cultural property they will introduce export certificates.[220] State parties are, of course, free to introduce export certificates for all of their cultural heritage if they so desire. However, they may also introduce export certificates solely for particular pieces of cultural property, such as those objects specifically designated in accordance with Article 1 of the Convention.

Another issue discussed that is controversial in the context of export certificates is their effect on import. Some authors link Article 6 with Article 7 (b) (i), which stipulates that state parties undertake to prohibit the import of cultural property stolen from a museum or a religious or secular public monument or similar institution in another state party after the entry into force of the convention for the states concerned, provided that such property is documented as appertaining to the inventory of that institution.[221]

They argue that, Article 7 (b) (i) e contrario, state parties with regard to cultural property not covered by this provision, are under no obligation to introduce any import prohibitions. This would mean that Article 6 has no impact on import

[219]Cf., for example, Bator (1982), p. 377. For a broader perspective on the topic of border controls concerning cultural property see Paterson (2011), pp. 287ff.

[220]Cf. O'Keefe (2007), p. 55.

[221]As in the case of the export certificates, the dimension of the obligation imposed by Article 7 (b) (i) of the Convention is controversial. Some authors understand the provision as imposing strict border control obligations. Considering that even in cases of illegal trafficking of arms and narcotics states generally rely on selective controls at the border and other methods like international exchange of information, such a far-reaching requirement seems inappropriate in the case of illicitly transferred cultural material. State parties have a free hand concerning the selection of their methods to implement the import prohibition. Cf. O'Keefe (2007), pp. 57ff; cf. also Steinbrück (2012), pp. 65ff.

matters.[222] For two reasons such an interpretation of this provision seems inadequate. Firstly, Article 7 (b) (i) owes itself to the previously mentioned idea that different cultural objects have different significance for different nations. The fact that Article 7 (b) (ii) constitutes a separate, advanced regime to reclaim these artefacts indicates that these cultural objects are of particular value to state parties. Therefore, Article 7 (b) (i) has to be understood as establishing a higher level of protection for these items due to their particular significance. State parties are, hence, already obliged to prohibit the import of cultural property stolen from the institutions mentioned, both private and public,[223] if they were documented as part of the inventory of that institution.[224] In the case of these cultural objects, state parties are not allowed to establish further requirements with regard to the implementation of import prohibitions. This does not mean, however, that under the 1970 UNESCO Convention, in the case of all other cultural property, state parties have no obligation to impose import restrictions. It only means that they may set higher requirements for introducing such restrictions. In the case of other cultural objects they are permitted, for example, to make the introduction of an import restriction conditional[225] to a prior special designation in accordance with Article 1.[226]

Secondly, according to Article 31 (1) of the Vienna Convention on the Law of the Treaties, a treaty shall be interpreted in good faith in accordance with the ordinary meaning to be given to the terms of the treaty in their context and in the light of its object and purpose. An interpretation denying export certificates any effect at all on matters of import clearly interferes with the convention's objective to prevent and annul illicit transfers. Thus, such an interpretation restricting the application of Article 6 of the 1970 UNESCO Convention cannot be considered to be done in good faith and is, therefore, not to be favoured in the light of Article 31 (1) of the Vienna Convention on the Law of the Treaties.[227]

Hence, Article 6 of the 1970 UNESCO Convention must be understood to have some consequences for import matters. Therefore, this provision has to be viewed as obliging a state party to introduce an import prohibition equivalent to the export prohibition of another state party.[228] However, considering the fact that each state party is free to decide which cultural property is required to have an export

---

[222] von Schorlemer (1992), p. 433; cf. also Stamatoudi (2011), p. 45 which implies this argumentation.

[223] Raschèr (2000), p. 58; Kurpiers (2005), p. 156 requires that the collection is meant for and accessible by the general public.

[224] This is why other authors relate Article 6 closely to Article 3 of the Convention. Cf., for example, Weidner (2001), p. 235.

[225] Odendahl (2005), p. 134 argues that state parties are obliged to acknowledge the export restrictions per se.

[226] Hönes (2010), p. 92.

[227] Stamatoudi (2011), p. 46 also reasons that Article 31 (1) of the Vienna Convention on the Law of Treaties requires such an interpretation.

[228] With the same interpretation Stamatoudi (2011), p. 46; Xi (2012), p. 858 does not seem to make any distinction between the different kinds of cultural material.

certificate and which cultural objects may be exported without such a certificate, committing other state parties which are not aware of the national legislation of the respective state party to investigate all cultural material without a certificate and, where necessary, deny entry, seems a relatively high administrative burden to the importing party. Therefore, state parties establishing an export certificate system must be required to inform other state parties about cultural property that is required to have such an export certificate. Only in the case of such a prior notification are state parties then obliged to check according to the provided list if the cultural property in question is required to have an export certificate and when necessary deny entry.[229]

Another clause which has to be mentioned in this regard is Article 8. It is one of the two provisions of the convention referring to punishment.[230] However, it does not provide a general system of punishment hence imposing an obligation on state parties to sanction private parties for every possible violation of convention regulations that state parties have to adopt. It does not even require state parties to establish a system for all violations in the context of export certificates.

State parties are only obligated to impose penalties or administrative sanctions on any person responsible for infringing the prohibitions referred to under Articles 6 (b) and 7 (b). Thus, state parties have solely to impose some sort of punishment for exporting cultural property from their territory unless accompanied by an above-mentioned export certificate (Article 6 (b)) and for importing cultural property stolen from a museum or a religious or secular public monument or similar institution in another state party after the entry into force of the treaty for the states concerned, provided that such property is documented as appertaining to the inventory of that institution (Article 7 (b) (i)). They also have to do so in any case where someone interferes with the appropriate steps to recover and return any such cultural property imported after the entry into force of the convention in both states concerned or at another point mentioned in Article 7 (b) (ii).

While most countries already have specific provisions imposing punishment in the case of the illicit export of their own cultural heritage, the same cannot be said for the illicit import of cultural property of other states.[231] However, Article 8 does

[229]China and the USA, for example, adopted a Memorandum of Understanding (MOU) under Article 9 of the 1970 UNESCO Convention in January 2009. The MOU aims at establishing means of cooperation to reduce the incentives for archaeological pillage and illicit trafficking in cultural objects that threaten China's ancient heritage by imposing restrictions on the importation of certain categories of archaeological materials from China, namely all undocumented artefacts from the Palaeolithic Era through the end of the Tang Dynasty as well as elements of monumental sculpture and other wall art that are at least 250 years old. The agreement provides a detailed list of categories of archaeological materials which may enter the US only if they are accompanied by an export permit issued by the appropriate authority in the Government of China. China, on the other hand, agreed to promote long-term loans of archaeological objects to museums. See http://www.state.gov/documents/organization/122226.pdf; for further MOUs between governments and museums see Lyons (2014), pp. 251–265.

[230]The other one is the second part of Article 10 (a) of the Convention.

[231]The USA, for example, has no law specifically for import, but rather one for the receipt and transportation of illegally transferred cultural material. O'Keefe (2007), p. 67.

not oblige state parties to introduce new, specific legislation on the topic, if the existing regulations are adequate to cover the issue.[232] Thus, it is sufficient for a state party to meet its obligation under this provision, if, for example, it already has a law which was originally adopted for another purpose, but which can also be applied to the illicit import of cultural property.

The provision also does not specify the punishment state parties have to impose. Thus, they may impose administrative sanctions such as fines, or penalties such as imprisonment. Hence, state parties are free to choose between a wide range of possibilities as long as they establish an effective system.[233]

2.2.6.3 Acquisition Restrictions for Cultural Institutions

Addressees to the 1970 UNESCO Convention are, as previously mentioned, solely state parties. Only they are bound by the obligations constituted by the treaty.[234] Since state parties have, however, understood that cultural institutions such as museums play a crucial role in the fight against the illicit trafficking of cultural property,[235] they have stipulated various means to involve these institutions in this endeavour.[236] One way state parties have chosen in this context is Article 7 (a),[237] according to which state parties must take the necessary measures to prevent museums and similar institutions within their territories from acquiring cultural property illegally exported from another state. Furthermore, they are obliged, whenever possible, to inform a state of origin of an offer of such cultural property.

---

[232]Stamatoudi (2011), p. 54.

[233]The original draft, however, only spoke of penalties, which is why von Schorlemer (1992), p. 433 deems the version of the final treaty as weakened.

[234]On the addressees of the 1970 UNESCO Convention cf. pp. 21; however, also see the exception to this rule provided in Chapter 2, n 117.

[235]Cf. Raschèr (2000), p. 57.

[236]Cf., for instance, Article 5 (e) of the 1970 UNESCSO Convention: "To ensure the protection of their cultural property against illicit import, export and transfer of ownership, the States Parties to this Convention undertake, as appropriate for each country, to set up within their territories one or more national services, where such services do not already exist, for the protection of the cultural heritage, with a qualified staff sufficient in number for the effective carrying out of the following functions: (e) establishing, for the benefit of those concerned (curators, collectors, antique dealers, etc.) rules in conformity with the ethical principles set forth in this Convention; and taking steps to ensure the observance of those rules".

[237]Article 7 (a) of the 1970 UNESCO Convention: "The States Parties to this Convention undertake: (a) To take the necessary measures, consistent with national legislation, to prevent museums and similar institutions within their territories from acquiring cultural property originating in another State Party which has been illegally exported after entry into force of this Convention, in the States concerned. Whenever possible, to inform a State of origin Party to this Convention of an offer of such cultural property illegally removed from that State after the entry into force of this Convention in both States;".

Though the obligation is not restricted to cultural property stolen from a museum or a religious or secular public monument or similar institution, as in case of Article 7 (b),[238] it still faces important restrictions. Firstly, Article 7 (a) speaks of cultural property originating in another state party and of informing a state party of origin. Thus, both states have to be party to the convention for the obligation to be effective. The provision constitutes no obligation of a state party towards a non-party.

Additionally, in compliance with the convention's general approach to retroactivity,[239] the obligation only covers cultural objects transferred after its entry into force in the states concerned. Hence, the provision does not impose any obligation on state parties concerning cultural property illegally transferred before the entry into force of the convention or cultural artefacts illicitly transferred after entry into force only in one of the involved state parties.[240]

However, the greatest controversy arises in the context of the clause which states "consistent with national legislation". This phrase, incorporated due to a request from the USA,[241] has to be comprehended as a compromise between a weak amendment not requiring state members to impose any legal obligation on museums but rather to win their support, and a strong amendment requiring state parties to make cultural institutions subject to a legally binding acquisition prohibition regarding cultural objects illicitly transferred.[242]

However, also based on the US declaration that this phrase would be interpreted as limiting the effect of the provision to museums whose acquisition policy is controlled by the government,[243] some authors read the provision as not imposing any legal obligation to introduce national laws beyond those already existing.[244] Interestingly, both limiting the obligation to museums whose acquisition policy is controlled by the government and interpreting the article as introducing no further-reaching legal obligations seems questionable.

First of all, the wording of the provision does not limit the obligation to certain cultural institutions, but covers all cultural institutions within a state's territories. Furthermore, making only certain cultural institutions subject to this prohibition and not others would arbitrarily discriminate between different museums which differ only slightly in terms of levels of governmental control and put public cultural institutions in an inferior position.[245]

---

[238]Steinbrück (2012), p. 72.

[239]On the issue of retroactivity in context of the 1970 UNESCO Convention cf. pp. 22f.

[240]Stamatoudi (2011), p. 47.

[241]Weidner (2001), p. 237.

[242]Nafziger (1975), pp. 388–389.

[243]O'Keefe (2007), p. 56; cf. also Streinz (1998), p. 86.

[244]Bator (1982), p. 380.

[245]This idea is also reflected in O'Keefe (2007), p. 51 in context of the commentary on Article 5 (e) of the 1970 UNESCO Convention.

With regard to the question of whether the provision imposes an obligation to introduce new, far-reaching obligations on state parties or not, it has to be considered that a contrary interpretation of the provision would contradict the spirit of the convention and thus is to be discarded, especially in light of the interpretive rule that an interpretation allowing for a larger scope is to be preferred.[246]

Pursuant to this, when one considers that new treaties are primarily adopted to accept new obligations and not simply to reaffirm old ones, the term "consistent with national legislation" cannot be interpreted as not requiring state parties to adopt new obligations into their national laws.[247] This phrase has to be read as taking the difference in the state parties' legal systems into consideration. State parties do not have to adopt a particular prescribed measure which might contradict their existing general legal system, but rather they are free in their choice of measures.[248] This allows the introduction of measures which perfectly integrate into their legal system and harmonise with other laws.

One possible measure, for example, is to make the compliance with certain codes of ethics[249] a precondition for funding or tax relief for cultural institutions acquiring cultural material rather than issuing acts and statutes.[250] This path of offering rewards rather than penalties can also prove to be a more effective way of influencing the acquisition policy of cultural institutions not controlled by the government.

2.2.6.4 International Cooperation and UNESCO's Role

A fundamental principle of international law is the concept of cooperation which is also strongly reflected in the 1970 UNESCO Convention.[251] In Particular, Articles 9, 15, and 17 address the issue of international cooperation.

While Articles 9 and 15, however, are concerned with cooperation between state parties to the convention, Article 17 addresses the involvement of UNESCO in this context.[252] The difference between Articles 9 and 15, on the other hand, lies in the differing framework of the cooperation. Article 9 is concerned with cooperation within the framework of the 1970 UNESCO Convention, whereas Article

[246] Stamatoudi (2011), pp. 47f with similar arguments.

[247] Stamatoudi (2011), p. 48.

[248] Stamatoudi (2011), p. 48 argues that no particular method of fulfilment is required, but rather an effective result.

[249] The ICOM Code of Ethics for Museums adopted by the 15th General Assembly of ICOM on 4 November 1986 is perhaps the most important such soft law instrument in this context. Cf. also Raschèr (2000), p. 57.

[250] Nafziger (1975), pp. 391–392.

[251] Stamatoudi (2011), p. 54.

[252] Stamatoudi (2011), p. 54.

15 addresses the cooperation beyond or outside the 1970 UNESCO Convention and the relation of such treaties with the 1970 UNESCO Convention.

According to Article 9 (1), any state party whose cultural patrimony is in jeopardy from pillage of archaeological or ethnological materials may call upon other state parties who are affected. In this context, several points are in need of clarification. While it is unambiguous that only states which are party to the treaty may invoke the provision, the term cultural patrimony is used for the first[253] and only time in the convention and thus is in need of interpretation and clarification. Considering that Article 9 itself again speaks later of cultural heritage[254] and that the versions of the treaty in the other authentic languages[255] use the corresponding words for cultural property and heritage,[256] which are generally and repeatedly used in the convention, it has to be assumed that no general change in meaning was intended[257] and that the wording is simply a product of an oversight in the drafting process.[258] However, one detail could indicate that it has a slightly different meaning than heritage. While in English the word heritage conveys a more general idea of tradition and other non-material aspects of culture, the term patrimony is connected more closely to the notion of a material inheritance.[259] This idea of materiality would also fit to the fact that Article 9 only covers archaeological or ethnological materials, but no other forms of heritage.[260]

For the provision to be applicable, furthermore, the cultural patrimony of the invoking state party has to be in jeopardy from pillage.[261] The provision itself does not define the term jeopardy. Though some authors understand the article as an emergency provision for crisis situations and thus interpret jeopardy as requiring a severe state of emergency,[262] a dictionary definition of jeopardy provides no such

[253]O'Keefe (2007), p. 69.

[254]Sentence 3 of Article 9 of the Convention: "Pending agreement each State concerned shall take provisional measures to the extent feasible to prevent irremediable injury to the cultural heritage of the requesting State.".

[255]According to Article 18 of the Convention, authentic languages are English, French, Russian, and Spanish.

[256]O'Keefe (2007), p. 69.

[257]Stamatoudi (2011), pp. 54f.

[258]Bator (1982), p. 379 claims that the provision is "a direct descendant of the 'crisis' provision contained in the United States alternative draft".

[259]O'Keefe (2007), p. 69.

[260]The USA attempted to restrict those even further. O'Keefe (2007), p. 69.

[261]Kaplan (1986), p. 146 implies that the provision's purpose is "the deterrence of a situation of pillage threatening the cultural heritage, not just of a single State, but of all mankind". Even though national heritages form part of the common heritage of mankind and thus, a threat to the heritage of a single nation is at least a partial threat to the common heritage of mankind, such an interpretation is not supported by the wording of the provision. The provision explicitly refers to state parties "whose cultural patrimony is in jeopardy". See also O'Keefe (2007), p. 69.

[262]Williams (1978), p. 186; Gordon (1971), p. 552; Abramson and Huttler (1973), p. 962.

indication.[263] Instead, taking into consideration the fact that the original proposal reads "critical jeopardy" and the term "critical" was voted out,[264] "jeopardy" has to be understood simply as danger and does not require an increased degree of emergency.[265]

The term "pillage" as well has not to be interpreted in a narrow sense, but as containing any form of misappropriation, in particular, the abstraction of cultural property of high value and the repeated theft of archaeological or ethnological materials. Hence, it has to be assumed that cultural patrimony is in jeopardy from pillage especially where the remains of a particular civilisation are threatened with destruction or extensive movement abroad or when the state of certain archaeological objects on the international market triggers a significant campaign of clandestine excavations leading to the destruction of important archaeological sites.[266]

Yet another point of contention arises in connection with the phrase "may call upon". Some state parties require in this regard bilateral agreements as a basis for further actions.[267] It is difficult to find any basis for this interpretation in the wording of Article 9 of the Convention.[268] In fact, coordination between the requesting state and the state called upon are favourable,[269] but this does not hinder state parties to take other actions, even unilateral ones, to improve the situation once having been called upon.[270]

The last point in this context is that states have to call upon state parties who are affected. Even though the provision itself does not supply any definition, this phrase has to refer to state parties capable of improving the situation, thus primarily market states,[271] but also to state parties known for their cultural property black markets or for being transit states for such material.

---

[263] Stamatoudi (2011), p. 55; cf. also Gerstenblith (2012), p. 650.

[264] DuBoff et al. (1976), pp. 124f.

[265] So also Raschèr (2000), p. 59 and O'Keefe (2007), p. 71.

[266] Fraoua (1986), p. 80.

[267] Switzerland and the USA are two such countries. DuBoff et al. (1976), p. 105; Schönenberger (2009), pp. 86ff; Kouroupas (2010), p. 156 for the specific requirements set up by the USA. See also Lanciotti (2012), p. 318; see also Prott (2011a), p. 455 for a number of countries having no such requirement; see Gerstenblith (2011), p. 396 for an overview of countries with which Switzerland and the USA have concluded bilateral agreements.

[268] Similar Stamatoudi (2011), p. 56.

[269] The MOU signed under Article 9 of the 1970 UNESCO Convention between China and the United States in January 2009 is a good example of what such cooperation may look like and what source nations can achieve with bilateral agreements. For further information on the MOU see Chapter 2, n 229; cf. also for further MOUs entered into by the USA Nafziger et al. (2014), pp. 379ff.

[270] Australia and Canada are two quite progressive states in this regard. Canada imposed controls on cultural materials that have been illegally exported from other states party to an international agreement relating to the prevention of illicit international traffic in cultural heritage. Australia does not even require the other state to be a party to an international convention. O'Keefe (2007), p. 72.

[271] Stamatoudi (2011), p. 55.

Once the requirements mentioned in the first sentence of Article 9 are met and the state party invokes the provision, the state parties involved ought to participate in a concerted international effort to determine a course of action and carry out the necessary concrete measures, including the control of exports and imports and international commerce in the specific materials concerned.

In this context it is important to see that participating in a "concerted international effort" requires on the one hand state parties to work together and act jointly, but, on the other, only obliges them to a genuine effort of contribution, not to a certain result. Another notable aspect here is that the "concerted international effort" is not limited to states that are party to the convention. Convincing market and/or transit states which are not party to the convention to contribute to the cause can also be subsumed under a "concerted international effort".[272] However, the concerted international effort has to aim at determining and carrying out the necessary concrete measures to improve the situation. The provision itself provides with the control of exports and imports and the international commerce in specific materials for a non-exclusive exemplary list of measures which could be taken in this regard.[273] Although state parties are free in their choice of measures and can, instead of enacting "hard" laws or relying on already existing ones, rely on "soft" activities such as educational measures[274] and public campaigns[275] to increase the awareness of the threat trade in cultural property without provenance can pose for the cultural heritage of the invoking state,[276] either way the measures taken have to be effective.

With this in mind, the joint determination and implementation of adequate measures often takes some time in which the cultural heritage of the state invoking Article 9 might be lost for good. Therefore, Article 9 stipulates that pending agreement each state concerned shall take provisional measures to the extent feasible to prevent irremediable injury to the cultural heritage of the requesting state. The article thus encourages state parties, both the one requesting and those called upon to take unilateral measures,[277] but with two important constraints. First, unilateral measures are only to be taken pending agreement. If after an agreement is reached it becomes apparent that the provisional measures are somehow interfering with the agreement or are in open contradiction to it, they have to be repealed. However, the provisional measures may also be incorporated into the final agreement or support it, in which case they can be maintained.

The second constraint refers to their extent. Unilateral provisional measures are only permissible to the extent feasible to prevent irremediable injury to the cultural

[272] O'Keefe (2007), p. 72.

[273] Stamatoudi (2011), p. 55.

[274] O'Keefe (2007), pp. 72f.

[275] Stamatoudi (2011), p. 56.

[276] Stamatoudi (2011), p. 56.

[277] Sentence 3 of Article 9 of the Convention reads "each State concerned" in contrast to sentence 2 which speaks of a "concerted international effort".

heritage of the requesting state. An irremediable injury has to be assumed in cases in which the reversal of the injury is either impossible as such, from an administrative or financial point of view excessive or the excavation site itself is destroyed. This is, for example, the case when due to extensive clandestine excavations the provenance of certain cultural objects, and thus their significance for the cultural identity of the requesting state, which relies, inter alia, on the contextual information such as the place of origin of an artefact,[278] is lost or when cultural objects from an excavation site are appearing on (black) markets all over the world.

In addition to Article 9, the treaty also contains a second provision addressing in particular the issue of international cooperation: Article 15. While Article 9 is concerned with cooperation within the framework of the 1970 UNESCO Convention, Article 15 by contrast addresses the cooperation beyond the convention and the relation of such external agreements with the 1970 UNESCO Convention.

According to Article 15, nothing in the convention shall prevent state parties from concluding special agreements among themselves or from continuing to implement agreements already concluded regarding the restitution of cultural property removed, whatever the reason, from its territory of origin, before the entry into force of the convention for the states concerned. This provision, on the one hand, clarifies that the 1970 UNESCO Convention does not affect international treaties already existing when the former came into force.[279] Furthermore, it emphasises that state parties may continue to conclude new such agreements regarding the restitution of cultural property.[280] It also provides reasons as to why state parties may be eager to do so by referring to two points which are commonly seen as weaknesses of the 1970 UNESCO Convention. State parties are free to adopt agreements regarding the restitution of cultural property removed, whatever the reason, from its territory of origin, before the entry into force of the treaty. Hence, state parties might conclude bilateral or regional treaties with a retroactive effective to overcome the temporal limitation of the 1970 UNESCO Convention.[281] However, they could also adopt agreements to extend the scope of the legal basis to reclaim cultural property provided for in Article 7 (b) (ii), which is restricted to cultural property stolen from a museum or a religious or secular public monument or similar institution, to other cases and categories of objects, such as cultural property stolen from private parties.

Nevertheless, it has to be understood that these special agreements do not discharge state parties from their obligations under the 1970 UNESCO Convention. The special agreements act as a supplement to the convention, not a substitute for it.[282]

[278]Schaffrath (2007), p. 30.

[279]O'Keefe (2007), p. 89.

[280]Stamatoudi (2011), p. 56.

[281]On the issue of retroactivity in the context of the 1970 UNESCO Convention cf. pp. 22f.

[282]O'Keefe (2007), p. 89; Stamatoudi (2011), p. 56.

The third clause of the 1970 UNESCO Convention dealing with international cooperation is Article 17. While Articles 9 and 15 are concerned with cooperation between state parties, Article 17 addresses the involvement of UNESCO in this context. The provision contains three types of regulations. First, it clarifies that state parties may call on the technical assistance of UNESCO. Secondly, it states that UNESCO may undertake certain measures on its own initiative. And lastly, it includes a sort of alternative dispute settlement mechanism.

According to Article 17 (1), state parties may call on the technical assistance of UNESCO, particularly as regards information and education, consultation and expert advice, as well as coordination and good offices. It is important to note that the measures referred to are only of an exemplary character.[283] State parties may utilise UNESCO's technical assistance also in regard to other measures.

UNESCO likewise has freedom to act and may on its own initiative conduct research and publish studies on matters relevant to the illicit movement of cultural property (Article 17 (2)) and, to this end, call on the cooperation of any competent non-governmental organisation (Article 17 (3)). Furthermore, according to Article 17 (4) it may, on its own initiative, make proposals to state parties for its implementation.

Exercising this initiative right and as form of technical assistance to state parties, UNESCO has undertaken several activities including publishing national laws on cultural heritage[284] and establishing an electronic database of these legislations.[285] Additionally, UNESCO has published a study on the workings of national controls,[286] a Handbook of National Regulations Concerning the Export of Cultural Property,[287] a commentary on the 1970 UNESCO Convention,[288] a resource handbook for the implementation of the 1970 UNESCO Convention,[289] a study of the trade in antiquities[290] and educational material.[291]

Besides these publications, UNESCO has additionally provided expertise to support state parties in the drafting of national legislation[292] and conducted workshops in cooperation with INTERPOL and ICOM on fighting illicit trafficking.[293] Furthermore, UNESCO has established the Intergovernmental Committee for Promoting the Return of Cultural Property to Its Countries of Origin or Its Restitution

[283]The exemplary character is owed to the phrase "particularly as regards" used in the provision.

[284]Cf. the "red leaflet" series: UNESCO Docs CLT-85/WS.

[285]http://www.unesco.org/culture/natlaws/.

[286]Prott and O'Keefe (1983).

[287]Prott and O'Keefe (1988).

[288]Fraoua (1986), p. 53.

[289]Askerud and Clément (1997).

[290]O'Keefe (1997).

[291]Stamatoudi (2011), p. 57.

[292]O'Keefe (2007), p. 92.

[293]Stamatoudi (2011), p. 57.

in Case of Illicit Appropriation (ICPRCP), which itself has proven to be a valuable asset in providing assistance to state parties.[294]

Last but not least, Article 17 (5) stipulates that at the request of at least two state parties which are engaged in a dispute over its implementation, UNESCO may extend its good offices to reach a settlement between them. Thus, state parties may call upon UNESCO to settle their dispute regarding the implementation of the 1970 UNESCO Convention. Whilst this seems appropriate, since UNESCO has the required expertise for this task,[295] the organisation should not be mistaken for a court. The clause clearly refers to the good offices mentioned and thus to technical assistance. Hence, UNESCO's role corresponds more to that of a mediator than a judge.

The intention of the drafters not to assign UNESCO the decisive role of a court can also be deduced from a systematic approach to the provision.[296] In most agreements with clear rules on dispute settlement, these are generally arranged in a separate article of the treaty.[297] Unlike in such conventions, this regulation was not afforded its own article, but it was incorporated only as the fifth paragraph of Article 17.[298]

Nevertheless, state parties are of course free to bring their dispute to court if they decide to do so. They may, for example, submit it to the International Court of Justice (ICJ),[299] if both parties accept its jurisdiction or are subject to it due to already existing prior consent.[300] Another way to involve the ICJ would be for UNESCO, as a specialised agency of the United Nations, to ask for its advisory opinion.[301]

2.2.6.5 Educational Measures

Since state parties have understood that in the fight against the illicit trafficking of cultural property they rely on the cooperation of people involved in various steps of

---

[294] On the ICPRCP cf. pp. 127ff.

[295] Stamatoudi (2011), p. 60.

[296] Similar O'Keefe (2007), p. 93.

[297] Within the World Trade Organization system there is even a highly detailed separate agreement regarding the dispute settlement. Cf. https://www.wto.org/english/res_e/booksp_e/analytic_index_e/dsu_01_e.htm.

[298] According to O'Keefe (2007), p. 93 this might reflect a hostility of the states of Marxist ideology concerning the International Court of Justice at the time of drafting.

[299] The International Court of Justice has so far ruled only once on a dispute involving cultural heritage (Cambodia v. Thailand), I.C.J. Reports 1962, pp. 6ff.

[300] Stamatoudi (2011), p. 61.

[301] Article V (12) of the UNESCO Constitution: "Between sessions of the General Conference, the Executive Board may request advisory opinions from the International Court of Justice on legal questions arising within the field of the Organization's activities.".

the international trading chain, but also on the general public,[302] Article 10 of the Convention was formulated. This provision aims to increase the awareness of the threat illicit trafficking poses to cultural heritage and thus fight illicit trafficking by educational measures. Hence, according to the first part of Article 10 (a), state parties undertake to restrict by education, information, and vigilance, movement of cultural property illegally removed from any state party.

Two points in this context are worth noting. First, the aim of the norm is not limited to the restriction of the movement of cultural property removed from the state party undertaking the educational measures, but as in the case of Article 5 (f), is directed at the restriction of the movement of cultural property removed from any state party. Secondly, the obligation is not restricted by a phrase such as "appropriate for each country". The latter may result from the fact that the obligation per se leaves a high level of discretion to state parties with regard to the measures undertaken. They may, for example, encourage journalists and relevant experts to circulate information about particular cultural property which has been stolen and/or illicitly traded.[303] They may also use films, conduct courses in cultural institutions,[304] and/or provide informational material to make customs officials and the public and in particular tourists visiting the countries of origin of these stolen cultural properties, aware of the dangers of souveniring cultural artefacts.[305] In general, state parties are free to adopt any measure, in particular those proposed by cultural experts,[306] as long as these are contributing to the goals of the provision. Even though the provision gives state parties virtually a free hand in determining the measures, the clause nevertheless imposes a clear obligation on states to undertake effective measures.[307]

Article 10 (b) even stipulates a broader obligation on state parties not limited to the restriction of the movement of cultural property illegally removed from any state party. State parties ought to endeavour by educational means to create and develop in the public mind a realisation of the value of cultural property and the threat to cultural heritage created by theft, clandestine excavations, and illicit exports.

Again, state parties are free to determine the measures.[308] They may rely on the same measures already mentioned above, in particular those proposed by cultural experts.[309] The measures only have to be adapted for the purpose of developing a

[302] Cf. also Stamatoudi (2011), p. 61.

[303] O'Keefe (2007), pp. 74f.

[304] Fraoua (1986), p. 83.

[305] O'Keefe (2007), p. 75.

[306] O'Keefe (2007), p. 75.

[307] The same view is also advocated by O'Keefe (2007), p. 77 and Stamatoudi (2011), p. 61. Bator (1982), p. 378, however, sees the obligation as an "unenforceable undertaking".

[308] Stamatoudi (2011), p. 61.

[309] See O'Keefe (2007), p. 77 for an exemplary list of measures.

general understanding in the public arena of the value of cultural property and the threat to it posed by the illegal activities mentioned.[310]

Institutions well-suited to determine the measures in the context of Article 10, as well as implement and supervise their operation, are the national services mentioned in Article 5, since they are already charged with the task of taking educational measures to stimulate and develop respect for the cultural heritage of all states.[311]

2.2.6.6 Register Requirement for Antique Dealers

Article 10 (a) (2nd Part) is the second provision of the treaty referring to sanctions. Unlike Article 8, however, it does not impose sanctions for the infringement of prohibitions referred to in other norms, but for the violation of an obligation constituted by the provision itself.

According to Article 10 (a) (2nd Part), state parties have to impose a quite detailed regulation on dealers to fight illicit trafficking.[312] Dealers not only have to maintain a register, but it has to include the origin of each item as well as the names and addresses of its supplier as well as a description and price of each item sold. Furthermore, dealers have to inform any purchaser of the cultural property of the export prohibition to which such property may be subject.[313] However, this obligation of state parties is limited in two aspects. First, they are only obligated "as appropriate for each country", which has to be understood as taking the different legal systems of state parties and their varying needs and conditions into consideration.[314] Thus, this phrase is not to be comprehended as imposing no binding obligation at all on state parties,[315] but as allowing them to implement the obligation in a manner consistent with their national legal system. With reference to the sanctions, this permits state parties also to determine and introduce the penal and/or administrative sanctions they are required to implement in compliance with their national legal system.[316]

The second aspect, however, seems to constitute a larger obstacle for the effectiveness of the provision. According to the wording of the provision, state

[310] Cf. O'Keefe (2007), p. 77.

[311] Cf. p. 49 on the obligation to introduce educational measures imposed by Article 5 (f) of the Convention.

[312] Raschèr (2000), p. 60.

[313] Article 10 (a) (2nd Part) of the Convention: "The States Parties to this Convention undertake: [...], as appropriate for each country, oblige antique dealers, subject to penal or administrative sanctions, to maintain a register recording the origin of each item of cultural property, names and addresses of the supplier, description and price of each item sold and to inform the purchaser of the cultural property of the export prohibition to which such property may be subject;".

[314] O'Keefe (2007), p. 76.

[315] von Schorlemer (1992), p. 434.

[316] Cf. Stamatoudi (2011), p. 62.

parties are only committed to oblige "antique dealers" to the register requirement. The term "antiques" only includes objects of the nearer past, starting certainly from the Middle Ages. Objects of previous periods are referred to as "antiquities".[317] Allowing for the fact that not all languages may possess this linguistic difference,[318] the use of this particular wording has not to be understood in a strict technical way. Hence, state parties are obligated to require all dealers of cultural property to keep a detailed and up to date register. The terminology is simply unfortunate.[319]

2.2.6.7 Transfer of Ownership

Article 13 (a) requires state parties to prevent by all appropriate means transfers of ownership of cultural property likely to promote the illicit import or export of such property. Thus, state parties are committed to enact or at least revise regulations in order to prevent those transfers of ownership which will likely facilitate the illicit import or export of cultural property.[320] However, this obligation is softened by three factors.

First of all, the obligation is limited by the words "consistent with the laws of each state". This does not automatically mean that the obligation has no legally binding effects at all. Rather, it has to be understood again as respecting the different legal systems and laws of state parties. Thus, state parties are not required to introduce any regulation inconsistent or even contrary to their existent legal regime.[321]

The obligation is furthermore tempered by the phrase "appropriate means". Thus, even if a measure may in principle be compliant with the legal order of a state party, it is nevertheless not obliged to impose it if it is deemed as inappropriate. This could well be the case when the measure requires what the state party considers as too much effort or financial burden compared to its benefit. By way of example here, requiring private parties dealing in artefacts to inform the authorities of each transaction, even involving artefacts of negligible value, may be considered as inappropriate.[322]

However, the factor softening the obligation to the greatest degree is the lack of a list of respective measures. Thus, state parties have in principle complete discretion

---

[317] O'Keefe (2007), p. 75.

[318] Cf. O'Keefe (2007), p. 75.

[319] However, many dealers are still quite reluctant when it comes to keeping registers bringing forth various arguments, such as confidentiality, data protection, and security from theft. Cf. Stamatoudi (2011), p. 62.

[320] O'Keefe (2007), p. 82.

[321] Similar O'Keefe (2007), p. 82 and Stamatoudi (2011), pp. 51f; Bator (1982), p. 378, however, interprets the wording as requiring no further action from states beyond what is already provided for in their laws.

[322] O'Keefe (2007), p. 83 e contrario.

with regard to the measures[323] as long as they are contributing to the aim of the provision to prevent the transfer of ownership of cultural property likely to promote the illicit import or export of such property.[324] Hence, they may ban the export of such material entirely or prohibit all trade in antiquities or of those of a certain period.[325] But, they may also just regulate the transfer and collection of certain classes of cultural property, for instance, those above a certain value, by requiring dealers to inform the authorities of the transfer of such objects.[326] However, despite the leeway granted in fulfilling the obligation regarding the measures, state parties are nonetheless legally bound to make an honest effort.[327]

2.2.6.8 Reporting Mechanism

Reporting mechanisms are nowadays a frequently encountered and well established instrument in the context of international organisations and treaty systems.[328] Article 16 introduces this system to the 1970 UNESCO Convention regime. According to this norm, state parties shall in their periodic reports submit to the General Conference of UNESCO, on dates and in a manner to be determined by it, information on the legislative and administrative provisions which they have adopted and other action which they have taken for the application of the convention, together with details of the experience acquired in this field. Thus, state parties are committed to include information on their progress in implementing the 1970 Convention in their periodic reports to UNESCO.

Unlike in the case of more recent UNESCO treaties, however, the provision does not itself provide for the establishment of an intergovernmental committee to oversee the operation of the reporting, which permits more immediate contact with state parties and thus more intimate knowledge but is in return more cost and effort intensive.[329] Nevertheless, while initially the ICPRCP primarily assumed this function,[330] the Meeting of State Parties to the 1970 UNESCO Convention has set up a subsidiary committee which, inter alia, now deals with this issue.[331]

[323]Weidner (2001), p. 241.

[324]Stamatoudi (2011), p. 52.

[325]O'Keefe (2007), p. 83.

[326]Stamatoudi (2011), p. 52.

[327]O'Keefe (2007), p. 82.

[328]An important example of such a reporting and monitoring system is the Universal Periodic Review undertaken by the United Nations Human Rights Council in accordance with UNGA Res 60/251, 15.03.2006, Article 5 (e).

[329]O'Keefe (2007), p. 91.

[330]O'Keefe (2007), p. 91.

[331]On the subsidiary committee cf. pp. 62ff.

Starting with Resolution 4.122 of the 19th session of the General Conference of UNESCO, reports have been requested from state parties.[332] Despite the fact that not all state parties submit reports and the reports are often of such quality that they do not contribute significantly to the knowledge concerning the effectiveness of the implementation of the treaty, UNESCO has published them—most recently in 2015.[333]

2.2.7 *The Institutional Framework of the 1970 UNESCO Convention: The Meeting of State Parties*

2.2.7.1 The Need for a Monitoring Body as the Key Factor Triggering the Institutionalisation

Since the 1970 UNESCO Convention itself does not provide for a clause establishing a periodic monitoring body, monitoring has been conducted by three different bodies: The Committee on Conventions and Recommendations of the UNESCO Executive Board, the Meeting of State Parties to the 1970 UNESCO Convention, which first took place in 2003 on the basis of a specific decision of the UNESCO Executive Board a year earlier,[334] and UNESCO's ICPRCP. The latter has become the main de facto monitoring body of the agreement.[335] Monitoring the implementation of the convention is of importance, since despite the increase in the number of states ratifying the convention its implementation into national legislation remains problematic; even source countries have failed to implement its norms,[336,337] impairing the effectiveness of the agreement's regulations in practice.

The 2nd Meeting of State Parties to the 1970 UNESCO Convention followed in 2012. In addition to a report of the secretariat on its activities and on the implementation of the 1970 UNESCO Convention by state parties,[338] the meeting

[332]http://unesdoc.unesco.org/images/0011/001140/114038e.pdf.

[333]The latest reports are available online: http://www.unesco.org/new/en/culture/themes/illicit-trafficking-of-cultural-property/1970-convention/periodic-reporting/. They are generally also incorporated into and evaluated in numerous documents. Annex to Part III of UNESCO Doc 187 EX/20, 19.09.2011, for instances, comprises a summary of the implementary measures. Until 2003, however, UNESCO published the reports itself. Cf. for example UNESCO GC 32 C/Resolution 38, 16.10.2003.

[334]http://www.unesco.org/new/en/culture/themes/illicit-trafficking-of-cultural-property/meeting-of-states-parties/.

[335]Shyllon (2012), p. 586.

[336]Cf. Shyllon (2014), p. 38.

[337]On the different methods of implementation undertaken by market states see Gerstenblith (2013), pp. 11–20.

[338]UNESCO Doc C70/12/2.MSP/5, 20.06.2012.

adopted its own rules of procedure.[339] Furthermore, different proposals for monitoring the implementation of the 1970 UNESCO Convention were discussed. The three possible legal modalities to advance the implementation of the 1970 UNESCO Convention discussed during the meeting were a revision of the convention, the creation of an additional instrument, and the creation of a monitoring body.[340] Finally, state parties reached agreement to establish a monitoring body in the form of a subsidiary committee to be elected at an extraordinary Meeting of State Parties to the 1970 UNESCO Convention convened in 2013.[341] The subsidiary committee subsequently had its 1st session later in 2013.[342]

In May 2015, at its 3rd session, the Meeting of State Parties to the 1970 UNESCO encouraged state parties—in the light of current events, such as the Syrian Civil War—to increase their efforts with regard to actions concerning the illicit trafficking of cultural property in the emergency situations of armed conflict or natural disaster[343] and invited the Director-General to establish a fund to support the implementation of the 1970 UNESCO Convention.[344]

2.2.7.2 The Leadership: The Meeting of State Parties

The Meeting of State Parties to the 1970 UNESCO Convention is regularly convened every two years[345] with, in general, public sessions.[346] Besides the states parties to the 1970 UNESCO Convention, a number of other entities[347] may send representatives to the meeting with other UNESCO member states leading the way. However, the latter do not have a voting right but solely observer status.[348]

---

339 http://www.unesco.org/new/en/culture/themes/illicit-trafficking-of-cultural-property/meeting-of-states-parties/.

340 UNESCO Doc C70/12/2.MSP/6, 20.06.2012.

341 UNESCO Doc C70/13/Extra.MSP/Resolutions, 01.07.2013.

342 http://www.unesco.org/new/en/culture/themes/illicit-trafficking-of-cultural-property/subsidiary-committee/1st-sc-session-2013/.

343 UNESCO Doc C70/15/3.MSP/Resolutions, May 2015, pp. 5f; cf. also for an overview of UNESCO safeguarding measures concerning Mali Manhart (2016), pp. 289f.

344 UNESCO Doc C70/15/3.MSP/Resolutions, May 2015, p. 6.

345 Article 14.1 of the Rules of Procedure of the Meeting of the State Parties.

346 Article 5 of the Rules of Procedure of the Meeting of the State Parties.

347 According to Articles 2.2 and 2.3 of the Rules of Procedure of the Meeting of the State Parties these entities are member states of UNESCO not parties to the 1970 Convention, associated members of UNESCO, permanent observer missions to UNESCO, the United Nations and its organisations, other intergovernmental organisations that have concluded mutual agreements with UNESCO, observers of intergovernmental and international non-governmental organisations, as well as representatives of observers invited by the Director-General.

348 Articles 1, 2.1–2.3 of the Rules of Procedure of the Meeting of the State Parties.

State parties to the 1970 UNESCO Convention on the other hand each have one vote[349] and decisions are taken by a simple majority of the members present and voting,[350] meaning that only affirmative or negative votes are counted.[351,352] The quorum consists of a simple majority of state parties.[353]

The meetings are moderated by the chairperson who is elected together with one or more vice-chairpersons[354] and a rapporteur by the meeting.[355] The chairperson opens and closes the plenary meetings, ensures the observance of the rules of procedure and directs the discussion including the right, order, and time-limit to speak.[356] Furthermore, he puts questions to a vote and announces decisions. Besides this, the chairman also rules on points of order and controls the proceedings and maintenance of order.[357]

However, during a discussion any delegation may raise a point of order which has to be immediately decided by the chairperson. An appeal may be made against the ruling of the chairman. Such an appeal is put to the vote immediately and the chairman's ruling stands unless overruled by a majority of the members present and voting.[358]

During a discussion, any delegation may also move the suspension or adjournment of the meeting or the adjournment or closure of a debate, and again the motion is put to a vote immediately.[359] In contrast, draft resolutions and amendments have to be transmitted by state parties to the 1970 UNESCO Convention in writing to the secretariat which has to circulate them sufficiently in advance to all other participants.[360] The secretariat, which consists of an official of the UNESCO Secretariat appointed by UNESCO's Director-General as well as other appointed officials,[361] is

[349]Article 12.1 of the Rules of Procedure of the Meeting of the State Parties.

[350]Article 12.2 of the Rules of Procedure of the Meeting of the State Parties.

[351]Article 12.3 of the Rules of Procedure of the Meeting of the State Parties.

[352]Voting is normally carried out by show of hands. When the result of a vote by show of hands is in doubt, the chairman may take a second vote by roll-call. A vote by roll-call is also taken if it is requested by no less than two delegations before voting takes place. (Article 12.4 of the Rules of Procedure of the Meeting of the State Parties).

Article 12 of the Rules of Procedure of the Meeting of the State Parties contains further detailed regulations on voting, like the order in which proposals have to be voted upon.

[353]Article 6.1 of the Rules of Procedure of the Meeting of the State Parties.

[354]In accordance with Article 4.2 of the Rules of Procedure of the Meeting of the State Parties the vice-chairpersons have the same powers and duties as the chairperson when replacing him due to his absence.

[355]Article 3 of the Rules of Procedure of the Meeting of the State Parties.

[356]Article 7 of the Rules of Procedure of the Meeting of the State Parties; Article 7.3 of the Rules of Procedure of the Meeting of the State Parties allows also observers to address the meeting.

[357]Article 4.1 of the Rules of Procedure of the Meeting of the State Parties.

[358]Article 8 of the Rules of Procedure of the Meeting of the State Parties.

[359]Article 9 of the Rules of Procedure of the Meeting of the State Parties.

[360]Article 11 of the Rules of Procedure of the Meeting of the State Parties.

[361]Article 13.2 of the Rules of Procedure of the Meeting of the State Parties.

furthermore charged with the tasks of receiving, translating, and distributing all official documents and performing any other task necessary for the proper conduct of the work of the Meeting of State Parties to the 1970 UNESCO Convention.[362]

2.2.7.3 The Executor: The Subsidiary Committee

2.2.7.3.1 Structure

The subsidiary committee has been established based on Article 14.2 of the Rules of Procedure of the Meeting of State Parties. It is comprised of 18 representatives of state parties to the 1970 UNESCO Convention, 3 per regional group,[363] which are elected by the Meeting of State Parties to the 1970 UNESCO Convention. The election has to obey the principles of equitable geographical representation and rotation.[364] In general, member states are elected for four years, though not all members of the committee are elected simultaneously. Half of the committee is in due course renewed every other year and member states are not immediately eligible for re-election.[365] Nevertheless, member states are free to choose their representatives who they delegate to the committee. They have to transmit to the secretariat in writing, the name, designation, and qualification of their representative.[366]

The committee is assisted by further entities—both permanent and temporary. While the bureau and the secretariat fall within the first category, the committee may also establish further subsidiary bodies. The bureau consists of a chairperson, four vice-chairpersons, and a rapporteur, again in conformity with the principle of equitable geographical representation.[367] It coordinates the work of the committee and performs the tasks set out in the Operational Guidelines for the Implementation of the Convention and any other task assigned by the committee.[368] For this purpose the bureau may meet as frequently as it deems necessary in sessions open to state members of the committee and other state parties to the 1970 UNESCO Convention.[369] In addition, the chairperson, or in his absence any vice-chairperson of the bureau, presides over the sessions, in particular, opens and closes the plenary

[362]Article 13.3 of the Rules of Procedure of the Meeting of the State Parties.

[363]The electoral groups being Western European and North American States, Eastern European States, Latin-American and Caribbean States, Asian and Pacific States, African States, and Arab States; cf. http://www.unesco.org/new/en/executive-board/members/.

[364]Article 14.4 of the Rules of Procedure of the Meeting of the State Parties.

[365]Article 14.5 of the Rules of Procedure of the Meeting of the State Parties.

[366]Rule 5.2 of the Rules of Procedure of the Subsidiary Committee.

[367]Rule 11.1 of the Rules of Procedure of the Subsidiary Committee.

[368]Rule 11.2 of the Rules of Procedure of the Subsidiary Committee.

[369]Rules 11.3 and 11.4 of the Rules of Procedure of the Subsidiary Committee.

meetings of the committee, directs the discussion including the right to speak,[370] ensures the observance of the rules of procedure and puts questions to a vote along with announcing decisions. Furthermore, it is also the bureau that rules on points of order and controls the proceedings and the maintenance of order.[371] It is elected anew by the committee every two years[372] among those committee members whose term of office continues throughout the ordinary session in compliance with the principle of geographic rotation.[373] Members of the bureau are eligible for immediate re-election to the same posts, provided that their country continues to be a member of the committee at least until the new term of office ends.[374] However, again, in the election of the bureau due regard has to be given to ensure equitable geographical representation and compliance with the principle of rotation.[375,376]

The secretariat, on the other hand, is not elected by the committee, but provided for by the Director-General of UNESCO, as part of his duty to assist the committee.[377] He appoints a member of the UNESCO Secretariat to act as secretary of the committee and other officials who together constitute the secretariat of the committee.[378] The secretariat performs all duties necessary for the proper conduct of the work of the committee; in particular, it receives, translates, and distributes all official documents of the committee[379] and arranges for the interpretation of discussions.[380]

Subsidiary bodies may be established by the committee as it deems necessary for the conduct of its work; however, membership to the subsidiary bodies is limited to member states of the committee.[381] Furthermore, their composition and terms of

---

[370] Regulations on the right to speak and its administration can be found in Rule 20 of the Rules of Procedure of the Subsidiary Committee.

[371] Rule 13.1 of the Rules of Procedure of the Subsidiary Committee.

[372] Rule 12.1 of the Rules of Procedure of the Subsidiary Committee speaks of "every second ordinary session". However, according to Article 14.3 of the Rules of Procedure of the Meeting of the State Parties the Committee is convened every year and thus every second ordinary session is every other year.

[373] Rule 12.1 of the Rules of Procedure of the Subsidiary Committee.

[374] Rule 12.2 of the Rules of Procedure of the Subsidiary Committee.

[375] Rule 12.3 of the Rules of Procedure of the Subsidiary Committee.

[376] Rules 13.2, 13.3, 14, and 15 of the Rules of Procedure of the Subsidiary Committee contain a number of regulations in case any member of the bureau is unable to attend (parts of) the sessions or may not be able to complete the term of his office.

[377] Rule 39.1 of the Rules of Procedure of the Subsidiary Committee.

[378] Rule 39.3 of the Rules of Procedure of the Subsidiary Committee.

[379] Rule 39.3 of the Rules of Procedure of the Subsidiary Committee regulates that documents relating to the items on the provisional agenda of each session of the committee have to be distributed to members of the committee not later than four weeks before the beginning of the session. They must be provided for in electronic form to state parties not members of the committee and to public or private organisations, individuals, and observers.

[380] Rules 39.5 and 39.4 of the Rules of Procedure of the Subsidiary Committee.

[381] This is, for instance, different in the case of the ad hoc subcommittees of UNESCO's ICPRCP. Membership to ad hoc subcommittees is explicitly also open to member states of UNESCO which are not represented in the ICPRCP. Cf. Article 6 (1) of the ICPRCP Statutes.

reference, including their mandate and duration of office, have to be defined by the committee at the time of their establishment. Again, in the appointing procedure due regard has to be given to the need to ensure an equitable representation of the different regions of the world.[382] Furthermore, the subsidiary body is subject to a quorum requirement with a quorum consisting of a majority of the state members of the body.[383]

2.2.7.3.2 Functions and Functioning

The subsidiary committee has been set up to promote the purposes of the 1970 UNESCO Convention, to review national reports presented to UNESCO's General Conference by its state parties, to exchange best practices and prepare and submit to the Meeting of State Parties to the 1970 UNESCO Convention recommendations and guidelines that may contribute to its implementation, to identify problem areas arising from its implementation, and to initiate and maintain coordination with UNESCO's ICPRCP.[384,385]

In order to fulfil these objectives, the committee is convened by the secretariat every year[386] with each session determining in general the date and location of the next session.[387] For this purpose, any member state of the committee may invite it to hold a session on its territory, as long as it covers the organisational costs.[388] However, in determining the place of the following session, due consideration has to be given to ensure an equitable rotation among the different regions of the world.[389]

In addition to this, the committee may also convene extraordinary sessions when deemed necessary.[390] This has to be done upon approval in writing by a two-thirds majority of the members of the committee[391] of a written request submitted via the secretariat by any member of the committee, any other state party to the 1970 UNESCO Convention or the Director-General of UNESCO.[392] Furthermore,

---

[382] Rule 19 of the Rules of Procedure of the Subsidiary Committee.

[383] Rule 16.2 of the Rules of Procedure of the Subsidiary Committee.

[384] On the ICPRCP cf. pp. 127ff.

[385] Article 14.6 of the Rules of Procedure of the Meeting of the State Parties.

[386] Article 14.3 of the Rules of Procedure of the Meeting of the State Parties.

[387] Rule 4.1 of the Rules of Procedure of the Subsidiary Committee reads: "The Committee shall determine at each session, in consultation with the Director-General, the date and place of the next session. The date and/or place may be changed, if necessary, by the Bureau, in consultation with the Director-General.".

[388] Rule 4.2 of the Rules of Procedure of the Subsidiary Committee.

[389] Rule 4.3 of the Rules of Procedure of the Subsidiary Committee.

[390] Rule 2.2 of the Rules of Procedure of the Subsidiary Committee.

[391] Rule 2.5 of the Rules of Procedure of the Subsidiary Committee.

[392] Rule 2.3 of the Rules of Procedure of the Subsidiary Committee.

details on the urgent matters the committee has been convened for have to be provided.[393]

For the convocation of the sessions, the chairperson of the committee is responsible in consultation with UNESCO's Director-General.[394] However, the latter, assisted by the secretariat, is in charge of the technical realisation of the convocation. He has to inform state members of the committee and other participants of the session of its date, place, and provisional agenda.[395,396] The secretariat, on the other hand, is in charge of performing all duties necessary for the proper conduct of the work of the committee, including receiving, translating, and distributing all official documents of the committee and arranging for the interpretation of the discussions.[397]

Although member states are free to send as many alternates, advisers, and experts assisting the representative as they deem necessary to the committee,[398] each member state has only one vote.[399] Decisions need to be taken by a simple majority of the members present and voting,[400] meaning that only affirmative or negative votes are counted.[401,402] The quorum consists of a majority of the state members of the committee.[403]

---

[393]Rule 2.4 of the Rules of Procedure of the Subsidiary Committee.

[394]Rule 3.1 of the Rules of Procedure of the Subsidiary Committee.

[395]Rules 8–10 of the Rules of Procedure of the Subsidiary Committee deal with the agenda. Rule 8 contains a quite detailed list of topics which have to be included into the provisional agenda of an ordinary session. In addition, it exercises restraint on the agenda of an extraordinary session by dictating that only those items for the consideration of which the session has been convened may be included in its agenda. Nevertheless, in accordance with Rule 9, in both cases the agenda has to be adopted at the beginning of the session and can in compliance with Rule 10 be amended or changed by a two-thirds majority of the state members present and voting.

[396]Rules 3.2 and 3.3 of the Rules of Procedure of the Subsidiary Committee. Rule 3.2 of the Rules of Procedure of the Subsidiary Committee also provides for specific deadlines in this regard: "The Director-General shall inform the States Members of the Committee of the date, place and provisional agenda of each session not less than sixty days in advance in the case of an ordinary session and, so far as possible, not less than thirty days in advance in the case of an extraordinary session.".

[397]Rules 39.5 and 39.4 of the Rules of Procedure of the Subsidiary Committee.

[398]Rule 5.1 of the Rules of Procedure of the Subsidiary Committee.

[399]Rule 33 of the Rules of Procedure of the Subsidiary Committee.

[400]Rule 35 of the Rules of Procedure of the Subsidiary Committee.

[401]Rule 36 of the Rules of Procedure of the Subsidiary Committee.

[402]Voting is normally by a show of hands unless a secret ballot is requested by one state member of the committee and seconded by two others. If there is any doubt concerning the result of a vote by a show of hands, the chairperson may take a second vote by roll-call. A vote by roll-call shall also be taken if it is requested by not less than two state members of the committee before the vote is taken (Rule 37 of the Rules of Procedure of the Subsidiary Committee). Rule 38 the Rules of Procedure of the Subsidiary Committee then contains a clause regulating the conduct of voting by secret ballot.

[403]Rule 16.1 of the Rules of Procedure of the Subsidiary Committee.

Other entities with other state parties to the 1970 UNESCO Convention and member states of UNESCO leading the way may participate in the sessions purely as observers and have no right to vote.[404] The committee may also invite entities with recognised competence in the areas of the protection of cultural heritage and combating illicit trafficking of cultural property, in order to consult them on specific matters.[405]

In any case, generally, the meetings are held in public.[406] When, in exceptional circumstances, the subsidiary committee decides to hold a private meeting, it has to determine persons who, in addition to representatives of state members of the committee and other state parties to the 1970 UNESCO Convention, the latter as observers, may be present.[407] The subsidiary committee has to present in written form at a subsequent public meeting any decision taken by it.[408] Other documents, such as the proceedings, may be made public immediately, but have to be publicised after a period of twenty years.[409]

The sessions are moderated by the bureau. The chairperson, or in his absence any vice-chairperson, of the bureau opens and closes the plenary meetings, ensures the observance of the rules of procedure and directs the discussion including the right to speak,[410] puts questions to a vote, and announces decisions. Furthermore, the chairperson also controls the proceedings and the maintenance of order.[411] He moreover has to decide immediately on any point of order which can be raised by any state member during the discussions. An appeal may be made against the ruling of the chairman with such an appeal put to a vote immediately and the chairman's ruling stands unless overruled by a majority of the members present and voting.[412]

---

[404] Article 14.8 of the Rules of Procedure of the Meeting of the State Parties; Rule 7 of the Rules of Procedure of the Subsidiary Committee. Unlike in the case of Article 14.8 of the Rules of Procedure of the Meeting of the State Parties, observers are furthermore categorised by Rule 7 of the Rules of Procedure of the Subsidiary Committee into three groups: (1) States parties to the 1970 UNESCO Convention which are not members of the committee which may participate in its sessions, and in those of its subsidiary bodies, (2) states not party to the 1970 UNESCO Convention that are member states of UNESCO, associate members or permanent observer missions to UNESCO as well as representatives of the UN and other organisations of the UN system and intergovernmental organisations with which UNESCO concluded mutual representation agreements which may participate in the work of the committee and (3) other intergovernmental organisations, non-governmental organisations, public and private organisations as well as individuals which need an authorisation of the committee in order to participate in the sessions of the committee.

[405] Article 14.9 of the Rules of Procedure of the Meeting of the State Parties.

[406] Rule 17 of the Rules of Procedure of the Subsidiary Committee.

[407] Rule 18.1 of the Rules of Procedure of the Subsidiary Committee.

[408] Rule 18.2 of the Rules of Procedure of the Subsidiary Committee.

[409] Cf. Rule 18.3 of the Rules of Procedure of the Subsidiary Committee.

[410] Regulations on the right to speak and its administration can be found in Rule 20 of the Rules of Procedure of the Subsidiary Committee.

[411] Rule 13.1 of the Rules of Procedure of the Subsidiary Committee.

[412] Rule 26 of the Rules of Procedure of the Subsidiary Committee.

However, member states of the committee may, during the discussion of any matter, propose the suspension or adjournment of a meeting as well as the adjournment or closure of a debate.[413]

Substantially, the committee has to address issues related to promoting the purposes of the 1970 UNESCO Convention, reviewing national reports presented to UNESCO's General Conference by its states parties, exchanging best practices, preparing and submitting recommendations and guidelines that may contribute to its implementation, identifying problem areas arising from its implementation as well as initiating and maintaining coordination with UNESCO's ICPRCP. For these purposes, the committee may adopt such decisions and recommendations as it deems appropriate.[414,415]

On the other hand, the subsidiary committee has to adopt a list of all decisions[416] and prepare a summary record of all statements made during the plenary meeting[417] which have to be distributed together with the final reports of the sessions by the Director-General of UNESCO to the members of the committee, the other state parties to the 1970 UNESCO Convention, and other observers of the session.[418] Furthermore, the committee must submit a report on its activities at each ordinary session of the Meeting of State Parties to the 1970 UNESCO Convention.[419]

Other UNESCO officials are integrated into the committee's work to the extent that the Director-General of UNESCO or his representative may make either oral or written statements on any question under consideration and may participate in the work of the committee and its subsidiary bodies.[420]

2.2.7.3.3 Accomplishments

Despite being a relatively new institution, the subsidiary committee has already proven quite productive. At its 1st session in July 2013, it not only adopted its own rules of procedure,[421,422] but based on its mandate, also decided to establish an informal working group to work on draft Guidelines for the Implementation of the

[413]Rules 27–31 of the Rules of Procedure of the Subsidiary Committee provide detailed regulations on the matter of procedures motions, including their consequences and the order in which they have to be voted.

[414]Rule 32.1 of the Rules of Procedure of the Subsidiary Committee.

[415]Rules 21–25 of the Rules of Procedure of the Subsidiary Committee contain a number of regulations regarding proposals, including rules on (order of) voting and withdrawal.

[416]Rule 42 of the Rules of Procedure of the Subsidiary Committee.

[417]Rule 43 of the Rules of Procedure of the Subsidiary Committee.

[418]Rule 44 of the Rules of Procedure of the Subsidiary Committee.

[419]Rule 45 of the Rules of Procedure of the Subsidiary Committee.

[420]Rule 39.2 of the Rules of Procedure of the Subsidiary Committee.

[421]UNESCO Doc C70/13/1.SC/Decisions, 24.07.2013, p. 2.

[422]The legal basis enabling it to do so is to be found in Article 14.7 of the Rules of Procedure of the Meeting of the State Parties.

1970 UNESCO Convention.[423] Subsequently, this informal working group met four times between November 2013 and April 2014 and prepared a final draft of the Operational Guidelines for the Implementation of the 1970 UNESCO Convention. This draft was later adopted and submitted by the 2nd session of the subsidiary committee to the 3rd Meeting of State Parties to the 1970 UNESCO Convention, which adopted it in May 2015.[424]

After a more technical extraordinary session in May 2015, which was convened in order to adopt the necessary documents for the 3rd Meeting of State Parties to the 1970 UNESCO Convention,[425] the subsidiary committee held its ordinary 3rd session in September 2015 in which it dealt with the national reports submitted by state parties on the measures taken to implement the 1970 UNESCO Convention.[426]

Furthermore, based on a decision taken by the 3rd session of the subsidiary committee,[427] its bureau and the Bureau of the Committee for the Protection of Cultural Property in the Event of Armed Conflict had a first joint meeting in December 2015 in which they exchanged information on the special threats cultural property faces in the event of armed conflicts and possible countermeasures. Moreover, both bureaus encouraged the Director-General of UNESCO to organise a meeting with the Chairpersons of the six UNESCO Cultural Conventions Committees during the 4th session of the Subsidiary Committee to the Meeting of States Parties to the 1970 Convention.[428]

2.2.8 *Evaluation*

Examining the 1970 UNESCO Convention over 40 years after its adoption, one might consider it to be outdated.[429] Not only do the moral standards and attitudes reflected in the treaty appear to be weak and outdated, such as the tendency towards cultural nationalism, for which the convention is under criticism,[430] but by now many states have enacted legislation going beyond what is required by the 1970

[423]UNESCO Doc C70/13/1.SC/Decisions, 24.07.2013, p. 3.

[424]UNESCO Doc C70/15/3.MSP/Resolutions, May 2015, p. 7. For the actual text of the Operational Guidelines see UNESCO Doc C70/14/2.SC/5, June 2014, pp. 5ff.

[425]Cf. UNESCO Doc C70/15/Extra.SC/Decisions, May 2015, p. 2.

[426]Cf. UNESCO Doc C70/15/3.SC/6, July 2015.

[427]Cf. UNESCO Doc C70/15/3.SC/Decisions, October 2015, p. 4.

[428]http://www.unesco.org/new/en/culture/themes/illicit-trafficking-of-cultural-property/subsidiary-committee/joint-bureaus-meeting/.

[429]von Schorlemer (1992), p. 443 even sees the convention as an inept instrument. For further points of general criticism cf. Posner (2007–2008), pp. 218ff.

[430]Taylor (2005), pp. 240f; Carleton (2007), pp. 23f.

UNESCO Convention.[431] Moreover, cooperation has reached a far more intensive level than required by the treaty, which has in particular been made possible by the tremendous developments in technology, most notably the advent of the Internet which allows the real time exchange of information globally. Today the discussion has shifted from a general debate on whether cultural heritage ought to be protected or not to a more profound discussion on the specific duties of states and the effectiveness of certain measures.[432]

To deem the 1970 UNESCO Convention, however, as insignificant would be an injustice to the treaty as the time and circumstances of its adoption have to be taken into consideration. The convention was negotiated and adopted at a time in which many source states had just gained their independence or were still in the process of becoming independent. The idea that the illicit transfer of cultural property threatens not only the heritage of the states of origin, but the cultural heritage of all mankind, was far from being well established.[433] Thus, the drafters of the convention had to reconcile strongly opposing positions, which led to many compromises within the treaty.[434]

Furthermore, it has to be taken into consideration that we have only reached the contemporary standard with respect to the protection and return of cultural material due to the foundations laid by the convention.[435] The 1970 UNESCO Convention has not only brought these issues to the attention of the international community, but it has also encouraged cooperation between states and promoted the understanding that cultural property ought to be protected from illicit trafficking.[436] One might even say that it has led to a shift in the burden of proof regarding the provenance of an object. Cultural artefacts appearing on the market after 1970 seem to be assumed to be of an illicit nature, unless their provenance can be established.[437]

The 1970 UNESCO Convention also eventually led to the enactment of codes of ethics[438] and the rise of an appreciation of the value of cultural property and awareness concerning its illicit trafficking in the minds of both the general public[439]

---

[431]Stamatoudi (2011), p. 64; Forrest (2010), p. 168; cf. also Meena (2009), p. 597.

[432]Stamatoudi (2011), p. 64.

[433]Stamatoudi (2011), pp. 64f.

[434]von Schorlemer (1992), p. 427.

[435]See Boos (2006), p. 51 for examples of the external effect of the convention; cf. also Prott (1997), p. 15 and Roodt (2015), p. 160.

[436]Cf. Raschèr (2000), p. 65.

[437]Cf. Fincham (2013), pp. 214ff.

[438]In this context the ICOM Code of Ethics for Museums adopted by the 15th General Assembly of ICOM on 4 November 1986 has to be mentioned as one of the most important soft law instruments in this regard. It explicitly references, for example, in its Article 7.2 to the 1970 UNESCO Convention. For further details on the ICOM Code of Ethics cf. pp. 146ff.

[439]For the specific effects of the treaty in the USA see Kouroupas (2010), p. 158; cf. also Prott (2011b).

and government[440] which is reflected in the changed attitude of states.[441] Thus, the convention has to be regarded as a pioneering legal instrument and milestone[442] as well as an advocate and catalyst in the international debate.

Nevertheless, there are certain flaws inherent to the convention which taint its achievements and which make it unable to deliver on the high hopes former colonies and source states originally placed in it. Firstly, the treaty has deficiencies concerning its material regulations. The legal basis it provides for the reclaiming of cultural property is limited to such objects stolen from specific institutions.[443] Furthermore, in particular with regard to the colonial heritage, the 1970 UNESCO Convention lacks retroactivity.

Secondly, despite the compromises the source states were willing to accept, for a long time most market states and former colonial powers were reluctant to accede to the convention. This attitude only began to change in the late 1990s. At that point an ever growing number of European states started ratifying the treaty.[444] However, as shown above, the actual implementation of the treaty still remains problematic.[445, 446] It can only be hoped that in the future, with the convention gaining ever more support, or at least ratifications, from (major) market states,[447] state parties will interpret the treaty in a more expansive way[448] and thus allow the 1970 UNESCO Convention as a living instrument to further contribute to the promotion of the protection and return of cultural property. The establishment of the institutional framework of the Meeting of State Parties to the 1970 UNESCO Convention with its subsidiary committee and the initiation of debates about finding better ways to implement the treaty, can be seen as a first positive step to bring the 1970 UNESCO Convention back onto the agenda and to reactivate debates concerning its deficiencies, even though this will most likely be insufficient to overcome the shortcomings concerning its material regulations.

440 Vigneron (2014), p. 127.

441 Weidner (2001), pp. 244f; Stamatoudi (2011), pp. 63f; cf. also Nafziger and Paterson (2014), pp. 26f; cf. further Prott (1996), p. 63; Prott (2011c), p. 441.

442 O'Keefe (2007), p. 166; Carleton (2007), p. 25.

443 With the same view Raschèr (2000), p. 65.

444 Cf. Gerstenblith (2013), p. 9.

445 Palmer (2013), p. 109 points out that local, or at times even regional legal principles which are effective in the territory in which the disputed object is located can block international measures.

446 Another deficiency in this context is the missing financial resource. There is, for instance, a great disparity between the resources allocated to the 1972 World Heritage Convention and the 1970 UNESCO Convention. Cf. Prott (2011c), p. 438.

447 Dromgoole (2013), p. 336.

448 O'Keefe (2007), p. 166.

References

Abramson RD, Huttler SB (1973) The legal response to the illicit movement of cultural property. Law Policy Int Bus 5:932–970

Askerud P, Clément E (1997) Preventing the illicit traffic in cultural property: a resource handbook for the implementation of the 1970 UNESCO Convention. UNESCO Publishing, Paris

Bator PM (1982) An essay on the international trade in art. Stanford Law Rev 34:275–384

Baufeld S (2005) Kulturgutbeschlagnahmen in bewaffneten Konflikten, ihre Rückabwicklung und der deutsch-russische Streit um die so genannte Beutekunst. Peter Lang, Frankfurt am Main

Blake J (2015) International cultural heritage law. Oxford University Press, Oxford

Boos S (2006) Kulturgut als Gegenstand des grenzüberschreitenden Leihverkehrs. Duncker & Humblot, Berlin

Brodie N (2015) Syria and its regional neighbors: a case of cultural property protection policy failure? Int J Cult Prop 22:317–335

Brodie N, Doole J, Watson P (2000) Stealing history: the illicit trade in cultural material. The McDonald Institute for Archaeological Research, Cambridge

Carleton A (2007) Piracy in the modern age: reviewing the mechanisms which combat pillage. Macquarie J Int Comp Environ Law 4:21–42

Chechi A (2013) Plurality and coordination of dispute settlement methods in the field of cultural heritage. In: Francioni F, Gordley J (eds) Enforcing international cultural heritage law. Oxford University Press, Oxford, pp 177–205

de Clippele MS, Lambrecht L (2015) Art law & balances: increased protection of cultural heritage law vs. private ownership: towards clash or balance? Int J Cult Prop 22:259–278

Dicke DC (1984) The instruments and the agencies of the international protection of cultural property. In: Council of Europe (ed) International legal protection of cultural property – proceedings of the thirteenth colloquy on European Law – Delphi, 2-22 September. Council of Europe Publications Section, Strasbourg, pp 17-43

Dromgoole S (2013) Underwater cultural heritage and international law. Cambridge University Press, Cambridge

DuBoff LD et al (1976) Proceedings of the panel on the U.S. enabling legislation of import, export and transfer of ownership of cultural property. Syracuse J Int Law Commerce 4:97–139

Fincham D (2008-2009) How adopting the Lex Originis rule can impede the flow of illicit cultural property. Columbia J Law Arts 32:111-150

Fincham D (2013) Social norms and illicit cultural heritage. In: Francioni F, Gordley J (eds) Enforcing international cultural heritage law. Oxford University Press, Oxford, pp 206–227

Fishman J (2010) Locating the international interest in international cultural property disputes. Yale J Int Law 35:347–404

Forrest C (2010) International law and the protection of cultural heritage. Routledge, London

Fraoua R (1986) Convention concernant les mesures à prendre pour interdire et empêcher l'importation, l'exportation et le transfert de propriété illicite des biens culturels (Paris, 1970): Commentaire et aperçu de quelques mesures nationales d'exécution. In: UNESCO Doc CC-86/WS/40, p 62

Friehe M (2013) Völkerrechtliche Haftung im Kulturgüterschutzrecht: Zugleich ein Beitrag zur Raub- und Beutekunstproblematik. Peter Lang, Frankfurt am Main

Gerstenblith P (2011) International art and cultural heritage. Int Lawyer 45:395–408

Gerstenblith P (2012) Art, cultural heritage, and the law: cases and materials, 3rd edn. Carolina Academic Press, Durham

Gerstenblith P (2013) Models of implementation of the 1970 UNESCO Convention: can their effectiveness be determined? In: Prott LV, Redmond-Cooper R, Urice S (eds) Realising cultural heritage law: Festschrift for Patrick Joseph O'Keefe. Institute of Art and Law, Builth Wells, pp 9–25

Gordon JB (1971) The UNESCO Convention on the illicit movement of art treasures. Harv Int Law J 12:537–556

Gornig GH (2007) Der internationale Kulturgüterschutz. In: Gornig GH, Horn H-D, Murswiek D (eds) Kulturgüterschutz: internationale und nationale Aspekte. Duncker & Humblot, Berlin, pp 17–63

Gruber S (2013) The fight against the illicit trade in Asian cultural artefacts: connecting international agreements, regional co-operation, and domestic strategies. Asian J Int Law 3:341–363

Herzog R (2001) Kulturgut unter Wasser: Schatzsucher, Das Seevölkerrecht und der Schutz des kulturellen Erbes. Shaker Verlag, Aachen

Hönes E-R (2006) Die UNESCO-Konvention über Maßnahmen zum Verbot und zur Verhütung der rechtswidrigen Einfuhr, Ausfuhr und Übereignung von Kulturgut vom 14. November 1970. Bayrische Verwaltungsblätter 165–173

Hönes E-R (2010) Internationaler Denkmal-, Kulturgüter- und Welterbeschutz. Deutsches Nationalkomitee für Denkmalschutz, Bonn

Hudson MO (1941) International legislation, vol VII (1935-1937) Numbers 402–505. Carnegie Endowment for International Peace, Washington

Hüfner K (2005) UNESCO im Überblick. In: Hüfner K, Reuther W (eds) UNESCO-Handbuch, 2nd edn. UNO-Verlag, Bonn, pp 15–43

International Law Association (2010) Draft report on national controls over the export of cultural material., http://www.ila-hq.org/en/committees/index.cfm/cid/13. Accessed 25 April 2016

Kaplan W (1986) Assistance under the 1970 UNESCO Cultural Property Convention: Canada's request to the United States. Stanford J Int Law 22:123ff

Kau M (2013) Der Staat und der Einzelne als Völkerrechtssubjekte. In: Graf Vitzthum W, Proelß A (eds) Völkerrecht, 6th edn. De Gruyter, Berlin, pp 131–235

Kouroupas MP (2010) Die UNESCO-Konvention von 1970: Die Erfahrungen der Vereinigten Staaten. Kunst und Recht 154–159

Kurpiers OR (2005) Die Lex Originis-Regel im internationalen Sachenrecht: Grenzüberschreitende privatrechtliche Ansprüche auf Herausgabe von abhanden gekommenen und unrechtmäßig ausgeführten Kulturgütern. Peter Lang, Frankfurt am Main

Lanciotti A (2012) The dilemma of the right to ownership of underwater cultural heritage: the case of the "Getty Bronze". In: Borelli S, Francioni F (eds) Cultural heritage, cultural rights, cultural diversity: New developments in international law. Martinus Nijhoff Publishers, Leiden, pp 301–326

Lyons CL (2014) Thinking about antiquities: museums and internationalism. Int J Cult Prop 21:251–265

Manhart C (2016) The intentional destruction of heritage: Bamiyan and Timbuktu. In: Logan W, Craith MN, Kockel U (eds) A companion to heritage studies. Wiley Blackwell, Chichester, pp 280–294

Meena T (2009) Nights at the museum: the value of cultural property and resolving the moral and legal problems of the illicit international art trade. Loyola Los Angel Int Comp Law Rev 31:581–614

Nafziger JAR (1975) Article 7(a) of the UNESCO Convention. In: DuBoff LD (ed) Art law: domestic and international. Fred B. Rothman & Co, South Hackensack, p 387ff

Nafziger JAR, Paterson RK (2014) International trade in cultural material. In: Nafziger JAR, Paterson RK (eds) Handbook on the law of cultural heritage and international trade. Edward Elgar, Cheltenham, pp 19–43

Nafziger JAR, Paterson RK, Renteln AD (2014) Cultural law: international, comparative, and indigenous. Cambridge University Press, Cambridge

O'Keefe PJ (1997) Trade in antiquities: reducing destruction and theft. UNESCO Publishing, Paris

O'Keefe PJ (2007) Commentary on the 1970 UNESCO Convention, 2nd edn. Institute of Art and Law, Leicester

O'Keefe R (2013) Protection of cultural property. In: Fleck D (ed) The handbook of international humanitarian law, 3rd edn. Oxford University Press, Oxford, pp 420–462

Ochoa Jiménez MJ (2011) Der Schutz materieller Kulturgüter in Lateinamerika: Universelles, regionales und nationales Recht. Universitätsverlag Göttingen, Göttingen

Odendahl K (2005) Kulturgüterschutz: Entwicklung, Struktur und Dogmatik eines ebenenübergreifenden Normensystems. Mohr Siebeck, Tübingen

Office International des Musées (1939a) Projet de convention internationale sur le repatriement des objets d'intérêt artistique, historique ou scientifique, perdus, volés ou ayant donné lieu à une aliénation ou exportation illicite. Art et Archéologie 1:51-52

Office International des Musées (1939b) Projet de convention internationale pour la protection des patrimoines historiques et artistiques nationaux. Art et Archéologie 1:69ff

Office International des Musées (1939c) Projet de convention internationale pour la protection des collections nationales d'art et d'histoire. Art et Archéologie 1:78ff

Pabst F (2008) Kulturgüterschutz in nicht-internationalen bewaffneten Konflikten. Duncker & Humblot, Berlin

Pallas NC (2004) Maritimer Kulturgüterschutz. Duncker & Humblot, Berlin

Palmer N (2013) Fetters and stumbling blocks: impediments to the recovery and return of unlawfully removed cultural objects: a common law perspective. In: Prott LV, Redmond-Cooper R, Urice S (eds) Realising cultural heritage Law: Festschrift for Patrick Joseph O'Keefe. Institute of Art and Law, Builth Wells, pp 97–110

Paterson RK (2011) Moving culture: the future of national cultural property export controls. Southwest J Int Law 18:287–294

Planche E (2010) Die UNESCO-Konvention von 1970: Anwendung auf internationaler Ebene. Kunst und Recht 143–147

Posner EA (2007-2008) The international protection of cultural property: some skeptical observations. Chicago J Int Law 8:213-231

Prott LV (1996) UNESCO and UNIDROIT: a partnership against trafficking in cultural objects. Uniform Law Rev 1:59–71

Prott LV (1997) Commentary on the UNIDROIT Convention on Stolen and Illegally Exported Cultural Objects 1995. Institute of Art and Law, Leicester

Prott LV (2009) The history and development of processes for the recovery of cultural heritage. In: Prott LV (ed) Witness to history: a compendium of documents and writings on the return of cultural objects. UNESCO Publishing, Paris, pp 2–18

Prott LV (2011a) "Illicit traffic in cultural objects: law ethics and the realities": workshop co-organized by the Institute of Advanced Studies and the Law School of the University of Western Australia, Perth, 4–5 August 2011. Int J Cult Prop 18:453–457

Prott LV (2011b) Strengths and weaknesses of the 1970 Convention: an evaluation 40 years after its adoption. In: UNESCO Doc CLT/2011/CONF.207/7, p 3

Prott LV (2011c) The fight against the illicit traffic of cultural property: the 1970 Convention: past and future, 15-16 March 2011. Int J Cult Prop 18:437-442

Prott LV, O'Keefe PJ (1983) Implementation of the 1970 UNESCO Convention on the Means of Prohibiting and Preventing the Illicit Import, Export and Transfer of Ownership of Cultural Property. In: UNESCO Doc CLT-83/WS/16

Prott LV, O'Keefe PJ (1988) Handbook of national regulations concerning the export of cultural property. In: UNESCO Doc CC.SS/WS/27

Prowda JB (2014) The perils of buying and selling art at the fair: legal issues in title. In: Vadi V, Schneider HEGS (eds) Art, cultural heritage and the market: ethical and legal issues. Springer, Heidelberg, pp 141–163

Raschèr AFG (2000) Kulturgüterschutz und Globalisierung – UNESCO-Konvention 1970 – UNIDROIT-Konvention 1995 – EG-Verordnung 3911/92 – EG-Richtlinie 93/7 – Schweizerisches Recht. Schulthess, Zürich

Renold M-A (2009) Stolen art: the ubiquitous question of good faith. In: Prott LV (ed) Witness to history: a compendium of documents and writings on the return of cultural objects. UNESCO Publishing, Paris, pp 309–313

Rietschel S (2009) Internationale Vorgaben zum Kulturgüterschutz und ihre Umsetzung in Deutschland: Das KGÜAG – Meilenstein oder fauler Kompromiss in der Geschichte des deutschen Kulturgüterschutzes? De Gruyter, Berlin

Roca-Hachem R (2005) UNESCO and UNIDROIT cooperation in the fight against illicit traffic in cultural property – conference celebrating the 10th anniversary of the UNIDROIT Convention on Stolen or Illegally Exported Cultural Objects – UNESCO, Paris (France) – 24 June 2005 – summary report. Uniform Law Rev 10:536–542

Roodt C (2015) Private international law, art and cultural heritage. Edward Elgar, Cheltenham

Schaffrath C (2007) Die Rückführung unrechtmäßig nach Deutschland verbrachten Kulturguts an den Ursprungsstaat. Peter Lang, Frankfurt am Main

Schmeinck S (1994) Internationalprivatrechtliche Aspekte des Kulturgüterschutzes. Duncker & Humblot, Berlin

Schnabel G, Tatzkow M (2007) Nazi-looted art: Handbuch Kunstrestitution weltweit. Proprietas Verlag, Berlin

Schnelle MA (2016) Der Abwanderungsschutz von Kulturgütern im Lichte der Freihandelsordnungen von AEUV und GATT. Nomos, Baden-Baden

Schönenberger B (2009) Restitution von Kulturgut: Anspruchsgrundlagen – Restiutionshindernisse – Entwicklung. Stämpfli Verlag, Bern

Schuschke-Nehen L (2008) Kulturgüterschutz in Deutschland und der Europäischen Union. University of Köln, Dissertation

UNIDROIT Secretariat (2001) UNIDROIT Convention on Stolen or Illegally Exported Cultural Objects: explanatory report. Uniform Law Rev 6:476–564

Shyllon F (2012) Second meeting of the states parties to the 1970 UNESCO Convention on the Means of Prohibiting and Preventing the Illicit Import, Export and Transfer of Ownership of Cultural Property. Int J Cult Prop 19:585–587

Shyllon F (2014) Legislative and administrative implementation of 1970 UNESCO Convention by African states: the failure to grasp the nettle. Int J Cult Prop 21:23–53

Siehr K (2005) Das UNESCO Übereinkommen vom 14.11.1970 über Maßnahmen zum Verbot und zur Verhütung der unzulässigen Einfuhr, Ausfuhr und Übereignung von Kulturgut – Inhalt des Übereinkommens und dessen geplante Umsetzung in Deutschland. Kunst und Recht 33–46

Siehr K (2011) Mystifizierung und Entmystifizierung von Kulturgütern und das Recht. Kunst und Recht 87–108

Slattery AJ (2012) To catch an art thief: using international and domestic laws to paint fraudulent art dealers into a corner. Villanova Sports Entertain Law J 19:827–871

Stamatoudi IA (2011) Cultural property law and restitution: a commentary to international conventions and European Union law. Edward Elgar, Cheltenham

Standrock O (1985) Foreign laws regulating the export of cultural property: the respect due to them by judge of the Lex Fori. In: Lalive P (ed) International sales of works of art. Institute of International Business Law & Practice, Paris, pp 457–478

Steinbrück C (2012) Die Umsetzung des UNESCO-Kulturgutübereinkommens in der Bundesrepublik Deutschland: Eine vergleichende Betrachtung mit der Umsetzung der Konvention in den Vereinigten Staaten von Amerika und der Schweiz. Carl Heymanns Verlag, Köln

Streinz R (1998) Internationaler Schutz von Museumsgut: Handbuch des Museumsrechts 4. Leske + Budrich, Opladen

Stumpf E (2003) Kulturgüterschutz im internationalen Recht unter besonderer Berücksichtigung der deutsch-russischen Beziehungen. Peter Lang, Frankfurt am Main

Taylor JM (2005) The rape and return of China's cultural property: how can bilateral agreements stem the bleeding of China's cultural heritage in a flawed system? Loyola Univ Chicago Int Law Rev 3:233–255

Thorn B (2005) Internationaler Kulturgüterschutz nach der UNIDROIT Konvention. De Gruyter, Berlin

Tucker RL (2011) Stolen art, looted antiquities, and the insurable interest requirement. Quinnipiac Law Rev 29:611–663

Vigneron S (2014) Protecting cultural objects: enforcing the illicit export of foreign cultural objects. In: Vadi V, Schneider HEGS (eds) Art, cultural heritage and the market: ethical and legal issues. Springer, Heidelberg, pp 117–139

Vogel J (2010) Kunstraub und Internationales Strafrecht. Juristenzeitung 1143–1150

von Schorlemer S (1992) Internationaler Kulturgüterschutz: Ansätze zur Prävention im Frieden sowie in bewaffneten Konflikten. Duncker & Humblot, Berlin

Vrdoljak AF (2008) International law, museums and the return of cultural objects. Cambridge University Press, Cambridge

Walter B (1988) Rückführung von Kulturgut im internationalen Recht. Übersee-Museum Bremen, Bremen

Weidner A (2001) Kulturgüterschutz als res extra commercium im internationalen Sachenrecht. De Gruyter, Berlin

Williams SA (1978) The international and national protection of movable cultural property: a comparative study. Oceana Publications, Dobbs Ferry

Xi L (2012) Contemporary observation on international protection of cultural property. Contemp Read Law Soc Justice 4:855–865

Yusuf A (2007) Standard-setting in UNESCO: conventions, recommendations, declarations and charters adopted by UNESCO (1948 – 2006), vol 2, vol UNESCO Publishing. Paris / Martinus Nijhoff Publishers, Leiden

Chapter 3
The Classical Approach: International Treaties—Part II

Abstract The 1970 UNESCO Convention on the Means of Prohibiting and Preventing the Illicit Import, Export and Transfer of Ownership of Cultural Property constitutes a milestone. It is the first treaty on an international scale exclusively devoted to the regulation of the return of cultural objects transferred in times of peace and hence, as one of its major achievements, the first globally-designated treaty to provide a legal basis to reclaim such items. Nevertheless, the 1970 UNESCO Convention has many shortcomings. Inter alia, it only raises questions of private law, but does not resolve them. Hence, the international community soon after its adoption realised the need for further action to overcome its flaws, particularly its missing private law dimension. This led to the adoption of the 1995 UNIDROIT Convention on Stolen or Illegally Exported Cultural Objects, which this chapter analyses in detail. Its purpose, scope and regulations, particularly those concerning the return of cultural objects, are broke down in the light of the convention's genesis as well as the different actors' positions and in comparison to the 1970 UNESCO Convention. Furthermore, the intertwining nature of both conventions is highlighted. The chapter concludes with an elaboration on the 1995 UNIDROIT Convention's relevance, as well as its strengths and weaknesses, before providing an overall evaluation of the treaties and the suitability of international treaties in general to solve controversies concerning claims for the return of cultural objects.

3.1 The 1995 UNIDROIT Convention on Stolen or Illegally Exported Cultural Objects

3.1.1 Introduction

Although the 1970 UNESCO Convention on the Means of Prohibiting and Preventing the Illicit Import, Export and Transfer of Ownership of Cultural Property constitutes a milestone regarding the return of illicitly transferred cultural objects, it proved not to be sufficient to prevent the illicit trafficking of artefacts

A. Taşdelen, *The Return of Cultural Artefacts*, DOI 10.1007/978-3-319-44060-6_3

and eliminate its consequences. One reason[1] for this insufficiency is surely the restriction of Article 7 (b) (ii) to cultural property stolen from a museum or a religious or secular public monument or similar institution. However, a more systematic issue is the fact that the 1970 UNESCO Convention is, due to the lack of a UNESCO mandate for matters of national law,[2] tailored towards administrative actions which are to be undertaken by state parties.[3] It only raises questions of private law, but does not resolve them.[4] The compatibility with national property law in practice has been disregarded.[5]

Thus, to overcome this deficiency and harmonise the various national private law regulations regarding the transfer of cultural objects, such as rules on time limitation,[6] on 24 June 1995 the self-executing UNIDROIT Convention on Stolen or Illegally Exported Cultural Objects was adopted as a follow-up agreement complementing the 1970 UNESCO Convention by bestowing a private law dimension to the question of the return of cultural property.[7] Both treaties are so closely intertwined that one might consider the 1995 UNIDROIT Convention to be a de facto protocol to the 1970 UNESCO Convention.[8]

3.1.2 From UNESCO's Request to the Adoption of the 1995 UNIDROIT Convention

Due to the lack of acceptance of the 1970 UNESCO Convention, which a UNESCO study in 1982 ascribed to the reasons mentioned above,[9] UNESCO decided to complement the 1970 UNESCO Convention—a public law and political instrument[10]—with private law structures.[11] Since compatibility with national property laws was considered to be of essential significance for the international acceptance

[1]Cf. Schönenberger (2009), p. 82; cf. also Gornig (2011), p. 124; cf. also Vrdoljak (2012), p. 121.

[2]Prott (1996), p. 60.

[3]Stamatoudi (2011), p. 68; cf. also von Schorlemer (2007), pp. 78f.

[4]Radloff (2013), p. 239.

[5]Weidner (2001), p. 249.

[6]Cf. Stamatoudi (2011), p. 68; cf. also Schneider (2010), p. 159.

[7]The complementing character of the 1995 UNIDROIT Convention is particularly evident in the last paragraph of its preamble: "RECOGNISING the work of various bodies to protect cultural property, particularly the 1970 UNESCO Convention on illicit traffic."; cf. also Kurpiers (2005), p. 101; Boos (2006), p. 56; Kienle and Weller (2004), p. 292; Kuprecht (2009), p. 178; Roehrenbeck (2010), p. 196.

[8]Shyllon (2012b), p. 586.

[9]Primarily the lack of compatibility with national property law in practice as well as the vagueness of the 1970 UNESCO Convention; Kurpiers (2005), pp. 101f; Beck (2007), p. 20; cf. also Pallas (2004), p. 57.

[10]Cf. von Schorlemer (2007), pp. 78f; cf. Blake (2015), p. 40.

[11]Cf. Schaffrath (2007), pp. 46f; cf. Pabst (2008), p. 78.

of the new regulations,[12] in 1984 UNESCO requested UNIDROIT,[13] which had already in 1968 and 1974[14] developed two relevant draft conventions providing a Uniform Law on the Acquisition in Good Faith of Corporeal Movables (LUAB),[15] to conduct a first study concerning the international protection of cultural objects particularly in light of the UNIDROIT LUAB of 1974 and the 1970 UNESCO Convention.[16]

This request was approved by the Governing Council of UNIDROIT in its 63rd session in May 1984[17] and followed by a second request by UNESCO in 1986.[18] These two studies[19] of independent experts came to the conclusion that an annex to Article 7 of the 1970 UNESCO Convention would not be an advisable course since it may not only endanger the ratification of the 1970 UNESCO Convention, but the elaboration of a uniform solution to the issue of the bona fide purchaser seemed unlikely.[20]

The reactivation of the 1974 LUAB, on the other hand, was discarded as its Article 11 constitutes that a purchaser of a stolen item cannot invoke bona fide per se which proved to be too much of an obstacle for the ratification of the LUAB

[12]Thorn (2005), p. 86.

[13]UNIDROIT was established as an auxiliary organ of the League of Nations in 1926 and today operates as an independent intergovernmental organisation studying needs and methods for modernising, harmonising, and co-ordinating private and in particular commercial law between states and groups of states as well as formulating uniform law instruments, principles, and rules to achieve those objectives. For further information on UNIDROIT see http://www.unidroit.org/about-unidroit/overview.

[14]Weidner (2001), p. 249.

[15]Cf. for the Projet de Convention d'UNIDROIT portant loi uniforme sur l'acquisition de bonne foi d'objets mobiliers corporels (LUAB de 1974) UNIDROIT Etude XLV-Doc 58, 1975; Schmeinck (1994), p. 122.

[16]Cf. UNIDROIT 1986 – Study LXX – Doc 1, December 1986: The Protection of Cultural Property – Study Request by UNESCO from UNIDROIT concerning the international protection of cultural property in the light in particular of the UNIDROIT Draft Convention providing a Uniform Law on the Acquisition in Good Faith of Corporeal Movables of 1974 and of the UNESCO Convention of 1970 on the Means of Prohibiting and Preventing the Illicit Import, Export and Transfer of Ownership of Cultural Property.

[17]Thorn (2005), p. 89.

[18]Cf. Kurpiers (2005), p. 102.

[19]Cf. UNIDROIT 1986 – Study LXX – Doc 1, December 1986: The Protection of Cultural Property – Study Request by UNESCO from UNIDROIT concerning the international protection of cultural property in the light in particular of the UNIDROIT Draft Convention providing a Uniform Law on the Acquisition in Good Faith of Corporeal Movables of 1974 and of the UNESCO Convention of 1970 on the Means of Prohibiting and Preventing the Illicit Import, Export and Transfer of Ownership of Cultural Property; cf. also UNIDROIT 1988 – Study LXX – Doc 4, April 1988: The International Protection of Cultural Property. Second Study Requested from UNIDROIT by UNESCO on the International Protection of Cultural Property with Particular Reference to the Rules of Private Law affecting the Transfer of Title to Cultural Property and in the Light of the Comments Received on the First Study.

[20]Weidner (2001), p. 249.

itself.[21] Hence, it seemed unlikely that a solution based on the LUAB would be adopted either. Rather, the two studies resulted in a first preliminary draft[22] which already dealt with matters of compensation[23] and the return of illegally transferred cultural objects,[24] but also excluded the return in certain cases such as the exercise of due diligence[25] or the acquisition by public auction.[26]

However, UNIDROIT decided to elaborate a new draft regulating the subject matter without becoming entangled in the legal terminology used so far and thereby avoiding the issues raised in the context of the other (draft) conventions.[27] For this purpose, at its 67th session in 1988, the Governing Council of UNIDROIT established an international commission[28] comprised of not only experts in the fields of the protection of cultural property, international law, and legal comparison but also lawyers representing museums, art dealers, and collectors, as well as representatives of UNESCO, INTERPOL, and the Council of Europe.[29] This commission held three meetings—in December 1988, April 1989, and January 1990[30]—which resulted in a Preliminary Draft Convention on Stolen or Illegally Exported Cultural Objects that already featured the two-part structure of the final convention distinguishing between stolen and illegally exported cultural material.[31]

This preliminary draft, which only contained the essence of the preceding scientific work in order to guarantee its political realisability,[32] was approved by the Governing Council on 23 April 1990 as the basis for further elaboration.[33] Subsequently, governmental experts of UNIDROIT member states elaborated further on the preliminary draft on four occasions.[34] At their last meeting, in October 1993, they presented a final draft. This final draft was the fundament for

[21] Thorn (2005), p. 89.

[22] UNIDROIT 1988 – Study LXX – Doc 3, June 1988: Preliminary Draft Convention on the Restitution of Cultural Property.

[23] Article 3 of the Preliminary Draft.

[24] Cf. Article 4 (1) of the Preliminary Draft.

[25] Article 2 (1) (a) of the Preliminary Draft.

[26] Article 2 (1) (b) of the Preliminary Draft.

[27] Cf. Odendahl (2005), p. 177; Thorn (2005), p. 89.

[28] Thorn (2005), p. 90.

[29] A full list of members of the commission can be found in the Appendix to UNIDROIT 1990 – Study LXX – Doc 19, August 1990: Preliminary Draft Convention on Stolen or Illegally Exported Cultural Objects approved by the UNIDROIT study group on the international protection of cultural property, with Explanatory Report.

[30] Beck (2007), p. 21, n 87.

[31] Asmuss (2011), p. 100; Beck (2007), p. 21.

[32] Reichelt (1994), p. 76.

[33] Thorn (2005), p. 90.

[34] Schaffrath (2007), p. 47.

the discussions at the final diplomatic conference in Rome where delegates of the UNIDROIT member states met between 7 and 24 June 1995.[35]

Though a variety of independent and governmental experts had already worked on the draft for a considerable time, at the conference in Rome the draft gave rise to considerable contention between market and source states. These included the possible retroactivity of the convention, the time limitation to be applied to any claim for return, the compensation for the bona fide purchaser, and the transnational effect of export regulations.[36]

As the source states outnumbered the market states, they were able to dominate the voting. However, quickly they realised that forcing their interests through decreased the likelihood that major market states would then ratify the convention and therefore limit its effectiveness. Hence, a working group comprised of delegates of source and market states was established on the initiative of Mexico.[37]

The compromise thus achieved was finally adopted on 24 June 1995 by the UNIDROIT member states with 37 to 5 votes and 17 abstentions.[38] The treaty was open for signature by all states until 30 June 1996[39] and is now open for accession.[40] The 1995 UNIDROIT Convention, however, entered into force in accordance with its Article 12 (1)[41] on 1 July 1998,[42] 6 months following the date of deposit of the fifth instrument of ratification, acceptance, approval or accession. Hitherto, 37 states have become parties to the convention, most recently Algeria.[43] However, the major art market states are yet to accede.

3.1.3 *The 1995 UNIDROIT Convention's Goals*

The aim of the treaty is clearly stated in its preamble. Accordingly, the 1995 UNIDROIT Convention was adopted to contribute effectively to the fight against the illicit trade in cultural objects by establishing common, minimal legal rules for

---

[35] Beck (2007), p. 22.

[36] Raschèr (2000), p. 68.

[37] Beck (2007), p. 23.

[38] Weidner (2001), p. 250; Beck (2007), p. 23; Carducci (2009), p. 79; Streinz (1998), p. 100.

[39] Cf. Article 11 (1) of the 1995 UNIDROIT Convention: "This Convention is open for signature at the concluding meeting of the Diplomatic Conference for the adoption of the draft UNIDROIT Convention on the International Return of Stolen or Illegally Exported Cultural Objects and will remain open for signature by all States at Rome until 30 June 1996.".

[40] Cf. Article 11 (3) of the 1995 UNIDROIT Convention: "This Convention is open for accession by all States which are not signatory States as from the date it is open for signature.".

[41] Article 12 (1) of the 1995 UNIDROIT Convention: "This Convention shall enter into force on the first day of the sixth month following the date of deposit of the fifth instrument of ratification, acceptance, approval or accession.".

[42] Raschèr (2000), p. 69.

[43] Cf. http://www.unidroit.org/status-cp.

the restitution and return of cultural objects between contracting states, with the objective of improving the preservation and protection of the cultural heritage.[44]

However, unlike the 1970 UNESCO Convention which was intended as a more comprehensive regulation of the subject matter,[45] the 1995 UNIDROIT Convention was ab initio only planned as a complementing instrument to the former[46] which would establish a harmonised minimum standard for the purposes of the preservation and protection of cultural heritage. This idea is particularly reflected in the fact that the state parties acknowledge that the convention will not by itself provide a solution to the problems raised by illicit trade, but that it initiates a process that will enhance international cultural cooperation and maintain a proper role for legal trading and inter-state agreements for cultural exchanges[47] and, furthermore, that its implementation should be accompanied by other effective measures for protecting cultural objects, such as the development and use of registers, the physical protection of archaeological sites and technical cooperation.[48]

Another remarkable point in this regard is that the state parties explicitly state that the adoption of the provisions of the convention for the future in no way confers any approval or legitimacy upon illegal transactions of whatever kind which may have taken place before the entry into force of the treaty.[49] The state parties thereby recognise that the 1995 UNIDROIT Convention has no effect of preclusion, especially in regard to colonial heritage, which can be seen as a clear concession to source states which tend to be former colonies. Equally, the statement that the provision of any remedies, such as compensation, needed to effect restitution and return in some states, does not imply that such remedies should be adopted in other states,[50] has to be understood as a good will gesture towards source states with limited financial means.

However, despite these concessions, the preamble is not representative of total victory for the source states, rather, it reflects a compromise.[51] It incorporates, for instance, a universalist approach to cultural heritage at several points. It declares that the protection of cultural heritage is of fundamental importance for the promotion of understanding between peoples and that the dissemination of culture is of significance for the well-being of humanity and the progress of civilisation.[52]

---

[44]Paragraph 4 of the Preamble of the 1995 UNIDROIT Convention.

[45]On the purpose of the 1970 UNESCO Convention cf. pp. 12ff.

[46]This is made clear especially by Paragraph 9 of the Preamble of the 1995 UNIDROIT Convention: "RECOGNISING the work of various bodies to protect cultural property, particularly the 1970 UNESCO Convention on illicit traffic and the development of codes of conduct in the private sector".

[47]Paragraph 7 of the Preamble of the 1995 UNIDROIT Convention.

[48]Paragraph 8 of the Preamble of the 1995 UNIDROIT Convention.

[49]Paragraph 6 of the Preamble of the 1995 UNIDROIT Convention.

[50]Paragraph 5 of the Preamble of the 1995 UNIDROIT Convention.

[51]Cf. Beck (2007), p. 23.

[52]Cf. Paragraph 2 of the Preamble of the 1995 UNIDROIT Convention.

Furthermore, according to the preamble, the preservation and protection of cultural heritage is in the interest of all.[53] Additionally, the convention was adopted deeply concerned by the illicit trade in cultural objects and the irreparable damage frequently caused by it, both to these objects themselves and to the cultural heritage of not only national, tribal, indigenous or other communities, but also to the heritage of all peoples, and in particular by the pillage of archaeological sites and the resulting loss of irreplaceable archaeological, historical, and scientific information.[54]

Moreover, the fact that the preamble contains the idea to maintain a proper role for legal trading and inter-state agreements for cultural exchanges[55] is also a manifestation of market state interests. Thereby they assured that not all trade in cultural objects was per se considered as morally contemptible and therefore illegalised, but that there was still capacity for their markets to operate.

3.1.4 The Ambit of the 1995 UNIDROIT Convention

3.1.4.1 Notion of "Cultural Objects"

According to Article 1 of the 1995 UNIDROIT Convention, the treaty applies to claims of an international character for the restitution of stolen cultural objects[56] and the return of cultural objects removed from the territory of a contracting state contrary to its law regulating the export of cultural objects for the purpose of protecting its cultural heritage, i.e. illegally exported cultural objects.

Thus, the definition of cultural objects is essential in order to determine the substantive scope of the agreement. In line with this, the definition of cultural object is contained in the very first part of the convention, in Article 2. Accordingly, for the purposes of the convention, cultural objects are those which, on religious or secular grounds, are of importance for archaeology, prehistory, history, literature, art or science and belong to one of the categories listed in the annex to the convention.[57]

Having in mind that the 1995 UNIDROIT Convention is meant to complement the 1970 UNESCO Convention, which is also reflected in Paragraph 9 of the

---

[53]Cf. Paragraph 4 of the Preamble of the 1995 UNIDROIT Convention.

[54]Paragraph 3 of the Preamble of the 1995 UNIDROIT Convention.

[55]Paragraph 7 of the Preamble of the 1995 UNIDROIT Convention.

[56]Article 3 (2) of the 1995 UNIDROIT Convention extends the term stolen to unlawfully excavated or unlawfully retained cultural objects: "For the purposes of this Convention, a cultural object which has been unlawfully excavated or lawfully excavated but unlawfully retained shall be considered stolen, when consistent with the law of the State where the excavation took place.".

[57]Cf. Article 1 of the 1970 UNESCO Convention: "For the purposes of this Convention, the term 'cultural property' means property which, on religious or secular grounds, is specifically designated by each State as being of importance for archaeology, prehistory, history, literature, art or science and which belongs to the following categories:".

Preamble of the 1995 UNIDROIT Convention,[58] and that many states had issued national legislation using its wording,[59] it is not surprising that Article 2 of the 1995 UNIDROIT Convention quotes almost verbatim the first sentence of Article 1 of the 1970 UNESCO Convention.[60] Moreover, the annex referred to in Article 2 of the 1995 UNIDROIT Convention is identical to the enumerative list contained in Article 1 of the 1970 UNESCO Convention.[61]

---

[58]Paragraph 9 of the Preamble of the 1995 UNIDROIT Convention reads: "RECOGNISING the work of various bodies to protect cultural property, particularly the 1970 UNESCO Convention on illicit traffic and the development of codes of conduct in the private sector".

[59]Forrest (2010), p. 199.

[60]Cf. Article 1 of the 1970 UNESCO Convention:

"For the purposes of this Convention, the term 'cultural property' means property which, on religious or secular grounds, is specifically designated by each State as being of importance for archaeology, prehistory, history, literature, art or science and which belongs to the following categories:"

and Article 2 of the 1995 UNIDROIT Convention:

"For the purposes of this Convention, cultural objects are those which, on religious or secular grounds, are of importance for archaeology, prehistory, history, literature, art or science and belong to one of the categories listed in the Annex to this Convention.".

[61]Article 1 of the 1970 UNESCO Convention:

(a) "Rare collections and specimens of fauna, flora, minerals and anatomy, and objects of palaeontological interest;
(b) property relating to history, including the history of science and technology and military and social history, to the life of national leaders, thinkers, scientists and artist and to events of national importance;
(c) products of archaeological excavations (including regular and clandestine) or of archaeological discoveries ;
(d) elements of artistic or historical monuments or archaeological sites which have been dismembered;
(e) antiquities more than one hundred years old, such as inscriptions, coins and engraved seals;
(f) objects of ethnological interest;
(g) property of artistic interest, such as:

  (i) pictures, paintings and drawings produced entirely by hand on any support and in any material (excluding industrial designs and manufactured articles decorated by hand);
  (ii) original works of statuary art and sculpture in any material;
  (iii) original engravings, prints and lithographs ;
  (iv) original artistic assemblages and montages in any material;

(h) rare manuscripts and incunabula, old books, documents and publications of special interest (historical, artistic, scientific, literary, etc.) singly or in collections ;
(i) postage, revenue and similar stamps, singly or in collections;
(j) archives, including sound, photographic and cinematographic archives;
(k) articles of furniture more than one hundred years old and old musical instruments."

Annex to 1995 UNIDROIT Convention:

(a) "Rare collections and specimens of fauna, flora, minerals and anatomy, and objects of palaeontological interest;

Hence, like in the case of the 1970 UNESCO Convention, for cultural objects to fall within the scope of the 1995 UNIDROIT Convention, they also have to fall under the abstract definition provided for in Article 2 of the 1995 UNIDROIT Convention as well as under one of the categories of its annex[62] as both are complementary. This approach has to be attributed to the same compromise concluded in the case of the 1970 UNESCO Convention.[63] While especially former colonial powers and major art market states were reluctant to accept a purely general definition out of fear that such a definition would escalate the scope of the agreement, the countries of origin advocated the former.[64] In the end both were incorporated. What seems to be again a compromise at first glance, proves to be a triumph for the importing countries since the definition is now even more restrictive than if it were purely enumerative as objects now have to satisfy the general definition in addition to be part of the enumerative list,[65] which again has an exhaustive character and is not of exemplary nature.

On closer consideration, however, there are two differences between the general definitions of cultural objects of the 1995 UNIDROIT and the 1970 UNESCO Conventions. Firstly, the 1995 UNIDROIT Convention uses the term "object" instead of "property". This is owed to the fact that by 1995 the term "property" was considered outdated since it was conceived as stressing the aspect of ownership too much and the fact that cultural artefacts are objects which can be traded as any other good. The term "heritage", which was gaining ground at that time, was on the

---

(b) property relating to history, including the history of science and technology and military and social history, to the life of national leaders, thinkers, scientists and artist and to events of national importance;
(c) products of archaeological excavations (including regular and clandestine) or of archaeological discoveries ;
(d) elements of artistic or historical monuments or archaeological sites which have been dismembered;
(e) antiquities more than one hundred years old, such as inscriptions, coins and engraved seals;
(f) objects of ethnological interest;
(g) property of artistic interest, such as:

(i) pictures, paintings and drawings produced entirely by hand on any support and in any material (excluding industrial designs and manufactured articles decorated by hand);
(ii) original works of statuary art and sculpture in any material;
(iii) original engravings, prints and lithographs ;
(iv) original artistic assemblages and montages in any material;

(h) rare manuscripts and incunabula, old books, documents and publications of special interest (historical, artistic, scientific, literary, etc.) singly or in collections ;
(i) postage, revenue and similar stamps, singly or in collections;
(j) archives, including sound, photographic and cinematographic archives;
(k) articles of furniture more than one hundred years old and old musical instruments.".

[62]Stamatoudi (2011), p. 73.

[63]UNIDROIT Secretariat (2001), p. 496.

[64]Stamatoudi (2011), p. 72, n 118.

[65]Raschèr (2000), p. 71.

other hand opposed by certain countries as being emotive.[66] However, the French version uses the term "biens culturels"—the same term used in the 1970 UNESCO Convention. This evidences that eventually the change in terminology should not be understood as a change in content.[67] And secondly, as a more significant distinction, the 1995 UNIDROIT Convention does not require an object to be "specifically designated"[68]—a requirement leading to quite some discussion in the context of the 1970 UNESCO Convention.[69]

Consequently, the 1995 UNIDROIT Convention does not allow contracting states to define their own national treasures, but aims at establishing an autonomous and uniform definition of cultural heritage.[70] One could argue that due to the quite distinct historical, cultural and religious background of different states, each state will have very distinct ideas of what might be of importance for another state or its citizens and, therefore, contracting states seem to be naturally the only competent authority to determine their own cultural treasures.[71] This approach would be further strengthened by the fact that permitting states to determine what is of importance to them increases the likelihood for the convention to be accepted.

However, this would undermine the 1995 UNIDROIT Convention, as it aims at establishing a harmonised minimum standard for the purpose of the preservation and protection of cultural heritage.[72] Furthermore, the convention also aims at protecting the ownership of private parties and relies on private action.[73] If the treaty required states to specially designate artefacts to benefit from the protection of the convention, this would allow states to exclude certain objects which might be of particular value for certain groups or individuals.[74] And finally, certain states do not have a tradition or system of classification. The special designation requirement would disadvantage them and in particular their citizens.[75] Hence, it was a necessary step to exclude this special designation requirement. In addition, waiving the requirement of special designation broadens the substantive scope of the treaty[76] by also allowing the convention to cover unregistered and uninventoried cultural objects.[77]

---

[66]Forrest (2010), p. 200; Prott (1997), p. 17.

[67]Cf. UNIDROIT Secretariat (2001), p. 488.

[68]Article 1 of the 1970 UNESCO Convention: "For the purposes of this Convention, the term 'cultural property' means property which, on religious or secular grounds, is *specifically designated by each State* as being of importance for archaeology, prehistory, history, literature, art or science and which belongs to the following categories:".

[69]On the dispute in the context of the 1970 UNESCO Convention cf. pp. 18f.

[70]Weidner (2001), p. 250.

[71]Cf. Stamatoudi (2011), p. 75.

[72]Cf. Beck (2007), p. 157.

[73]Prott (1996), p. 62; Campfens (2014), p. 68.

[74]Cf. Rietschel (2009), p. 54.

[75]Prott (1997), pp. 26f.

[76]So also Thorn (2005), p. 112.

[77]Cf. also Roodt (2015), p. 113.

3.1.4.2 Addressees

In compliance with the general arrangement of the 1995 UNIDROIT Convention, the personal scope differentiates between stolen and illegally exported cultural objects. For illegally exported cultural objects Article 5 (1) constitutes explicitly that only contracting states may request a court or other competent authority of another contracting state to order the return of a cultural object illegally exported from the territory of the requesting state. Thus, in the case of illegally exported cultural objects only a contracting state may be claimant and defendant.[78]

With regard to stolen cultural artefacts, however, the convention only states in Article 3 (1) that the possessor of a cultural object which has been stolen shall return it. Hence, the treaty only clarifies the defendant: the possessor. It is important in this context to understand that in the light of the aims of the 1995 UNIDROIT Convention to prevent the theft and facilitate the restitution of stolen cultural objects the term "possessor" does not correspond to a specific term used in any particular jurisdiction, but has to be interpreted in a broad, convention-inherent sense.[79]

Article 3 (1) does, however, not specify the claimant. Since the object has been stolen it is obvious that the property owner is a legitimate claimant, regardless of his nationality. This means that in the spirit of the convention even citizens of countries which are not party to the treaty may invoke the rights provided for in it.[80] In addition, the provision can also be invoked by the contracting state itself if it is the rightful owner.[81] Further to this though, besides the legitimate property owner, the rightful possessor may also invoke the provisions concerning stolen cultural objects.[82] Since he is also affected in his own rights he may even claim the stolen cultural object if the legitimate property owner does not intend to do so.

Another relevant issue here is the relationship between both possible causes of action. While private parties can only act in the case of stolen cultural property, in certain cases states may have a cause of action on the basis of the rules on illegally exported cultural objects as well as the norms on stolen ones. This is the case when the cultural object has not only been stolen, but also illegally exported and the contracting state is the property owner. The convention does not grant any precedence to either of the two legal bases.[83] Thus, a state can decide on which grounds it will reclaim the cultural object; or it may even invoke both. Furthermore, as the state is infringed in its own rights when cultural property is exported illegally, it has

[78]In this context, Asmuss (2011), p. 98ff, 130ff has to be mentioned, who discusses whether or not indigenous groups have the equivalent right as state parties to invoke Article 5 (1) of the UNIDROIT Convention directly, but eventually argues for an analogous application of Article 5 (1) of the UNIDROIT Convention which takes the special needs and interests of indigenous peoples into account.

[79]Cf. Beck (2007), p. 162.

[80]Beck (2007), p. 161.

[81]Beck (2007), p. 161.

[82]See Halsdorfer (2009), p. 309 for further discussion.

[83]Thorn (2005), p. 96.

the right to reclaim it on these grounds, even if the property owner does not take action based on the regulations regarding stolen cultural objects.[84]

3.1.4.3 Territorial Scope

While the first intention was to create a uniform law covering all claims for the restitution of stolen cultural objects,[85] the drafters of the convention soon realised that this would require massive interference with the various national property laws of state parties, since the fundamental concepts established by the convention are quite foreign to a multitude of national legislations.[86] Hence, the convention was restricted to claims of international character.[87] However, as a consequence, the drafters accepted a dual system. Cases of international character fall within the scope of the convention and thus in these cases the claimant can rely on the benefits of the treaty, whereas cases with a merely domestic character are only subject to national legislation[88]—a situation known from European Union (EU) law.

As a product of this distinction the determination of the international character of a case is of crucial importance. While in cases of illegally exported cultural objects international character is intrinsic to the case, since the cultural object must have crossed the border,[89] in the case of stolen cultural objects the question of whether or not this requirement is met sometimes raises issues. In principle, the disputable cases can be divided into four categories: (1) Cases in which the stolen objects have been returned to the country in which the theft occurred, (2) cases in which the transfer of property has already taken place within the country where the theft took place, (3) cases in which only the nationality of the owner and the thief or purchaser differ, and (4) cases in which the theft occurred in a country that is not party to the 1995 UNIDROIT Convention.

When a cultural object is stolen in one state and brought to another where it is sold, this is clearly a case with international character.[90] An interesting question arises though if the purchaser is a national of the source country and brings the

---

[84]Thorn (2005), p. 96.

[85]Cf. UNIDROIT 1992 – Study LXX – Doc 30 – Appendix III, June 1992, Article 1: "This Convention applies to claims for the restitution of stolen cultural objects and for the return of cultural objects removed from the territory of a Contracting State contrary to its export legislation." The draft does not include any restriction to "claims of an international character".

[86]Beck (2007), p. 145.

[87]Cf. UNIDROIT Secretariat (2001), p. 492.

[88]Beck (2007), p. 29.

[89]Cf. Thorn (2005), p. 97.

[90]Kurpiers (2005), p. 103.

cultural object back to the country in which it had been stolen. Does this re-import annul the international character of the case?

Some might argue that when, for example, a Greek purchaser re-imports to Greece a cultural object which was stolen from there and which he bought from the Greek thief in another state party to the 1995 UNIDROIT Convention, there is no longer a case with international character, since at the moment of the claim, the claimant and the opponent are Greek nationals and the cultural object is located within Greece, the place where the theft took place.[91]

It must be admitted that not every tenuous foreign element should be considered sufficient to meet the international character requirement, since this would render the distinction between purely domestic cases and those with international character practically obsolete by basically leaving no more space for entirely domestic cases. However, cases in which the object has been physically removed from the territory of origin and sold in another state do meet the international character requirement and are thus covered by the convention.[92]

This approach is particularly supported by the purpose of the convention; the treaty aims not only at the restitution of stolen cultural objects, but also at protecting them. Annulling the international character of the mentioned cases would only be beneficial to those laundering works of art.[93] Thus, once international character has been established it is not lost if the stolen cultural object at some point in time returns to the country in which the theft occurred. Therefore, cases in which the stolen object is back in the country in which the theft took place are still ones with an international character.[94]

Another issue causing debate is the transfer of property within the country where its theft occurred to someone who acted in good faith. The question is whether this former purely domestic case obtains an international character or not when this bona fide purchaser conveys the cultural object to another country, despite the fact that at the time of crossing a national border he had already acquired ownership according to the laws of the country in which the object was stolen.

There is no clause within the treaty explicitly precluding such cases from the scope of the convention.[95] Thus, for example, if an Italian in good faith buys a cultural object stolen in Italy and obtains ownership of it in accordance with the Italian laws on bona fide, once this purchaser transfers the item to another country, the person the cultural object was stolen from could invoke the convention.

However, such a revival of the possibility to reclaim stolen cultural property would not only seriously undermine the distinction between purely domestic cases and those with an international character, it would also constitute a serious intrusion into the national rules on bona fide purchases by opening up the possibility to

---

[91] Cf., for example, Stamatoudi (2011), pp. 71f.

[92] Beck (2007), p. 147.

[93] Cf. Kurpiers (2005), p. 103.

[94] Weidner (2001), p. 250; so also Kurpiers (2005), p. 103.

[95] Beck (2007), p. 149.

circumvent them.[96] Furthermore, permitting private parties, and in particular a state, to invoke the convention when according to the national laws of that particular state the purchaser has already obtained ownership seems inexplicable. When, therefore, a bona fide purchaser transfers a (once) stolen[97] cultural object he has acquired ownership of according to the laws of the country in which it was stolen to another territory, this may not be referred to as a case having international character.[98]

A difference in the nationality between a thief and the property owner is the third case in need of clarification. In the case mentioned above, if the thief or the bona fide purchaser were Brazilian instead of Italian, one might hesitate as to whether the case would have international character or not, since nationals of two different states are involved.

However, as the stolen cultural object has not been physically removed from the country where the theft took place, the lex rei sitae is the most adequate instrument to solve the matter[99]; in particular, considering that in a globalised world with regions, such as the European Union, where people can easily cross borders and relocate from one country to another, in praxis the number of cases involving only citizens of the same state is minimal. Therefore, such a wide interpretation of the internationality of the case's character would effectively leave no room for domestic cases. Hence, these cases have to be considered as domestic cases with regard to the convention. They have to be resolved by applying national legislation, including regulations on the conflict of laws.[100]

A more delicate and complex matter are cases in which the theft has occurred in a third country; for example, when a cultural object belonging to a Turkish citizen is stolen in England by a German national and sold to a Belgian national in Sweden, at first glance, one may intuitively think that neither Turkey, nor England, Germany or Belgium are party to the convention and therefore the issue does not fall within the scope of the treaty. However, Sweden is state party to the 1995 UNIDROIT Convention.

As a general principle, states not party to a convention and their citizens are not bound by it and the obligations it establishes. On the other hand, they may not invoke the rights the convention provides for.[101] However, the drafters of the 1995 UNIDROIT Convention foresaw this issue and have elaborated on it. Article 1 of the Draft of the Governmental Experts required stolen cultural objects to be removed from the territory of a contracting state.[102] Hence, according to that

---

[96]Cf. Kurpiers (2005), p. 104.

[97]Some argue that the object loses its characteristic as "stolen", cf. Beck (2007), p. 150.

[98]Schaffrath (2007), p. 49; so also Kurpiers (2005), p. 104.

[99]Also Beck (2007), p. 151.

[100]Stamatoudi (2011), pp. 71f comes to the same conclusion, however, with a different argumentation.

[101]Cf. Graf Vitzthum (2013), pp. 120f.

[102]UNIDROIT 1990 – Study LXX – Doc 19, August 1990.

draft the scenario above would not fall within the scope of the 1995 UNIDROIT Convention. However, this passage was not adopted into the final convention. Article 10 (1) of the 1995 UNIDROIT Convention constitutes that the provisions of Chapter II shall apply only in respect of a cultural object that is stolen after the convention enters into force in respect of the state where the claim is brought, provided that the object was stolen from the territory of or is located in a contracting state after the entry into force of the convention for that state. Article 10 (1) (b), therefore, suggests that the mentioned case above falls within the scope of the treaty.[103]

However, one important restriction has to be made. If a bona fide purchaser obtains ownership of a stolen cultural object according to the national legislation of a country the object was located in before it reached the contracting state where the claim is brought, the case is excluded from the scope of the convention. Otherwise, a person whose cultural property was stolen in a contracting state in which a bona fide purchaser obtains ownership in accordance with the laws of that state would be in a more unfavourable situation than a person whose cultural property is sold in that state after being stolen in a non-contracting state. This would be the case, since as mentioned above in the context of the second case, the former cannot benefit from the 1995 UNIDROIT Convention, whereas the latter could.

In conclusion then, in order for a case to have an international character it has to fulfil two conditions. First, the stolen cultural object has to physically cross the border and leave the country where the theft occurred and, secondly, the prior rightful property owner must not have forfeited ownership to, in particular, a bona fide purchaser in the country of the theft or, in cases where the such occurred in a country which is a non-contracting party, before the stolen cultural object enters the contracting state party where the claim is brought.

3.1.4.4 The Crux Again: Retroactivity

Similar to the case of the 1970 UNESCO Convention, whether or not the 1995 UNIDROIT Convention ought to have a retroactive effect was one of the most controversial matters during the negotiations.[104] Again, the same groups formed to oppose each other; on the one hand, those countries most affected by the theft and illicit export of their cultural heritage and, on the other hand, major art market states dreading not only that a retroactive effect would lead to an inestimable number of claims depleting the collections of their national museums and collectors, but also for the general principle of free trade.[105] Since a retroactive effect of the convention

---

[103] Cf. Stamatoudi (2011), p. 70.

[104] Blake (2015), p. 47; Sheng (2010), p. 67.

[105] Thorn (2005), p. 96; cf. also Vrdoljak (2008), p. 273.

would have furthermore caused serious conflicts with constitutional guaranties existing in a significant number of states,[106] overall, the 1995 UNIDROIT Convention being retroactive would have made the convention unacceptable, particularly for major art market states.

As such, a compromise similar to the one in the context of the 1970 UNESCO Convention was struck. The 1995 UNIDROIT Convention is silent with regard to retroactivity and thus, in accordance with Article 28 of the Vienna Convention on the Law of the Treaties, it does not have a general retroactive effect.[107] For illegally exported cultural objects, Article 10 (2) clarifies furthermore that the provisions shall apply only in respect of a cultural object that is illegally exported after the convention enters into force for the requesting state as well as the state where the request is brought.[108] Thus, for the convention to be applicable in the case of illegally exported cultural objects, both, the state from where it has been exported illicitly and the state into which it has been imported have to be state parties to it.

The issue is, however, a little more complex for stolen cultural heritage. In the case of these objects, Article 10 (1) stipulates that the provisions apply only in respect to a cultural object that is stolen after the convention enters into force in respect of the state where the claim is brought, provided that the object was stolen from the territory of or is located in a contracting state after the entry into force of the convention for that state.

Thus, in the case of stolen cultural objects the convention always must have entered into force in the country of the claim at the time when a cause of action is brought. If the cultural object has been stolen in a contracting party, the 1995 UNIDROIT Convention must have additionally entered into force in this particular state at the time of the theft. However, it is also sufficient if instead the stolen cultural object has been imported into the state where a cause of action is brought after the convention entered into force for that state.[109]

However, as in the case of the 1970 UNESCO Convention, as compensation for not bestowing a general retroactive effect on the agreement, Article 10 (3) clarifies that the 1995 UNIDROIT Convention does not in any way legitimise any illegal transaction of whatever nature which has taken place before its entry into force or which is excluded under its Article 10 (1) and (2), nor limit any right of a state or other person to make a claim under remedies available outside the framework of the

---

[106]Beck (2007), p. 163.

[107]Thorn (2005), p. 97; cf. also von Schorlemer (1998), pp. 320f; Article 28 of the Vienna Convention on the Law of the Treaties: "Unless a different intention appears from the treaty or is otherwise established, its provisions do not bind a party in relation to any act or fact which took place or any situation which ceased to exist before the date of the entry into force of the treaty with respect to that party.".

[108]Prott (1996), p. 68 draws attention to the fact that earlier drafts had provisions explicitly expressing the non-retroactive character of the convention. This was abandoned as this seemed to expressly legitimise transfers prior to the entry into force of the convention, especially during colonial times.

[109]Cf. Kurpiers (2005), p. 105.

convention for the restitution or return of a cultural object stolen or illegally exported before the entry into force of the agreement.[110] Hence, state parties are not only free to conclude further reaching arrangements on which ground they may return cultural objects stolen or illegally exported before the entry into force of the treaty, but they may also simply return these based on national legislation.

3.1.5 The 1995 UNIDROIT Convention's Regulations on Restitution and Return

The dichotomy drawn between the restitution of stolen cultural objects and illegally exported ones in Article 1 of the Convention is reflected throughout the treaty. Chapter II contains the regulations for stolen cultural objects, whereas the provisions on illegally exported cultural artefacts are comprised by Chapter III of the 1995 UNIDROIT Convention.

3.1.5.1 Chapter II: Restitution of Stolen Cultural Objects

Articles 3 and 4 of the Convention contain the central provisions regarding the restitution of stolen cultural objects. Besides a general rule to restitute these objects, the chapter also deals with matters of time limitation[111] and compensation.[112]

3.1.5.1.1 The Unconditional Obligation to Restitute Stolen Cultural Objects

Article 3 (1) of the Convention establishes that the possessor of a cultural object which has been stolen shall return it. Thus, it constitutes a general obligation under private law to restitute stolen cultural objects.[113] This statement appears simple and natural at first glance. However, upon closer examination, it is quite striking. Not only does it impose a general obligation on the possessor to return the stolen cultural objects, it also completely disregards the legal construct of the bona fide purchaser common to civil law jurisdictions.[114]

---

[110]Cf. Article 15 of the 1970 UNESCO Convention: "Nothing in this Convention shall prevent States Parties thereto from concluding special agreements among themselves or from continuing to implement agreements already concluded regarding the restitution of cultural property removed, whatever the reason, from its territory of origin, before the entry into force of this Convention for the States concerned.".

[111]Cf. Article 3 (3)–(8) of the 1995 UNIDROIT Convention.

[112]Cf. Article 4 of the 1995 UNIDROIT Convention.

[113]Cf. Kurpiers (2005), p. 105.

[114]Cf. Raschèr (2000), pp. 76f; cf. also Thorn (2005), p. 120.

To facilitate the free movement of goods,[115] civil law jurisdictions, with different peculiarities,[116] concede the bona fide purchaser a title and position protected by law even with regard to the former legitimate owner or possessor of an object.[117] Hence, they accept that there may be situations in which a legitimate title bearer might not regain possession or even title which he has lost unlawfully. Equally, they acknowledge that a person may obtain a legally valid title from a non-entitled person.

Article 3 (1) of the Convention, with its lapidary statement, overturns this entire legal construct by imposing a general obligation to restitute in any case. Moreover, the convention employs the term "possessor" rather than "holder" or "owner". This means that it does not matter if in a certain jurisdiction the physical holder of the object has or has not obtain ownership. Using the more neutral term "possessor" guarantees that anyone who physically has the object, whether only as a holder or as an owner, is obligated to return it.[118]

However, imposing this general commitment, which is most favourable for achieving the goals of the convention, to increase the level of protection of cultural objects and the number of restitutions and returns of these artefacts, has only been made possible by the fact that the common law jurisdictions follow the Roman legal principle of nemo dat quod non habet ("no one gives what he does not have") meaning that no one can transfer a title he does not own and, therefore, repudiating the legal construct of the bona fide purchaser.[119]

A second important point in regard to the general obligation to restitute established by Article 3 (1) is the precise content of the obligation. The provision simply stipulates that the stolen cultural object has to be returned. It does not specify what is meant by this obligation. Does it only require the new possessor to physically give the object back or does it also imply that the possessor is obliged to procure property to the former legitimate owner?[120]

A first point of reference in order to solve this issue may be the fact that Article 3 (1) uses the term "restitute" in contrast to the phrase "return" found in the chapter about illegally exported cultural objects. One may be lead to believe that the utilisation of different terminology suggests different obligations[121]; that one means the pure obligation to provide possession and the other may imply a legal

---

[115]Thorn (2005), p. 118.

[116]For instance, in Italy the title is immediately acquired, whereas in France further requirements have to be met. Thorn (2005), p. 118; Hartung (2005), p. 360.

[117]Cf. Renold (2009), pp. 309f; cf. also Schnabel and Tatzkow (2007), ch I for more specific regulations of various countries concerning this matter with a focus on cultural objects looted during World War II.

[118]Cf. Prott (1997), p. 31.

[119]Cf. Thorn (2005), pp. 117f.

[120]Cf. Kurpiers (2005), p. 106; cf. also Thorn (2005), p. 123.

[121]Cf. Beck (2007), p. 171.

duty to procure ownership in addition. However, a consideration of the preliminary work of the study group reveals the use of terminology aimed primarily at distinguishing between the different natures of the claims under Chapter II (stolen cultural objects) and Chapter III (illegally exported cultural objects), the former being of a private law nature and the latter of a public law character.[122] The preliminary work gives no indication that the intention of the drafters of the 1995 UNIDROIT Convention was to impose different obligations by using different terminology in the two distinct chapters concerning stolen and illegally exported cultural objects.[123]

A systematic approach using Chapter III, however, is of assistance in determining the obligation imposed by Article 3 (1). As a general rule, in the case of an illegal export, the possessor of the cultural object must procure title and is entitled to compensation. Only as an exception, and with the consent of the requesting state party, may he retain ownership of the object.[124] Chapter II has a parallel structure[125]; the possessor has to restitute the stolen object and, in the case of good faith, is entitled to compensation.[126] Hence, the obligation of the possessor must be the same: to procure ownership where he has it.

This interpretation of the possessor's obligations under Article 3 (1) of the 1995 UNIDROIT Convention is also supported by the goals of the treaty. The 1995 UNIDROIT Convention aims at preserving cultural heritage by protecting the property of the legitimate owner. Not granting him the title would give rise to a legally unfavourable situation. Either the previous legitimate owner would regain possession, but due to a lack of ownership could potentially face claims from the possessor from whom he reclaimed the stolen object, or he would be protected from such claims by law which would leave the possessor with the property, which would be, however, hollow and worthless. Hence, although Article 3 (1) of the Convention does not ipso jure grant ownership to the former legitimate owner, it imposes on the possessor the obligation to bestow upon him the title.[127]

However, the provision does not indicate how to procure ownership specifically. In order not to be overly intrusive into the legal order of state parties it leaves this matter to their discretion. Thus, the possessor must procure ownership to the former legitimate owner in compliance with the legal system of the state in which the stolen cultural object is located.

---

[122] UNIDROIT 1990 – Study LXX – Doc 18, May 1990: The International Protection of Cultural Property. Summary report on the third session of the UNIDROIT study group on the international protection of cultural property, Paragraphs 16ff.

[123] Beck (2007), p. 172.

[124] Article 6 (3) (a) of the UNIDROIT Convention: "Instead of compensation, and in agreement with the requesting State, the possessor required to return the cultural object to that State, may decide: (a) to retain ownership of the object;".

[125] Cf. Beck (2007), pp. 172f.

[126] Cf. Sheng (2010), p. 66.

[127] Cf. Beck (2007), p. 174.

Another important point with regard to the general obligation to restitute is that although it covers all cultural objects, it is only applicable to stolen items. That having been said though, the 1995 UNIDROIT Convention itself does not provide for a definition of the term "stolen".[128] In order to clarify the meaning of "stolen", the drafting history with the preparatory work leading the way has to be taken into consideration.

The first drafts state that when a person has been dispossessed of cultural property by theft, conversion, fraud, intentional misappropriation of lost property or any other culpable act assimilated thereto by a court, the possessor of such property shall make restitution to the dispossessed person.[129] Since the drafters, however, came to the agreement that only theft was a criminal act recognised by all jurisdictions and that it would be inappropriate to extend the application of a uniform law to less clearly defined cases, the enumeration was restricted to stolen cultural objects.[130] In order to compensate for this, the drafters allowed member states at first to extend the provisions of Chapter II to acts other than theft whereby the claimant has been wrongfully deprived of possession of the object.[131] Hence member states could, for example, apply the rules on stolen cultural objects also to cases of conversion and fraud.

However, in the final version, all that is left of this is Article 9 (1) of the 1995 UNIDROIT Convention which clarifies that nothing in the convention shall prevent a contracting state from applying any rules more favourable to the restitution or the return of stolen or illegally exported cultural objects than provided for by the

[128]Halsdorfer (2009), p. 308.

[129]Cf. UNIDROIT 1988 – Study LXX – Doc 3, June 1988: Preliminary draft Convention on the restitution of cultural property, Article 2 (1): "When a person has been dispossessed of cultural property by theft, conversion, fraud, intentional misappropriation of lost property or any other culpable act assimilated thereto by a court [...], the possessor of such property shall make restitution of it to the dispossessed person".

[130]Cf. UNIDROIT 1990 – Study LXX – Doc 18, May 1990: The International Protection of Cultural Property. Summary report on the third session of the UNIDROIT study group on the international protection of cultural property 12: "One of the first problems which it encountered was that of whether only cases of theft should be regulated or whether on the other hand there should be an extension to any other similar act sanctioned by the criminal law. Some members were of the view that only theft should be dealt with, as this was a criminal act in all legal systems, and that it would be most imprudent to extend the application of the uniform law to less clearly defined cases which were treated differently from one country to another.".

[131]UNIDROIT 1990 – Study LXX – Doc 18, May 1990: The International Protection of Cultural Property. Summary report on the third session of the UNIDROIT study group on the international protection of cultural property, Appendix III, Article 11 (a) (i): "Each Contracting State shall remain free in respect of claims brought before its courts or competent authorities:

(a) for the restitution of a stolen cultural object:

(i) to extend the provisions of Chapter II to acts other than theft whereby the claimant has wrongfully been deprived of possession of the object;".

convention. Thus, state parties may still issue more favourable laws themselves or allow their courts to apply more favourable foreign laws using the rules on the conflict of laws. On the other hand, keeping in mind the drafting history, the term "stolen" has to be interpreted in a narrowly defined manner as not including fraud, conversion or similar cases, but solely theft in the narrow sense of the word.[132]

However, even theft is not always theft; various jurisdictions define this criminal act in quite different ways and require distinct legal prerequisites.[133] Here, the aim of the 1995 UNIDROIT Convention to establish a uniform law and the minutes of the Third Meeting of Governmental Experts have to be taken into consideration. Thus, for the purpose of the convention, the notion of theft is not a restrictive one based on certain national laws, but rather a broader, autonomous one.[134]

Article 3 (2) furthermore stipulates that for the purposes of the convention, a cultural object which has been unlawfully excavated or lawfully excavated but unlawfully retained shall be considered stolen, when consistent with the law of the state where the excavation took place. This provision thus allows contracting parties to extend the rules of Chapter II to unlawful excavation and containment by equating these to theft.[135] On the other hand, for determining what comprises an excavation, the 1956 UNESCO Recommendation on the International Principles Applicable to Archaeological Excavations has to be consulted.[136] Accordingly, an archaeological excavation is any research aimed at the discovery of objects of archaeological character, whether such research involves digging of the ground or systematic exploration of its surface or is carried out on the bed or in the sub-soil of inland or territorial waters.[137]

---

[132]Cf. Weidner (2001), p. 253.

[133]Cf. Beck (2007), p. 166.

[134]Cf. Thorn (2005), p. 117; Prott (1997), p. 31 states that the study group argued that the state parties' courts could either apply their own law or such other law according to their rules of private international law.

[135]However, Fincham (2008–2009), pp. 139f questionably considers this provision as one of the major stumbling blocks for market states to ratify the convention.

[136]Stamatoudi (2011), p. 79.

[137]Article I (1) of the 1956 UNESCO Recommendation on the International Principles Applicable to Archaeological Excavations: "For the purpose of the present Recommendation, by archaeological excavations is meant any research aimed at the discovery of objects of archaeological character, whether such research involves digging of the ground or systematic exploration of its surface or is carried out on the bed or in the sub-soil of inland or territorial waters of a Member State.".

3.1.5.1.2 The Time Limitation Issue

The subject matter of a time limitation for claims based on Article 3 (1) of the Convention was, as in the case of the 1970 UNESCO Convention, highly controversial.[138] Again, two polarised opinions were advocated. On the one side, market states argued in favour of a short time limitation in order to ensure maximum marketability, safety in transactions, and stability in the presumptions that were publicly created.[139] Source states, by contrast, campaigned for no time limitation at all, primarily based on moral principle, the idea of justice, and in order to combat the illicit trade in cultural objects by preventing the legitimisation of stolen objects in the long term.[140]

Once again a compromise was struck: Article 3 (3)–(8) of the Convention contain quite a complex body of different time limitations; they not only stipulate relative and absolute time limitations, but there is also a distinction drawn in the provisions between ordinary and specific cultural objects, for which different rules apply. As a general principle, Article 3 (3) requires that any claim for restitution shall be brought within a period of 3 years from the time when the claimant knew the location of the cultural object and the identity of its possessor. Considering the complexity of cases involving stolen cultural property—often the stolen artefact passes through various hands in different countries before it reaches the final purchaser—a time limitation of 3 years appears quite short.[141] A mitigating factor here is that the period only begins once the former possessor knows not only the location of the cultural object, but also the identity of its possessor. Hence, the period only begins when the former possessor may justly and reasonably be expected to take action. The 3 year time limitation, thus, must be seen as a manifestation of the legal concept of forfeiture[142]—a person not demanding his right within an appropriate time frame may not be worthy of protection any longer.

Nevertheless, Article 3 (3) also establishes, besides this relative time limitation of 3 years, an absolute time limitation of 50 years. Hence, the former possessor has to claim the stolen object in any case within a period of 50 years from the time of the theft. This absolute time limitation is longer than corresponding time limitations in most national legislations.[143] Even though it does appear quite long and may have some discouraging effect on thieves and art dealers trading with stolen cultural objects due to concerns of reclaims, one important point has to be kept in mind: cultural objects generally gain value over time. Not being able to openly present and market a certain stolen cultural object may not appear as much of an obstacle for theft if the thief can reasonably rely on an exorbitant rise in the market value of a

[138] O'Keefe (2006), p. 228.

[139] Stamatoudi (2011), p. 79.

[140] Weidner (2001), p. 257.

[141] Cf. O'Keefe (2006), pp. 230f.

[142] Weidner (2001), p. 256.

[143] Cf. Raschèr (2000), p. 79.

particular cultural object within the time period.[144] However, for reasons of legal certainty and in particular to protect the good faith of bona fide purchasers[145] an absolute time limitation seems appropriate—at least for certain objects.

For other objects, such a time limitation does not appear suitable due to their invaluable nature. Hence, Article 3 (4) stipulates that a claim for the restitution of a cultural object forming an integral part of an identified monument or archaeological site, or belonging to a public collection, shall not be subject to time limitations other than a period of 3 years from the time when the claimant knew the location of the cultural object and the identity of its possessor. Thus, for these cultural objects the absolute time limitation does not apply; they are only subject to the relative time limitation of 3 years. This provision has to be ascribed to the fact that in many jurisdictions (certain) cultural objects are deemed to be of such superior value that they are inalienable and the entitlement to them cannot be legally lost under any circumstance.[146]

However, a remarkable point in this regard is the fact that the agreement does not refer to any national legislation. Hence, even if the national rules do not acknowledge the concept of inalienability,[147] the former possessor may reclaim the stolen cultural object on the grounds of the treaty.

The definition of a public collection is found in Article 3 (7) of the Convention. Thus, for the purposes of the convention, a public collection consists of a group of inventoried or otherwise identified cultural objects owned by a contracting state, a regional or local authority of a contracting state, a religious institution in a contracting state or an institution that is established for an essentially cultural, educational or scientific purpose in a contracting state and is recognised in that state as serving the public interest. Hence, in order to benefit from the special protection offered by Article 3 (4) of the Convention, the cultural objects must be inventoried or otherwise identified—a requirement previously laid down in a similar manner in the 1970 UNESCO Convention. The question arising in this context is what "a group of cultural objects" is. Considering the aim of the convention, the term has to be understood broadly. Thus, two objects are sufficient to constitute a group.[148]

Article 3 (8) of the 1995 UNIDROIT Convention does exempt from the inventory requirement sacred or communally important cultural objects belonging to and used by a tribal or indigenous community in a contracting state as part of that community's traditional or ritual use[149] and thereby equates these objects to those

---

[144]Cf. Stamatoudi (2011), p. 82.

[145]Similar Meena (2009), p. 598.

[146]Cf. Kurpiers (2005), p. 108.

[147]Cf. Weidner (2001), p. 258.

[148]Same O'Keefe (2006), p. 236.

[149]Article 3 (8) of the 1995 UNIDROIT Convention: "In addition, a claim for restitution of a sacred or communally important cultural object belonging to and used by a tribal or indigenous community in a Contracting State as part of that community's traditional or ritual use, shall be subject to the time limitation applicable to public collections.".

belonging to a public collection due to their overwhelming spiritual value for such mentioned communities.

However, the fact that these cultural objects are in principle only subject to the relative time limitation of 3 years was possibly seen as being too burdensome for certain states and hence considered to likely impair the acceptability of the convention. Hence, Article 3 (5) allows contracting states to declare that a claim is subject to a time limitation of 75 years or such longer period as is provided in its law. Thus, contracting parties may render the inalienability of certain cultural objects partly inoperative by making them subject to a time limitation of 75 or more years, which has to be seen as an accommodation for state parties unfamiliar with the concept of inalienability.[150] However, this declaration, which has to be made at the time of signature, ratification, acceptance, approval or accession,[151] cuts both ways; once a state party makes such a declaration, its own claims made in other contracting states are also subject to the same time limitation.[152] This is an expression of the general concept of reciprocity inherent to international relations and international law.

Another important subject is the effect of the time limitation. The convention itself does not specify whether the time limitation is only of procedural nature or a material dimension[153]—does the right to reclaim the cultural object perish or is it just hindered?

Since the text remains silent on this matter, this legal loophole has to be filled. As the convention aims at establishing a harmonised uniform minimum standard for the purposes of the preservation and protection of cultural heritage, a uniform interpretation of the legal effect of the time limitation autonomous to the treaty appears appropriate. However, neither the preliminary work provides any sign of such an interpretation, nor is there a clear concept evident common to all contracting parties. In different jurisdictions the time limitation has quite different outcomes. Hence, although this could lead to some fragmentation, the effect of the time limitation has to be determined according to the legislation of the forum state, including the rules on the conflict of laws.[154]

150Cf. Weidner (2001), pp. 258f.

151Article 3 (6) of the 1995 UNIDROIT Convention: "A declaration referred to in the preceding paragraph shall be made at the time of signature, ratification, acceptance, approval or accession.".

152Article 3 (5) (2) of the 1995 UNIDROIT Convention: "A claim made in another Contracting State for restitution of a cultural object displaced from a monument, archaeological site or public collection in a Contracting State making such a declaration shall also be subject to that time limitation.".

153Cf. Beck (2007), p. 181; cf. also O'Keefe (2006), pp. 232f.

154Beck (2007), p. 181.

3.1.5.1.3 The Compensation Requirement

Article 3 (1) of the Convention establishes an unconditional obligation on the possessor to return stolen cultural objects. Hence, despite potential good faith which would grant ownership to the possessor of a stolen object and entitle him to keep it, especially in civil law jurisdictions, the possessor has to return the artefact under all circumstances.

However, in compensation for this unconditional obligation to return the stolen cultural object, Article 4 (1) of the Convention stipulates that—regardless of his good or bad faith at the time of the claim[155]—the possessor of a stolen cultural object required to return it shall be entitled, at the time of its restitution, to payment of fair and reasonable compensation provided that the possessor neither knew nor ought reasonably to have known that the object was stolen and can prove that it exercised due diligence when acquiring the object. Interestingly, the convention uses the term "due diligence" which is a term of art in US law, whereas in general the drafters were quite conscious to avoid such terms of art from certain jurisdictions, such as bona fide purchaser, in order to avoid confusion.[156]

Nevertheless, this compromise[157] between the two extreme views, one protecting comprehensively the title obtained by a good faith purchaser and the other advocating no protection and thus no compensation,[158] requires two conditions to be met in order for the possessor to be entitled to compensation.[159] As a subjective[160] condition the possessor must have neither actually known nor could reasonably be expected to have known that the object was stolen. In addition, Article 4 (1) constitutes an objective criterion by requiring the possessor to prove that he exercised due diligence when acquiring the object. Article 4 (4) specifies how to assess whether the required due diligence was met; in determining whether the possessor exercised due diligence, regard shall be given to all the circumstances of the acquisition, including the character of the parties, the price paid, whether the possessor consulted any reasonably accessible register of stolen cultural objects, and any other relevant information and documentation which he could reasonably have obtained, and whether the possessor consulted accessible agencies or took any other step that a reasonable person would have taken in the circumstances.

---

[155]Boos (2006), p. 59; Schaffrath (2007), p. 51; cf. also Lalive (2009), p. 322.

[156]Prott (1997), p. 46.

[157]Ochoa Jiménez (2011), p. 47.

[158]Thorn (2005), p. 117; Weidner (2001), pp. 254f.

[159]See further for the tension between cultural heritage protection and private ownership rights and approaches to reconcile both interests using the example of Belgium de Clippele and Lambrecht (2015), pp. 259–278.

[160]Cf. Raschèr (2000), p. 82.

Hence, Article 4 (4) provides for a quite profound and non-exhaustive[161] list of circumstances which may be considered when determining whether or not due diligence has been exercised,[162] such as an unusual place of transfer or undue haste being involved.[163] At the same time, this provides the purchaser with quite a detailed list of options he can make use of in order to assure the legality of the transaction. However, the most remarkable feature of Article 4 (1) of the Convention is the fact that, while in most jurisdictions that follow the concept of a good faith purchaser the good faith is assumed, the provision actually requires the possessor to prove that he exercised due diligence when acquiring the object.[164] This shift in the burden of proof[165] seems to be attributed to the idea that in any particular case the purchaser is from a practical point of view the person who can ensure the legality of the transaction the easiest.[166] While the claimant, as the victim of the theft, has no influence on the transaction between the dealer and purchaser, generally he is not even aware of it and thus cannot hinder it, for the purchaser it is a relatively trivial matter to determine whether or not a transaction is, or at least appears, legal.[167] Furthermore, by shifting the burden of proof to the purchaser, the general goal of the convention to fight illegal transactions of cultural objects is promoted as traders faced with more cautious purchasers will less likely find customers for stolen cultural objects which will in turn decrease the demand for such artefacts and in the long run lessen the number of thefts.[168]

Having said that, the treaty also recognises that there are persons more culpable than the purchaser: thieves and bad faith intermediaries. Therefore, Article 4 (2) of the 1995 UNIDROIT Convention provides that without prejudice to the right of the possessor to compensation, reasonable efforts shall be made to have the person who transferred the cultural object to the possessor, or any prior transferor, pay the compensation where to do so would be consistent with the law of the state in which the claim is brought. Furthermore, Article 4 (3) states that payment of compensation to the possessor by the claimant, when this is required, shall be without prejudice to the right of the claimant to recover it from any other person. Hence, state parties may pass on their duty to compensate to those third parties being in bad faith, but may also recover the amount paid in compensation from these persons.

[161]The non-exhaustive character of the list is emphasised by the usage of the term "including" in Article 4 (4) of the 1995 UNIDROIT Convention.

[162]Fincham (2008–2009), p. 137 however criticises that the provision could have been more specific about what actions should be taken and that the buyer should be required to consult impartial experts and major art theft databases.

[163]Prott (1997), p. 47.

[164]Weidner (2001), p. 255; Kurpiers (2005), p. 109; Renold (2009), p. 313.

[165]Hoffman (2009), p. 90.

[166]Kurpiers (2005), p. 110; Thorn (2005), p. 119.

[167]Cf. Raschèr (2000), p. 84.

[168]Similar Thorn (2005), p. 107.

In this regard the greatest problem with these provisions seem to be that they do not link the right of the possessor to claim compensation to any sort of duty on his part to contribute to trace the person the state party can pass on its duty to compensate the possessor or recover its loss from. Hence, since the possessor will obtain his compensation in any case, it is unlikely that in practice he will go to extremes to help the state party to locate such individuals.[169] A possible solution to provide incentive for the possessor to help trace the bad faith intermediary would be to implement laws granting him a further-reaching right to compensation against the latter than against the claimant state. In doing so, the purchaser would have an interest in locating the bad faith intermediary as he could claim any losses from him exceeding the compensation he can demand from the claimant.

Regarding the amount of the compensation, as is the case in the 1970 UNESCO Convention, the compensation has to be "fair and reasonable". This likewise raises the question of whether the compensation has to be paid according to the current value or the value at the time of purchase.[170] For the same reasons given in the context of the 1970 UNESCO Convention—predominantly that a good faith purchaser should neither have a loss nor a gain due to the purchase—the compensation does not have to meet the current value of the artefact, which might have increased tremendously since the purchase, but may also not just be symbolic in nature.[171] Rather, it has to consist of the purchase price, the costs related to the purchase, and any expenditure made on preservation,[172] assuming they were necessary and adequate.[173] Under this regime potential purchasers also cannot speculate on making at least some profit even if a cultural object should turn out to be stolen.

The idea that the possessor ought not to gain from obtaining a stolen cultural object is also reflected in Article 4 (5). According to this clause, the possessor shall not be in a more favourable position than the person from whom he acquired the cultural object by inheritance or otherwise gratuitously. Hence, the possessor must accept the bad faith of his predecessor he obtained the object from gratuitously as if he would himself have been in bad faith at the time of gaining the object. Thus, a possessor who has obtained the object gratuitously from a bad faith possessor is not entitled to compensation.[174]

3.1.5.2 Chapter III: Return of Illegally Exported Cultural Objects

Articles 5, 6, and 7 of the 1995 UNIDROIT Convention govern the central provisions regarding the return of illegally exported cultural objects.

---

[169]Cf. Stamatoudi (2011), p. 91.

[170]Cf. Weidner (2001), p. 255; cf. also Kurpiers (2005), p. 109.

[171]Thorn (2005), p. 151.

[172]Also Kurpiers (2005), p. 109.

[173]For more details on the matter of just compensation cf. pp. 27ff.

[174]Stamatoudi (2011), p. 94.

3.1.5.2.1 The Restricted Obligation to Return Illegally Exported Cultural Objects

The obligation to return illegally exported cultural objects established in Article 5 (1) of the Convention[175] is distinct from the duty to restitute stolen cultural objects dictated by Article 3 (1)[176] in several ways. Besides being written in softer language—Article 3 (1) reads "shall return it", whereas Article 5 (1) only speaks of "may request"—the very nature of the obligations differ. While Article 3 (1) creates a basis for a cause of action under private law, Article 5 (1) is more reminiscent of an administrative assistance treaty,[177] especially since only contracting states may invoke this provision and they can address in addition to courts also any other competent authority of another contracting party.

During the drafting of the 1995 UNIDROIT Convention states primarily affected by the illegal export of their cultural heritage advocated for a general obligation to return all cultural objects exported in violation of any national provisions regarding the transfer of cultural material. However, the market states in particular did not favour this idea, not only since they were campaigning for the free movement of goods,[178] including cultural objects, but also as this would require them to disregard the general principle of territoriality of laws by bestowing an extraterritorial effect to foreign states' national public laws by having to enforce them.[179] In light of the wide acceptance concerning the general application of foreign national public laws[180] nowadays and the fact that, in practice, it is the courts of the requested states which ultimately decide on the return of illegally exported cultural objects,[181] this fear of the market states seems unfounded.

However, a compromise was again eventually struck. In principle, a breach of a contracting state party's national public law forms the basis for the obligation to return.[182] This accrues from Article 1 (b) of the Convention that defines illegally exported cultural objects as such items removed from the territory of a contracting state contrary to its law regulating the export of cultural objects for the purpose of

---

[175] Article 5 (1) 1995 UNIDROIT Convention: "A Contracting State may request the court or other competent authority of another Contracting State to order the return of a cultural object illegally exported from the territory of the requesting State.".

[176] Article 3 (1) 1995 UNIDROIT Convention: "The possessor of a cultural object which has been stolen shall return it.".

[177] Cf. Boos (2006), p. 60; Weidner (2001), p. 259.

[178] Raschèr (2000), p. 90; Thorn (2005), p. 139.

[179] Cf. Boos (2006), p. 60; cf. also Thorn (2005), p. 146; cf. also Nafziger et al. (2014), p. 411.

[180] Stamatoudi (2011), p. 96 refers in this context to several international conventions such as the EEC Rome Convention on the Law Applicable to Contractual Obligations.

[181] Weidner (2001), pp. 260f expresses even the fear that in practice it is more likely that courts will interpret Article 5 (3) of the Convention quite restrictively in order to protect national interests such as the free movement of goods.

[182] Cf. Schaffrath (2007), p. 54; cf. also Kurpiers (2005), p. 110; Thorn (2005), p. 137.

protecting its cultural heritage.[183] Hence, contracting states are in some measure obliged to enforce foreign national public laws.[184] However, a breach of a contracting state party's national public law in itself is insufficient to lead to the return of a cultural object.

For a start, Article 1 (b) only defines such cultural objects as illegally exported that were removed contrary to the laws regulating the export of cultural objects for the purpose of protecting its cultural heritage of the respective state. Hence, only the breach of national laws specifically passed to protect cultural objects activate the obligation under Article 5 (1). The violation of provisions, which only casually or coincidentally happen to protect cultural objects, is insufficient to initiate the obligation established by the provision.[185]

Besides, unlike in the case of stolen cultural objects in which the former legal possessor or owner can reclaim the stolen cultural object as long as the state in which it is currently located is a contracting party and thus despite the fact whether or not the territory from which it has been stolen is a party to the convention,[186] Articles 5 (1) and 1 (b) have a narrower scope. Firstly, only contracting states are allowed to request the return of illegally exported cultural objects. Private parties cannot invoke Article 5 (1). Furthermore, the right only exists with regard to those cultural objects that have been illegally exported from the territory of the requesting state. However, this has the positive side effect that the 1995 UNIDROIT Convention avoids the complicated determination of the question of whose cultural heritage a certain object belongs to by bestowing the right to reclaim it to the contracting party from whose territory it has first been illegally exported.[187]

Another restriction to the right to request the return of illegally exported cultural objects is to be found in Article 5 (3). This provision establishes a number of conditions which have to be met in addition to the breach of national laws protecting cultural heritage in order to benefit from Article 5 (1).[188] Accordingly, a court or other competent authority of the state addressed shall order the return of an illegally exported cultural object if the requesting state establishes that the removal of the object from its territory significantly impairs (a) the physical preservation of the object or of its context, (b) the integrity of a complex object, (c) the preservation of information of, for example, a scientific or historical character and/or (d) the traditional or ritual use of the object by a tribal or

[183]In this regard, Article 17 of the UNIDROIT Convention has to be mentioned which establishes that "(e)ach Contracting State shall, no later than six months following the date of deposit of its instrument of ratification, acceptance, approval or accession, provide the depositary with written information in one of the official languages of the Convention concerning the legislation regulating the export of its cultural objects. This information shall be updated from time to time as appropriate.".

[184]Weidner (2001), p. 260.

[185]Cf. Raschèr (2000), p. 88; cf. also Thorn (2005), pp. 138f.

[186]Cf. Beck (2007), p. 161.

[187]Cf. Schaffrath (2007), pp. 54f.

[188]Cf. Schaffrath (2007), pp. 53f.

indigenous community or if the requesting state establishes that the object is of significant cultural importance for the requesting state.

Hence, in order for a contracting state to regain its cultural object, in addition to the breach of one of its own national laws specifically protecting cultural objects, at least one of the (further) autonomous requirements established by Article 5 (3) of the Convention has to be fulfilled.[189] However, in this context, it is of importance to fully grasp the difference in character between the two alternatives presented to the claimant by Article 5 (3); (a)–(d) provide for an enumerative list of interests which is in principle exhaustive,[190] but may be extended in accordance with Article 9 (1)[191] by each contracting party.[192] The impairment of these interests grants the contracting party the right to reclaim a specific cultural object. However, all these interests do not directly constitute a part of the relationship between the specific state and the particular artefact. In contrast, the second alternative provided for in Article 5 (3) requires the object itself to be of significant cultural importance to the state in question and thus provides grounds for a claim to return fundamentally based on the state-cultural object relationship itself.[193]

The significant cultural importance of a specific object, however, may not only originate from the particular craftsmanship or the scientific or aesthetic value of the item, but also from its rarity.[194] Hence, the final example of a specific art movement or period may, despite its inadequacies regarding craftsmanship, be nevertheless of significant cultural importance for the contracting state party.[195]

Another issue raised in the context of Article 5 (3) is how to interpret the requirement that the interests listed in (a)–(d) have to be impaired. A literal interpretation would require an actual adverse effect on the particular interest.[196] However, keeping the aims of the treaty in mind, to foster the protection of cultural objects and the return of such artefacts illicitly transferred, such an interpretation seems inadequate. A wider interpretation permitting claims on the grounds of a serious threat of damage to the listed interests appears more harmonious with the aims of the treaty.[197] However, Article 5 (3) demands a significant impairment of the interest. Hence, too broad an interpretation was not intended by the drafters and therefore the requirement of Article 5 (3) is met when the threat is sufficiently

[189] Cf. Schaffrath (2007), p. 54; Raschèr (2000), p. 90.

[190] Cf. Beck (2007), p. 195.

[191] Article 9 (1) 1995 UNIDROIT Convention: "Nothing in this Convention shall prevent a Contracting State from applying any rules more favourable to the restitution or the return of stolen or illegally exported cultural objects than provided for by this Convention.".

[192] Thorn (2005), pp. 140f.

[193] Raschèr (2000), p. 90 distinguishes in this context similarly between reasons lying outside the object itself and those connected to it.

[194] Thorn (2005), p. 141.

[195] Thorn (2005), p. 141.

[196] Beck (2007), p. 196.

[197] Beck (2007), p. 197.

qualified. The occurrence of damage has to be certain and the adverse effect on the interests has to be severe. Furthermore, the harm has to be imminent in order for Article 5 (3) to be fulfilled.[198]

However, with regard to this, it is also important to realise that the complainant has either to establish that the removal of the object impairs one of the interests mentioned in Article 5 (3) (a)–(d) of the Convention or that the object is of significant cultural importance. Hence, both options are available. It is enough that the contracting state party can establish one; it is not required to establish both.[199] When thus the cultural object is of significant cultural importance, the illegal export does not additionally have to impair one of the listed interests and vice versa.

Another point weakening the right to reclaim a cultural object based on Article 5 (1) of the Convention compared to a claim grounded on Article 3 (1) is to be found in Article 5 (4). According to this clause, any request made under Article 5 (1) shall contain or be accompanied by such information of a factual or legal nature as may assist the court or other competent authority of the state addressed in determining whether the requirements of Article 5 (1)–(3) have been met.

Hence, unlike in the case of stolen cultural objects, the 1995 UNIDROIT Convention does not stipulate with regard to illegally exported cultural objects a shift in the burden of proof towards the purchaser of the object,[200] but adheres to the general principle that each party to an action has to prove those facts which are beneficial to it. Even though some authors criticise Article 5 (4) by arguing that it restricts the convention's application with regard to illegally exported cultural objects without any apparent good reason,[201] this argument seems flawed. For a start, theft is a universally regulated crime accepted by everyone as an offence and well known even to laymen, whereas the laws regarding the protection of cultural objects vary significantly from country to country[202] and generally are too complex to be fully comprehensible to people without legal training. Furthermore, the right to reclaim stolen cultural objects according to Article 3 (1) of the Convention is based on a strong, universally accepted legal fundament: the concept of property. Claims grounded in Article 5 (1) are on the other hand based on a breach of legislation protecting cultural objects and hence on a quite particular interest.

By contrast, Article 7 is a provision more obviously excluding certain objects from the scope of Article 5 (1). According to this norm, the provisions of Chapter III shall not apply where the export of a cultural object is no longer illegal at the time at which the return is requested or the object was exported during the lifetime of the person who created it or within a period of 50 years following the death of that person.

---

[198] Beck (2007), p. 197.

[199] Thorn (2005), p. 140.

[200] Cf. Beck (2007), p. 260.

[201] Cf. Stamatoudi (2011), p. 97.

[202] Cf. Boos (2006), p. 61.

Article 7 (1) (a) reflects an idea well known from the field of criminal law; if between the criminal act and the court case the law has changed in favour of the defendant, he shall benefit from this change.[203] The same is true for the purchaser of illegally exported cultural objects. If the law in the contracting party has changed, he shall benefit from this. Furthermore, in consideration of the general reluctance of many states to enforce foreign states' national public laws, it also seems adequate that state parties do not have to enforce those laws which the state of origin has itself dismissed for some reason, in particular for being too restrictive with regard to the export of certain cultural objects.[204]

However, the restriction stipulated in Article 7 (1) (b), that objects exported during the lifetime of the person who created it or within a period of 50 years following the death of that person do not fall within the scope of Article 5 (1) of the Convention, is justified by UNIDROIT with the argument that the non-recognition of foreign law in this case constitutes a liberal response to the need to promote contemporary art in that it enables living artists to build a reputation abroad and that this exception is already accepted in most national legislations.[205] Nevertheless, this is still criticised by certain authors.[206]

Article 7 (2) of the Convention, on the other hand, arranges for an exception of the restriction stipulated by Article 7 (1) (b). Accordingly, notwithstanding the latter provision, Chapter III shall apply where a cultural object was made by a member or members of a tribal or indigenous community for traditional or ritual use by that community and the object will be returned to that community. Hence, contracting states have to enforce foreign national laws where cultural objects created by members of tribal or indigenous communities are concerned, despite the time of the creation of the particular object or in other words, even if the cultural object has been exported within the lifetime of the creator or within 50 years of his or her death.

Another provision enlarging the scope of Article 5 (1) is Article 5 (2). According to this norm a cultural object which has been temporarily exported from the territory of the requesting state, for purposes such as exhibition, research or restoration, under a permit issued according to its law regulating its export for the purpose of protecting its cultural heritage and not returned in accordance with the terms of that permit shall be deemed to have been illegally exported. Hence, cultural objects legally exported, but retained in violation of the export permit are also deemed to be illegally exported and therefore benefit from Article 5 (1).

A last point of discussion in regard to the obligation to return illegally exported cultural objects is the precise content of the obligation. Besides ordering the physical return of the illegally exported object, does the court also has to order the transfer of ownership?

---

[203]Cf. Wessels et al. (2015), p. 19.

[204]Thorn (2005), p. 141.

[205]UNIDROIT Secretariat (2001), p. 540.

[206]Stamatoudi (2011), p. 98.

According to Article 6 (3) (a), instead of compensation and in agreement with the requesting state, a possessor required to return a cultural object to that state, may decide to retain ownership of the object. Thus, only as an exception and only with the consent of the requesting state party may the possessor retain ownership of the object. Hence, in contrast to this, as a general rule, the possessor of the cultural object must procure ownership.

It is important in this context to note that Article 6 (3) (a) of the Convention reads "instead of compensation". Compensation is a right to which only good faith owners are entitled.[207] Thus, an exception to the general obligation to transfer ownership can only be applicable for good faith purchasers. Bad faith purchasers may under no circumstances retain ownership.[208]

3.1.5.2.2 The Time Limitation Rules

The regulations on time limitation with regard to illegally exported cultural objects are much less complex than the respective arrangements in the context of stolen cultural objects.[209] They are regularised in a single paragraph, in Article 5 (5). According to this norm, any request for return shall be brought within a period of 3 years from the time when the requesting state knew the location of the cultural object and the identity of its possessor and in any case within a period of 50 years from the date of the export or from the date on which the object should have been returned under a permit referred to in Article 5 (2). Hence, with regard to illegally exported cultural objects, only the relative time limitation of 3 years and the absolute time limitation of 50 years already familiar from the context of stolen cultural objects[210] are applicable.[211,212]

However, in the case of illegal exportation, there are no special rules on cultural objects forming an integral part of an identified monument or archaeological site or belonging to a public collection, as in Article 3 (4), (5), and (7) of the Convention or for sacred or communally important cultural objects belonging to and used by a tribal or indigenous community, such as in Article 3 (8) of the Convention.[213]

---

[207] Cf. Article 6 (1) of the 1995 UNIDROIT Convention: "The possessor of a cultural object who acquired the object after it was illegally exported shall be entitled, at the time of its return, to payment by the requesting State of fair and reasonable compensation, provided that the possessor neither knew nor ought reasonably to have known at the time of acquisition that the object had been illegally exported.".

[208] For the distinct treatment of bad and good faith purchasers with further arguments see Beck (2007), pp. 243ff.

[209] Beck (2007), p. 256.

[210] Cf. Article 3 (3) of the 1995 UNIDROIT Convention.

[211] Cf. Schaffrath (2007), p. 56.

[212] Cf. p. 117 for the explanations made in that context regarding the issue of time limitation.

[213] Cf. Kurpiers (2005), p. 111; Weidner (2001), p. 261.

Though on first glance this may appear surprising and give rise to criticism, as expressed by certain authors,[214] on closer inspection this renouncement of special regulations proves to be quite adequate. The cases in which cultural objects belonging to a public collection are exported illegally from the territory of a contracting party—not taking into account cases of theft—can essentially be divided into two categories. Firstly, either the object has been exported by a person to whom it has been entrusted by the curator of the public collection or the curator himself or, secondly, the object only becomes illegally exported in accordance with Article 5 (2) since it has not been returned in accordance with the terms of its export permit.

However, unlike in the case of theft, in these two scenarios the officials in charge of the public collection know at least the first person who has conducted the wrongful act. Therefore, for these officials and thus the contracting party, it is much easier to instigate and follow through with investigations into the whereabouts of the illegally exported cultural object. Hence, an extension of the generally applicable time limitation rules is not necessary.

On the other hand, concerning sacred or communally important cultural objects belonging to and used by a tribal or indigenous community, the extension of time limitations in the case of theft is owed to the idea that these communities are in need of special protection.[215] However, in cases of illegally exported cultural objects only the state is permitted to reclaim an object; the communities themselves cannot invoke Article 5 (1) of the Convention. Granting the contracting party an extension under these circumstances could only be justified if the state can be seen as a proxy for the tribal or indigenous community. It is important here to keep in mind that in most cases in which sacred or communally important cultural objects belonging to and used by a tribal or indigenous community are illegally exported—again disregarding cases of theft—either a member of the community or someone it has been entrusted to by the community will have illegally exported the cultural object.[216] Thus, the wrongful act was either conducted by the protected entity itself, one of its members or it is relatively easy for the victims to trace the lost item. Therefore, these communities either warrant no special protection or are not in need of a further reaching time limitation.

3.1.5.2.3 The Requirement to Compensate

Analogous to the case of the possessors of stolen cultural objects, the 1995 UNIDROIT Convention, as redemption for the loss of his legal position,[217] entitles

[214]Cf. Kurpiers (2005), p. 111; Weidner (2001), pp. 261f.

[215]Cf. Beck (2007), p. 257.

[216]Beck (2007), p. 257.

[217]Schaffrath (2007), p. 55 however interprets the compensation as an equilibrium for the intrusion into the national legal order.

the possessor of an illegally exported cultural object to compensation. However, there are slight but significant differences between the two compensatory regulations. According to Article 6 (1) of the Convention the possessor of a cultural object who acquired the object after it was illegally exported shall be entitled, at the time of its return, to payment by the requesting state of fair and reasonable compensation, provided that the possessor neither knew nor ought reasonably to have known at the time of acquisition that the object had been illegally exported.

Hence, while in the case of stolen cultural objects all possessors who are required to return are entitled to compensation,[218] in the case of illegally exported cultural objects the scope of the provision is narrowed down to only those possessors who acquired the object after it was illegally exported. This might appear frustratingly incongruous at first glance. But on further examination this restriction proves to be reasonable. If the scope of those eligible for compensation was not restricted to those who acquired the object after it was illegally exported, under certain circumstances even the person who exported the cultural object illegally may be entitled to compensation,[219] since unlike theft, the misconduct of illegal export does not necessarily require intent[220] and thus cases in which the owner of a cultural object negligently illegally exports the very same are, even though unlikely, easily conceivable.

Another fundamental difference between the restitution of stolen cultural objects and the return of illegally exported ones is the reason for giving the artefacts back and thus the aim of the provisions. While in the case of stolen cultural objects this lies in the dispossession of the former owner and thus it aims at the reconstitution of his position, in the case of illegally exported cultural objects the aim is to physically relocate the object to the country of origin, but not necessarily the restoration of the ownership.[221] Hence, Article 6 (3) determines that instead of compensation and in agreement with the requesting state, the possessor required to return the cultural object to that state, may decide to retain ownership of the object or to transfer ownership against payment or gratuitously to a person of its choice residing in the requesting state who provides the necessary guarantees.

Some authors claim the provision to be owed to the fact that especially the common law countries would not accept a provision which could be seen as constituting a confiscation of private property and which thus would interfere with private interests. They furthermore argue that these states would enter into such an obligation only if and in so far as it results from an agreement between the

[218]Article 4 (1) 1995 UNIDROIT Convention.

[219]See UNIDROIT 1994 – Study LXX – Doc 49, December 1994, No. 109: "A proposal to the effect that in the absence of such a certificate the bad faith of the possessor should be irrebuttably presumed was rejected by most delegations on the ground that it assumed the possessor's knowledge of the export legislation of each country and would have the effect of rendering virtually impossible the acquisition in good faith of any cultural object.".

[220]Cf. Thorn (2005), p. 138.

[221]Cf. Thorn (2005), p. 153; cf. also Schaffrath (2007), p. 55.

possessor and the claimant state party.[222] Such an interpretation of the provision, however, seems quite doubtful since the agreement depends on the state party. Thus, the state party regains the object in any case; the only difference is that if the state does not consent, it has to pay compensation.

Thus, the provision has to be seen as an endeavour to facilitate the physical return of illegally exported cultural objects to the country of origin by allowing, in particular, financially weaker state parties to permit the possessor to retain ownership or sell the object to a person residing in the requesting state for being in return released of their obligation to compensate the possessor.[223]

One remarkable point in this context is that Article 6 (3) (b) reads "transfer ownership against payment". Thus, the possessor may sell the illegally exported cultural object to a person of his choice for any agreed upon price. Hence, unlike the possessor of a stolen cultural object, he could theoretically make a profit with the object he obtained based on wrongful grounds.[224]

In addition, some authors raise another issue in the context of Article 6 (3). They cite res extra commercium, i.e. those cultural objects which are according to the law of the state of origin inalienable state property. The right of the possessor to sell illegally exported cultural objects to a person of his choice residing in the requesting state would in practice be undermined by the fact that as soon as the object returns to the state of origin it would automatically become state property again.[225]

This fear seems without cause principally for two reasons. First, the number of relevant cases seems to be relatively small, since in cases of res extra commercium the object has always and thus also prior to the illegal export been state property and an illegal export of state property in most cases is based on the theft of the cultural object, which is why states in such cases will rather reclaim the object based on Article 3 (1).

The second and more profound reason is that Article 6 (3) of the Convention itself makes such cases unlikely. According to the norm, the sale has to be in agreement with the requesting state. A requesting state party will be unlikely to permit the possessor to sell a cultural object it deems to be inalienable state property or will change the object's status before doing so.[226]

Another section of the provision that is somewhat puzzling and perhaps gives greater cause for concern is the requirement of the purchaser to provide the necessary guarantees. The agreement does not specify which guarantees these have to be, nor does it say anything about what might be the consequences if the guarantee is breached or suspended at a later point.[227] However, as the purchase has

[222]Cf. Stamatoudi (2011), pp. 100f.

[223]Schaffrath (2007), p. 55 comes to the same conclusion.

[224]Cf. Stamatoudi (2011), pp. 101f.

[225]Cf. Weidner (2001), p. 263.

[226]Weidner (2001), p. 263.

[227]Stamatoudi (2011), p. 101.

to take place in agreement with the requesting state, it has to be assumed that the convention surrenders the right to define which guarantees it deems to be necessary and what the consequences of a breach of such guarantees are to the respective state party who may determine them on a case-by-case basis.

Another significant difference between Articles 6 (1) and 4 (1) is the missing explicit obligation of the possessor of an illegally exported cultural object to prove that he or she exercised due diligence when acquiring the object[228] in order to be entitled to compensation. The meaning of this omission gives rise to some controversy. Some argue that the burden of proof is determined by the lex fori.[229] However, considering the aim of the treaty, to create a minimum standard for purposes of the preservation and protection of the cultural heritage by a uniform law, the omission can only be interpreted as imposing the burden of proof, as a general rule, on the requesting state. Hence, in the case of illegally exported cultural goods the claimant has, in accordance with general rules, to prove the mala fide of the possessor.[230]

Some authors argue that this unjustly improves the situation of the possessor of an illegally exported cultural good in comparison to the possessor of a stolen one and, in light of the goals of the treaty, wrongly punishes the possessor according to his predecessor's crime.[231] Although such a distribution of the burden of proof seems most unfortunate in light of the aims of the convention, it has to be considered that in the cases of illegally exported and stolen cultural objects the interests the treaty has to address are distinct and hence the convention needs to treat such cases differently. While in both types of cases the interest contradicting the return or restitution is the title of the current possessor, in the case of an illegally exported cultural object the return is "solely" based on a breach of a certain country's export regulations, whereas in the case of stolen cultural objects the ownership of the former possessor is put in the balance, which is a ground carrying much more legal weight in most jurisdictions. Thus, imposing the burden of proof on the claimant state party in the case of illegally exported cultural objects seems reasonable. Nevertheless, state parties may, in accordance with Article 9 (1),[232] enact national provisions more favourable for the return of illegally exported cultural objects, such as norms passing the burden of proof to the possessor.[233]

That having been said, Article 6 (2) holds the criterion for determining the bona fide of the possessor. Thus, in determining whether the possessor knew or ought reasonably to have known that the cultural object had been illegally exported,

[228] Article 4 (1) of the 1995 UNIDROIT Convention.

[229] For example Thorn (2005), p. 155.

[230] Beck (2007), p. 254.

[231] Stamatoudi (2011), p. 100.

[232] Article 9 (1) of the 1995 UNIDROIT Convention: "Nothing in this Convention shall prevent a Contracting State from applying any rules more favourable to the restitution or the return of stolen or illegally exported cultural objects than provided for by this Convention.".

[233] Cf. Thorn (2005), p. 150.

regard shall be given to the circumstances of the acquisition, including the absence of an export certificate required under the law of the requesting state. Hence, all circumstances of the acquisition have to be taken into consideration, in particular the absence of an export certificate required under the law of the requesting state. However, this open formulation also enables the deciding body to have recourse to criteria provided for in Article 4 (4) of the Convention in the context of stolen cultural goods,[234] such as the character of the parties, the price paid, whether the possessor consulted any reasonably accessible register, and any other relevant information and documentation which it could reasonably have obtained, and whether the possessor consulted accessible agencies or took any other step that a reasonable person would have taken in the circumstances.[235]

Given these criteria, it is clear that professional art dealers with specific knowledge in their respective art sectors will be subject to a much higher standard than private lay collectors and hence it will be much easier to prove their mala fide, since, for example, export regulations can be regarded as commonly and clearly known among this circle of experts.[236] Moreover, even those private lay collectors who neglect to consult experts may run the risk of losing their eligibility for compensation. Furthermore, the higher standards indirectly also apply to people obtaining the illegally exported object by inheritance or otherwise gratuitously due to Article 6 (5) of the Convention.[237,238]

As this provision shows, there are also similarities between the regulations concerning compensation in the case of stolen and illegally exported cultural objects. In both cases, for instance, the possessor must have acquired the object by purchase,[239] since Article 6 (5) of the Convention stipulates also for cases of illegally exported cultural objects that the possessor shall not be in a more favourable position than the person from whom he acquired the cultural object by inheritance or otherwise gratuitously. Thus, possessors obtaining illegally exported cultural objects by inheritance or otherwise gratuitously from the person who exported it illegally are not entitled to compensation.

Another area where both chapters essentially harmonise is the amount of compensation to be paid. As in the case of stolen cultural objects, the payment is

[234] Stamatoudi (2011), p. 100.

[235] Article 4 (4) 1995 UNIDROIT Convention: "In determining whether the possessor exercised due diligence, regard shall be had to all the circumstances of the acquisition, including the character of the parties, the price paid, whether the possessor consulted any reasonably accessible register of stolen cultural objects, and any other relevant information and documentation which it could reasonably have obtained, and whether the possessor consulted accessible agencies or took any other step that a reasonable person would have taken in the circumstances.".

[236] Raschèr (2000), p. 95.

[237] Article 6 (5) of the 1995 UNIDROIT Convention: "The possessor shall not be in a more favourable position than the person from whom it acquired the cultural object by inheritance or otherwise gratuitously.".

[238] Thorn (2005), p. 156.

[239] Beck (2007), p. 253.

required to be "just and reasonable". However, a notable difference between Article 4 of the Convention and Article 6 (4) is that the latter clarifies that the cost of returning the cultural object shall be borne by the requesting state, without prejudice to the right of that state to recover costs from any other person.

Hence, despite the obligation of the claimant state party to bear the costs of the transfer for the same reasons given in the context of the 1970 UNESCO Convention, predominantly that a good faith purchaser should neither have a loss, but also not gain due to the purchase, the compensation does not have to meet the current open market value of the cultural object, which may have increased tremendously since the time of purchase, but conversely also may not just be symbolic in nature.[240] Rather, it has to consist of the purchase price, the costs related to the purchase, and any expenditure made on preservation,[241] assuming they were necessary and reasonable.[242] This way, potential purchasers cannot speculate on making some money even if the cultural object should turn out to be illegally exported and will therefore likely be more careful when buying such an object.

3.1.6 The Complementary Rules of the 1995 UNIDROIT Convention Promoting Restitution and Return

Aside from the norms regulating the restitution and return of cultural property itself, the 1995 UNIDROIT Convention furthermore contains in Chapter IV (Articles 8–10) on "General Provisions" and Chapter V (Articles 11–21), entitled "Final Provisions", a number of complementary provisions facilitating the claim for restitution and return by particularly regulating procedural matters.

3.1.6.1 Jurisdiction

Article 8 (1) of the 1995 UNIDROIT Convention stipulates for stolen and illegally exported cultural objects that a claim under Chapter II and a request under Chapter III may be brought before the courts or other competent authorities of the contracting state where the cultural object is located. Thus, for the first time in a multilateral agreement, the 1995 UNIDROIT Convention adopts the forum rei sitae for cultural objects and establishes the international jurisdiction of the place where the stolen or illegally exported cultural material is situated.[243] This jurisdiction continues even if the cultural artefact has been removed to another territory after the action has been filed.[244]

---

[240]Odendahl (2005), p. 151.

[241]Cf. Kurpiers (2005), p. 109.

[242]For more details on this issue cf. pp. 27ff.

[243]Thorn (2005), p. 164.

[244]Beck (2007), p. 263.

This regulation is extraordinary since normally a jurisdiction based on the forum rei sitae is only common in the case of immovable property.[245] Multinational agreements, in particular those concluded between civil law jurisdictions, do not normally apply the forum rei sitae to movable property.[246] For example, both the European Community (EC) Council Regulation 44/2001 of 22 December 2000 on Jurisdiction and the Recognition and Enforcement of Judgments in Civil and Commercial Matters, which applies between EU member states and replaces—except in relation to Denmark—the 1968 Brussels Convention on Jurisdiction and the Enforcement of Judgements in Civil and Commercial Matters, as well as the 2007 New Lugano Convention, which basically extends the applicability of Regulation 44/2001 to certain member states of the European Free Trade Association (EFTA), establish as a general rule the jurisdiction of the member state in which the person to be sued is domiciled.[247,248]

Nevertheless, in the case of cultural objects the forum rei sitae, in particular in light of the UNIDROIT Convention appears appropriate. It has to be taken into consideration that in practice most stolen cultural objects are not necessarily sold or auctioned in the country where the theft occurred or in which the current possessor is domiciled, but in order to gain greater profit in more established auction houses which are often located in third countries.[249] Therefore, Article 10 (1) of the 1995 UNIDROIT Convention declares the treaty applicable for cases in which the object is located in a contracting state after the entry into force of the convention for that state and hence for cases in which neither the country of origin, where the theft has taken place, nor the country in which the current possessor has his residence are party to the 1995 UNIDROIT Convention. This provision would become inoperative if the forum rei sitae was not applicable because the former possessor in that case could neither take legal action in the country of theft nor the state in which the current possessor is located due to a lack of jurisdiction in consequence of the non-ratification of the treaty by the respective states.[250]

Enabling the former possessor to take action at a court or other competent authority of the state party in which the cultural object is located, furthermore,

---

[245]Cf. Article 22 (1) of the EC Council Regulation 44/2001 and equally worded Article 22 (1) of the New Lugano Convention: "The following courts shall have exclusive jurisdiction, regardless of domicile: 1. in proceedings which have as their object rights in rem in immovable property or tenancies of immovable property, the courts of the State bound by this Convention in which the property is situate.".

[246]Cf. Stamatoudi (2011), pp. 102f; cf. also Prott (1997), p. 71.

[247]Article 2 (1) of the EC Council Regulation 44/2001 and equally worded Article 2 (1) of the New Lugano Convention: "Subject to this Regulation, persons domiciled in a Member State shall, whatever their nationality, be sued in the courts of that Member State.".

[248]However, the second sections of the EC Council Regulation 44/2001 and the equally worded New Lugano Convention contain lists of special jurisdictions which do not include the forum rei sitae.

[249]Cf. Beck (2007), p. 265.

[250]Cf. Stamatoudi (2011), p. 103.

increases the effectiveness of the provisions on restitution and return as the court or competent authority has direct access to the particular object[251] and may, for example, stop its further export and thus possible disappearance or halt its auction with the result that the cultural object cannot be transferred during the course of the court case so that the former possessor does not have to chase the object from country to country despite having obtained a valid verdict.[252] Otherwise, by the time a judgment is made the object may have been transferred to another person in another country and, by the time it can be located and the legitimate owner tries to enforce the decision, the object may have been exported again.

In addition to this, the court decision can be directly enforced. Since the state which has to enforce the judgment is at the same time the one which has issued it,[253] the claimant will not likely encounter problems having the decision enforced. This is particularly relevant as the 1995 UNIDROIT Convention itself does not provide for any regulation regarding the recognition and enforcement of foreign courts' holdings.[254] This matter is completely left to national legislation. Bi- and multilateral agreements, such as the EC Council Regulation 44/2001 and the 2007 New Lugano Convention which regulate this matter explicitly in relation of the EU and EFTA countries, are thus desirable, if not inevitable.[255]

However, such bi- and multilateral agreements carry another risk in that they may establish other jurisdictions and thereby come into conflict with the regulations of the 1995 UNIDROIT Convention. As mentioned above, neither the EC Council Regulation 44/2001, or its predecessor the 1968 Brussels Convention, nor the 2007 New Lugano Convention recognise forum rei sitae. However, as all three of these treaties are only applicable in civil and commercial matters,[256] discord with the 1995 UNIDTROIT Convention in matters of illegally exported cultural objects is precluded as the request for return of such artefacts in the context of the 1995 UNIDROIT Convention has a public law nature.[257]

A conflict between the 1968 Brussels Convention and the 2007 New Lugano Convention on one hand and the 1995 UNIDROIT Convention on the other has been avoided for cases of stolen cultural objects by the fact that both formerly mentioned treaties declare in their Article 67 (1) that the conventions shall not affect any conventions by which the contracting parties and/or the states bound by

[251] Cf. Thorn (2005), pp. 164f.

[252] On the possibility of provisional measures under the 1995 UNIDROIT Convention cf. pp. 117f.

[253] Stamatoudi (2011), p. 103.

[254] Beck (2007), p. 275.

[255] Similar Thorn (2005), p. 190.

[256] Article 1 (1) of the EC Council Regulation 44/2001 and equally worded Article 1 (1) of the New Lugano Convention: "This Convention shall apply in civil and commercial matters whatever the nature of the court or tribunal. It shall not extend, in particular, to revenue, customs or administrative matters.".

[257] See UNIDROIT 1990 – Study LXX – Doc 18, May 1990: The International Protection of Cultural Property. Summary report on the third session of the UNIDROIT study group on the international protection of cultural property, Paragraphs 16ff.

the conventions are bound and which in relation to particular matters, govern jurisdiction or the recognition or enforcement of judgments. Moreover, without prejudice to obligations resulting from other agreements between certain contracting parties, these conventions shall not prevent contracting parties from entering into such conventions.

When it comes to the EC Council Regulation 44/2001, however, the matter is more complicated. It contains in its Article 71 (1) a provision similar to that contained in the treaties mentioned before which reads that the regulation shall not affect any conventions to which the member states are parties and which in relation to particular matters, govern jurisdiction or the recognition or enforcement of judgments. However, it does not contain the forward-looking part allowing state parties to become members of such agreements. Due to the supremacy of EU law, state parties would be prevented from entering into such conventions.[258] They could also not do so based on the lex posterior idea which would normally leverage the later regulation. Hence, with regard to the scope of the EC Council Regulation 44/2001, which only applies between EU member states, there is a conflict between the regulation and the 1995 UNIDROIT Convention which would actually prevent EU member states that were not party to the 1995 UNIDROIT Convention at the time of the issuing of the regulation from entering it.[259] However, as the drafters of the 1995 UNIDROIT Convention have foreseen this issue, they have introduced Article 13 (3). According to these provisions in their relations with each other, contracting states which are members of organisations of economic integration or regional bodies may declare that they will apply the internal rules of these organisations or bodies and will not therefore apply as between these states the provisions of the convention the scope of application of which coincides with that of those rules. Thus, EU member states can become member to the 1995 UNIDROIT Convention as they are free to apply the rules of the EC Council Regulation 44/2001 among each other and apply the rules of the 1995 UNIDROIT Convention in relation to non-EU countries, where the regulation is not applicable.[260] However, Article 13 (3) of the 1995 UNIDROIT Convention requires the contracting party to actively make a respective declaration at the time of accession. This exception is not automatically applicable.[261]

Here we must note that the forum rei sitae jurisdiction is not exclusive according to the 1995 UNIDROIT Convention. Article 8 (1) stipulates for stolen and illegally exported cultural objects that a claim under Chapter II and a request under Chapter III may be also brought to the courts or other competent authorities otherwise having jurisdiction under the rules in force in contracting states. The question of whether or not a court or a competent authority of a country has

[258] Cf. Beck (2007), p. 268.

[259] Cf. Beck (2007), p. 268.

[260] Cf. Beck (2007), pp. 268f.

[261] Article 13 (3) of the 1995 UNIDROIT Convention explicitly requires the contracting parties to "declare that they will apply the internal rule".

jurisdiction is determined by respective national laws.[262] Therefore, and in particular, since there is no hierarchy between the various possible jurisdictions, such as the forum rei sitae, the jurisdiction of the state where the wrongful act took place or the current possessor has his domicile, the claimant is empowered with the right to freely choose between possible jurisdictions.[263] This gives rise to two important issues. Firstly, as alleged by the German delegation to the diplomatic conference, the claimant is free to take action in different jurisdictions simultaneously which may lead to contradictory judgments in the same case.[264] Whilst seemingly a valid concern, Germany could not gather sufficient support for the idea to introduce a hierarchy between the various jurisdictions by establishing the forum rei sitae as a general rule and the jurisdiction of the state party of domicile of the possessor as an exception for cases in which the location of the cultural object could not be determined.[265] Thus, in the case of parallel procedures and with regard to recognition and enforcement, the general rules of international civil procedure law are applicable.[266]

Another issue further to this is the fact that even if the claimant only brings one action in a single jurisdiction he is free to choose the one most favourable for him. This places the possessor of the cultural object at a disadvantage,[267] because by choosing the jurisdiction the claimant effectively also determines the applicable law of property. It is likely that he will prefer the jurisdiction which will apply, also based on the rules on the conflict of laws, the norms most favourable for him.[268] While generally common law countries try to restrict this so called forum shopping by taking recourse to principles such as forum non conveniens,[269] civil law jurisdictions recognise this right of the claimant.[270]

---

[262]Cf. Thorn (2005), p. 165.

[263]Cf. Stamatoudi (2011), p. 103.

[264]Cf. Diplomatic Conference for the Adoption of the Draft UNIDROIT Convention on the International Return of Stolen or Illegally Exported Cultural Objects, Rome, 7 to 24 June 1995, Acts and Proceedings, CONF. 8/5 Add. 2, April 1995, p. 80: "As the Convention deliberately leaves open the definitions of claimants and defendants, the likelihood of parallel cases regarding the same object arising in different Contracting States is even greater. In view of a possible multiplicity of actions the handing down of conflicting judgments cannot be ruled out.".

[265]Beck (2007), p. 265. For the exact wording of the proposal see Diplomatic Conference for the Adoption of the Draft UNIDROIT Convention on the International Return of Stolen or Illegally Exported Cultural Objects, Rome, 7 to 24 June 1995, Acts and Proceedings, CONF. 8/5 Add. 2, April 1995, p. 80: "A claim or a request under this Convention may only be brought before the courts of the Contracting State in which the cultural object is located at the time of lodging the claim or request. Should the cultural object not be located in a Contracting State or should its location be unknown to the claimant, the latter may have resort to the courts of the Contracting State in which the defendant has his customary domicile.".

[266]Beck (2007), p. 265.

[267]Stamatoudi (2011), p. 103.

[268]Cf. Thorn (2005), p. 166.

[269]Thorn (2005), p. 166.

[270]Cf., for example, the second sections of the EC Council Regulation 44/2001 and the equally worded New Lugano Convention.

In the case of the 1995 UNIDROIT Convention, however, the disadvantage of the possessor which goes hand in hand with the right of the claimant to determine the jurisdiction in which he will bring action is in accordance with the essential concept of the treaty,[271] as the convention aims at facilitating the restitution and return of the cultural objects. This approach is also supported by Article 9 (1) which allows member states to apply any rules more favourable to the restitution or the return of stolen or illegally exported cultural objects than provided for by the convention.

Furthermore, despite the fact that in practice the choice between jurisdictions will in most cases be limited to the forum rei sitae, the domicile country of the claimant or of the current possessor,[272] the 1995 UNIDROIT Convention itself establishes a minimum standard with regard to the restitution or the return of stolen or illegally exported cultural objects. Therefore, in practice it should not be feared that courts of different state parties will issue completely contradictory judgments.[273] Judgments will more likely in most cases only vary in terms of nuance.

A different situation exists concerning illegally exported objects where there is a restriction to the claimant's right to choose the jurisdiction he wants to take action in. According to Article 5 (1) of the Convention a contracting state may request the court or other competent authority of another contracting state to order the return of a cultural object illegally exported from the territory of the requesting state. Hence, in the case of illegally exported cultural objects the requesting state has to make its request at the court or other competent authority of another contracting state. The requesting state thus is not allowed to take action in its own courts or competent authorities. Otherwise the state would be both claimant and judge in its own case which could undermine its obligations under the convention, such as its burden to prove its case in accordance with Article 5 (3).[274] The same must apply in the case of stolen cultural objects. If a state reclaims a stolen object on the grounds of Article 3 (1) it is not permitted to take action in its own courts, but must do so in the forum rei sitae or the state in which the current possessor is domiciled.[275] However, this restriction does of course not apply to natural persons.

Finally, Article 8 (2) provides a final means to determine the jurisdiction by granting the parties the right to agree to submit the dispute to any court or other competent authority without restricting the choices to contracting parties. Hence, the parties may also submit the dispute to any court or competent authority of a state not party to the 1995 UNIDROIT Convention.

Any balanced consideration in the context of jurisdiction requires that Article 16 (1) and (2) be mentioned. Article 16 (1) establishes that each contracting state

[271] Thorn (2005), pp. 167f.

[272] Cf. Thorn (2005), p. 168.

[273] Similar Thorn (2005), p. 168 who argues that the minimum standard basically rules out forum shopping.

[274] Beck (2007), p. 270 with the same result.

[275] Beck (2007), p. 270.

shall at the time of signature, ratification, acceptance or accession, declare that claims for the return or restitution of cultural objects brought by a state under Article 8 may be submitted to it (a) directly to the courts or other competent authorities of the declaring state, (b) through an authority or authorities designated by that state to receive such claims or requests and to forward them to the courts or other competent authorities of that state and/or (c) through diplomatic or consular channels. Furthermore, according to Article 16 (2), each contracting state may also designate the courts or other authorities competent to order the restitution or return of cultural objects under the provisions of Chapters II and III.

Hence, contracting states are not only free to determine the competent courts or to establish, for example, for reasons of cost efficiency, special bodies or declare such bodies as competent, but may also choose to interpose an authority between the claimant and the competent courts or even refer the claimant to diplomatic or consular channels. They are moreover free in combining the different variations provided for in Article 16 (1) of the Convention.[276]

3.1.6.2 Arbitration

Submitting the dispute to a court or other competent authority is not the only way introduced by the 1995 UNIDROIT Convention to resolve the issue. Article 8 (2) of the Convention explicitly states that the parties may agree to submit the dispute to arbitration.

This provision was adopted without any controversy as the choice of submitting disputes to arbitration was considered a procedural freedom.[277] Furthermore, even though alternative dispute resolution, in particular arbitration, cannot be seen as a panacea, it is beneficial in promoting the goals of the convention for many reasons.[278] However, the 1995 UNIDROIT Convention only allows the possibility to resolve disputes over cultural objects by employing arbitration without providing any concrete provisions on how the arbitration procedure could or should actually be conducted.

3.1.6.3 Provisional Measures

Article 8 (3) of the Convention is the central provision with regard to provisional measures. It states that resort may be had to the provisional, including protective, measures available under the law of the contracting state where the object is located. A remarkable point in this context is that this may be done even when

[276]Cf. Thorn (2005), p. 178.

[277]Thorn (2005), p. 169.

[278]See on the benefits, but also obstacles of alternative dispute resolution pp. 176ff; for additional aspects on arbitration cf. Thorn (2005), pp. 169f and Beck (2007), p. 271.

the claim for restitution or request for return of the artefact is brought before the courts or other competent authorities of another contracting state. Hence, a claimant may submit the dispute to the court of one contracting state which has jurisdiction, but at the same time request for provisional, including protective measures, at the court of another contracting party. However, the right to apply for provisional measures is limited to the courts and competent authorities of the contracting state where the object is located. The claimant may not request such measures from courts and competent authorities located in other contracting states.[279]

Unfortunately, the provision contents itself with granting the right to provisional, including protective measures without defining them. This is in fact left to the national jurisdictions as the phrase "under the law of the Contracting State where the object is located" clarifies. Thus, the measures a claimant may take are determined not directly by the convention, but by the national law of the particular state in which the cultural material is situated.[280] The claimant may utilise all available measures the respective jurisdiction offers.

In this context the aim of the provision is the key point to be kept in mind. The norm aims at ensuring the effectiveness of the final court ruling in the matter by preventing the decision from becoming ineffective in practice due to certain developments, such as the destruction of the cultural object under dispute or its disappearance.[281] Therefore, the term "provisional, including protective measures" has to be understood in a broad sense. Hence, in order to protect the substance of the artefact, the claimant may, for example, ask for protective measures with the aim of ensuring the integrity and safety of the cultural object or its proper handling and storage.[282]

On the other hand, the courts or other competent authorities of the contracting state where the cultural object is located may, for purposes of inhibiting its disappearance, prohibit its further export or mandate its withdrawal from an auction.[283] This can be necessary and adequate in practice since auction houses regularly allow potential purchasers to remain anonymous and often the actual purchasers send proxies to auctions.[284]

3.1.6.4 The Application of more Favourable Rules and the Interpretative Guideline

Since the restitution and return of stolen and illegally exported cultural objects is politically a highly sensitive issue, even the establishment of a minimum standard

---

[279]Cf. Beck (2007), pp. 273f.

[280]Cf. Beck (2007), p. 274.

[281]Thorn (2005), p. 170.

[282]Beck (2007), p. 274f; Stamatoudi (2011), p. 103.

[283]Cf. Stamatoudi (2011), p. 103.

[284]Cf. Thorn (2005), p. 171.

in this regard, such as the 1995 UNIDROIT Convention, constitutes a major achievement.[285] However, the drafters of the agreement were aware of the fact that in the course of drafting the document they often had to find compromises in order to maximise the level of acceptability of the future treaty, and that this generally had a negative impact on the level of protection with regard to the restitution and return of cultural objects.[286] Therefore, they wanted to allow and give state parties incentives to enact further reaching regulations more favourable concerning the restitution and return of stolen and illegally exported cultural material.[287]

Hence, Article 9 (1) of the First Draft already contained a regulation allowing any state party to extend the protection of cultural property beyond that completed in the treaty, either by broadening the notion of cultural heritage or by making provision for its restitution in circumstances in which such restitution is not required by the convention by disallowing or restricting the right to compensation of the person in possession or in any other manner.[288] Article 11 of the 1990 Draft[289] extended the cases in which contracting parties were allowed to apply more favourable rules, but retained the listing principle. Thus, only in cases listed in Article 11 of the 1990 Draft were contracting parties permitted to apply more favourable rules. However, since the establishment of a comprehensive list of the circumstances under which contracting parties were allowed to make use of more favourable rules proved to be unfeasible due to the contradicting notions of the

---

[285]Thorn (2005), p. 171.

[286]Cf. Thorn (2005), p. 171.

[287]Cf. Stamatoudi (2011), p. 105.

[288]See UNIDROIT 1988 – Study LXX – Doc 3, June 1988, p. 4.

[289]See UNIDROIT 1990 – Study LXX – Doc 19, August 1990, pp. 5f: Article 11 of the 1990 Draft:

"Each Contracting Party shall remain free in respect of claims brought before its courts or competent authorities:

for the restitution of a stolen cultural object:

- to extend the provisions of Chapter II to acts other than theft whereby the claimant has wrongfully been deprived of possession of the object;
- to apply its national law when this would permit an extension of the period within which a claim for restitution of the object may be brought under Article 3 (2);
- to apply its national law when this would disallow the possessor's right to compensation even when the possessor has exercised the necessary diligence contemplated by Article 4 (1).

for the return of a cultural object removed from the territory of another Contracting State contrary to export legislation of that State:

- to have regard to interests other than those material under Article 5 (3);
- to apply its national law when this would permit the application of Article 5 in cases otherwise excluded by Article 7.
- to apply the Convention notwithstanding the fact that the theft or illegal export of the cultural object occurred before the entry into force of the Convention for that State.".

parties involved,[290] the concept of providing a list was discarded. Therefore, the final version of the provision, Article 9 (1) of the 1995 UNIDROIT Convention, establishes that nothing in the convention shall prevent a contracting state from applying any rules more favourable to the restitution or the return of stolen or illegally exported cultural objects than provided for by the agreement.

Nevertheless, the sample of cases listed in the preliminary drafts give a measure of insight into the circumstances under which more favourable regulations are imaginable. Hence, for these cases contracting states may apply more favourable rules or adopt such rules in the future. They may, for example

- apply the convention to artefacts which would not fall within the scope of the agreement by broadening the notion of cultural objects,[291]
- extend the provisions of Chapter II to acts other than theft whereby the claimant has wrongfully been deprived of possession of the object,[292]
- apply their national law when this would permit an extension of the period within which a claim for restitution of object may be brought,[293]
- apply their national law when this would disallow the possessor's right to compensation even when the possessor has exercised the necessary diligence,[294]
- have regard to interests other than those material under Article 5 (3) of the Convention,[295]
- apply their national law when this would permit the application of Article 5 in cases otherwise excluded by Article 7 of the Convention,[296]
- apply the convention notwithstanding the fact that the theft or the illegal export of the cultural object occurred before the entry into force of the convention for that state[297] and/or
- apply the convention to domestic cases.[298]

But it has to be kept in mind that the state whose court or competent authority is deciding the matter is permitted to apply the more favourable rules, but by no means is it required to do so. The claiming state, on the other hand, may not avail itself of Article 9 (1) of the Convention.[299]

In this context, Article 9 (2) supplies its reader with another questionable regulation. According to this norm, Article 9 (1) shall not be interpreted as creating an obligation to recognise or enforce a decision of a court or other competent authority

---

[290] Thorn (2005), p. 172.

[291] Article 9 of the First Draft.

[292] Article 11 (a) (i) of the 1990 Draft.

[293] Cf. Article 11 (a) (ii) of the 1990 Draft which only covers the case of stolen cultural objects.

[294] Cf. Article 11 (a) (iii) of the 1990 Draft which only covers the case of stolen cultural objects.

[295] Article 11 (b) (i) of the 1990 Draft.

[296] Article 11 (b) (ii) of the 1990 Draft.

[297] Article 11 (c) of the 1990 Draft.

[298] Cf. for the list of possible circumstances also Thorn (2005), p. 173.

[299] Thorn (2005), p. 173.

of another contracting state that departs from the provisions of the convention. This provision was included based on the French delegation's concern that due to the more favourable rules regulation provided for in Article 9 (1) claimants may systematically conduct forum shopping by bringing claims at courts or competent authorities of contracting states which do not recognise the right of the bona fide possessor to compensation.[300]

Closer examination reveals that the need for such a provision appears disputable. First, Article 9 (2) clarifies that contracting parties do not have to recognise or enforce decisions of other contracting parties that—as a result of the right to apply more favourable rules—depart from the provisions of the agreement. However, it is extremely difficult to imagine a case in which the right of one contracting state to apply more favourable rules with regard to the restitution or return of stolen or illegally exported cultural objects may be in conflict with the provisions of the 1995 UNIDROIT Convention.[301]

Furthermore, the ruling courts do not necessarily apply the lex fori. In accordance with international civil procedure law they commonly apply the law of other jurisdictions. Thus, the ruling court of a country not familiar with the idea of compensating the bona fide possessor may nevertheless grant him such right by applying the law of a state that does recognise the concept and vice versa.[302]

3.1.6.5 The 1995 UNIDROIT Convention's Relation to other Agreements

The "Final Provisions" of Chapter V of the 1995 UNIDROIT Convention contain a number of norms regulating the relation of the treaty with other agreements. Article 13 (1) of the Convention states that the treaty does not affect any international instrument by which any contracting state is legally bound and which contains provisions on matters governed by the 1995 UNIDROIT Convention, unless a contrary declaration is made by the states bound by such instrument. Hence, the treaty in particular does not affect the obligations of state parties with regard to the 1970 UNESCO Convention.

Furthermore, Article 13 (3) of the Convention determines that, in their relations with each other, contracting states which are members of organisations of economic integration or regional bodies may declare that they will apply the internal rules of these organisations or bodies and will not therefore apply as between these states the provisions of the convention the scope of application of which coincides with

[300]Cf. Diplomatic Conference for the Adoption of the Draft UNIDROIT Convention on the International Return of Stolen or Illegally Exported Cultural Objects, Rome, 7 to 24 June 1995, Acts and Proceedings, CONF. 8/C.1/S.R. 9 p. 233, CONF. 8/C.1/S.R. 10 p. 234 and CONF. 8/C.1/S.R. 19 p. 310.

[301]Thorn (2005), p. 174.

[302]Cf. Stamatoudi (2011), p. 108.

that of those rules. As previously mentioned, this norm is especially relevant in the case of the EC Council Regulation 44/2001 of 22 December 2000 on Jurisdiction and the Recognition and Enforcement of Judgments in Civil and Commercial Matters.[303] However, the provision also is of relevance to the Commonwealth States which have similarly adopted a model legislation concerning illicit export.[304]

Another provision with relevance to the EC Council Regulation 44/2001 is Article 16 (4) of the 1995 UNIDROIT Convention, which regulates that the provisions of Article 16 (1)–(3) do not affect bilateral or multilateral agreements on judicial assistance in respect of civil and commercial matters that may exist between contracting states. Hence, even if an EU member state designates certain courts or authorities in accordance with Article 16 (1) and (2) of the Convention for purposes of the restitution and return of stolen and illegally exported cultural objects in the context of the 1995 UNIDROIT Convention, this does not affect the designation in relation to other EU member states based on EC Council Regulation 44/2001.

3.1.6.6 Improving the Application of the 1995 UNIDROIT Convention through Agreements

Since the 1995 UNIDROIT Convention only aims to establish a minimum standard with regard to the restitution and return of stolen and illegally exported cultural objects, it does not restrict states from undertaking further reaching protective measures.[305] For this matter, they may also cooperate. In order to clarify this, the 1995 UNIDROIT Convention contains, just as the 1970 UNESCO Convention,[306] a provision on cooperation. A key difference exists though in that Article 13 (2) of the 1995 UNIDROIT Convention aims more narrowly to improve the application of the 1995 UNIDROIT itself. Thus, any contracting state may enter into agreements with one or more contracting states, with a view to improving the application of the 1995 UNIDROIT Convention in their mutual relations. However, the states which have concluded such an agreement are compelled to transmit a copy to the depositary.

3.1.6.7 Reservations

Article 18 of the Convention determines that no reservations are permitted except those expressly authorised in the agreement itself. At first glance, this norm appears unusual as no reservations are permitted under the agreement. However, the provision can be ascribed to certain events in the context of the drafting.

[303]For further details on the EC Council Regulation 44/2001 cf. pp. 112f.

[304]Stamatoudi (2011), p. 108.

[305]Stamatoudi (2011), p. 107.

[306]On cooperation in context of the 1970 UNESCO Convention cf. pp. 48ff.

At the diplomatic conference, first the US delegation suggested allowing states to opt out of Chapter III[307] and later the Japanese delegation proposed to permit states to opt out of either Chapter II or Chapter III.[308] The possibility to declare reservations with regard to certain provisions or even opt out of a whole chapter would have doubtlessly destroyed the close linkage between the distinct provisions as well as the fragile balance of the treaty.[309] Therefore, both US and Japanese delegations' proposals, together with the right to declare reservations, were rejected at the diplomatic conference.[310]

3.1.6.8 Review

The 1995 UNIDROIT Convention also provides for a review provision. Article 20 of the Convention permits the President of UNIDROIT at regular intervals or at any time at the request of five contracting states to convene a special committee in order to review the practical operation of the convention. Thus, the review cannot only be initiated by five contracting states; the norm also permits the President of UNIDROIT to do so. Moreover, the reviews may be undertaken at any time there is a specific indication that the convention is functioning poorly or at regular intervals.

The subject of the review is the practical operation of the agreement. This means that the reviewing body may not only examine national legislations issued based on the treaty, but may also revise national court rulings and decisions of the competent authorities. Based on this review the body may submit legally non-binding recommendations to increase the practical operation of the 1995 UNIDROIT Convention.[311]

[307]Cf. Diplomatic Conference for the Adoption of the Draft UNIDROIT Convention on the International Return of Stolen or Illegally Exported Cultural Objects, Rome, 7 to 24 June 1995, Acts and Proceedings, CONF. 8/C.1/S.R.19 p. 311.

[308]Cf. Diplomatic Conference for the Adoption of the Draft UNIDROIT Convention on the International Return of Stolen or Illegally Exported Cultural Objects, Rome, 7 to 24 June 1995, Acts and Proceedings, CONF. 8/C.1/S.R.19 p. 312.

[309]Stamatoudi (2011), p. 108; Thorn (2005), p. 179.

[310]Cf. Diplomatic Conference for the Adoption of the Draft UNIDROIT Convention on the International Return of Stolen or Illegally Exported Cultural Objects, Rome, 7 to 24 June 1995, Acts and Proceedings, CONF. 8/C.1/S.R.19 pp. 311–313 and CONF. 8/S.R. 6 pp. 354f.

[311]Cf. Thorn (2005), p. 179.

3.1.7 Assessment

As it is always the case when a certain topic is insufficiently regulated or even bereft of any legal regulation, any legal regularisation that appears constitutes a significant contribution.[312] To deem the 1995 UNIDROIT Convention, however, solely noteworthy due to the prior regulatory shortcomings concerning the topic of the restitution and return of stolen and illegally exported cultural objects, would do injustice to the agreement.

The 1995 UNIDROIT Convention features a number of (new) achievements regarding the subject matter of return. It not only ensures the right of the legitimate prior owner to pursue his claim for the stolen cultural object, but safeguards also the assertion of contracting parties' export regulations concerning cultural material.[313] Furthermore, the treaty strengthens the 1970 UNESCO Convention and complements it by establishing a set of minimum rules concerning the restitution and return of stolen and illegally exported cultural objects by bestowing a private law dimension to this arena.[314] How closely both treaties are intertwined is evidenced by the fact that on the First Meeting of the Special Committee to Review the Practical Operation of the 1995 UNIDROIT Convention on Stolen or Illegally Exported Cultural Objects held in June 2012, it was suggested that in the future the meetings of the monitoring bodies of both treaties should dovetail with each other, which would provide members the opportunity to compare practical experiences and any difficulties they may have encountered since the previous meetings.[315]

However, the greatest single achievement of the convention is Article 4 (4).[316] This provision not only lays the cornerstone of an international standard regarding the purchase of cultural objects by establishing objective and subsumable criteria, it also shifts the burden of proof onto the purchaser, forcing him to substantiate his exercise of due diligence concerning the purchase in question.

At the same time, this very provision is the major point of criticism brought forward by art traders and market states.[317,318] They argue that in particular this shift in the burden of proof creates an atmosphere irritating private collectors, bringing collectors, museums, and art traders into disrepute, and preventing cultural exchange.[319] However, a point often omitted or not considered by these critics is the

[312]Cf. also Stamatoudi (2011), p. 108.

[313]Fechner (2005), p. 496.

[314]Cf. Raschèr (2000), pp. 99f.

[315]Shyllon (2012a), pp. 583f.

[316]Same Raschèr (2000), p. 99; similar Fincham (2008–2009), pp. 135ff.

[317]Cf. Schaffrath (2007), pp. 57f.

[318]For further criticism see also Schaffrath (2007), pp. 57ff; Thorn (2005), pp. 191ff.

[319]Cf. Thorn (2005), p. 180; cf. also Schneider (2013), p. 127.

fact that the 1995 UNIDROIT Convention, according to its preamble, also acknowledges the role of cultural exchange for the understanding between people and aims therefore at inhibiting only the illicit trafficking of cultural objects.[320] The treaty by no means promotes the idea of inhibiting all trade in cultural material. And thereby, contrary to what the provision's critics argue, it actually benefits traders, collectors, and museums.[321]

Nevertheless, it has to be kept in mind that the 1995 UNIDROIT Convention represents a compromise between the source countries and the market states as well as between the continental European legal tradition and the Anglo-American legal system.[322,323] Hence, it contains on the one hand, the unconditional obligation to return stolen and illegally exported cultural objects, disregarding the legal concept of bona fide purchase common to continental European legal systems, while on the other hand, it provides provisions on compensation for the possessor, an obligation unfamiliar principally to common law jurisdictions.

It is due to this need for compromise in order to achieve a general acceptance of the agreement, the regulations established by the convention fail to achieve the optimum level of protection for cultural objects.[324] Moreover, some delicate issues, such as granting a general retroactive effect to the convention in order to regulate in particular matters of colonial heritage, could not be incorporated into the treaty at all. Rather, the convention contents itself, as did the 1970 UNESCO Convention,[325] with the clarification in Article 10 (3) that the agreement does not in any way legitimise any illegal transaction of whatever nature which has taken place before its entry into force, nor limit any right of a state or other person to make a claim under remedies available outside the framework of the treaty for the restitution or return of a cultural object stolen or illegally exported before the entry into force of the convention.

Overall, it can be noted that the 1995 UNIDROIT Convention has made a significant contribution to the fight against the illicit trade in cultural heritage and its restitution and return whilst simultaneously, with regard to regulations, has

[320]Cf. Paragraph 2 of the Preamble of the 1995 UNIDROIT Convention: "CONVINCED of the fundamental importance [...] of cultural exchange for promoting the understanding between peoples"; see Paragraph 4 of the Preamble of the 1995 UNIDROIT Convention: "DETERMINED to contribute effectively to the fight against illicit trade in cultural objects".

[321]Same Raschèr (2000), p. 100.

[322]Schaffrath (2007), p. 57.

[323]This is also why Schneider (2013), p. 126 calls the 1995 UNIDROIT Convention not only a legal, but also a cultural achievement.

[324]For a more detailed list of criticism see Prott (2009), pp. 216ff.

[325]Cf. Article 15 of the 1970 UNESCO Convention: "Nothing in this Convention shall prevent States Parties thereto from concluding special agreements among themselves or from continuing to implement agreements already concluded regarding the restitution of cultural property removed, whatever the reason, from its territory of origin, before the entry into force of this Convention for the States concerned.".

overcome many of the shortcomings of the 1970 UNESCO Convention with the important exception of retroactivity.

However, what the 1995 UNIDROIT Convention was able to achieve with regard to further the material regulations concerning the return of cultural objects, it has thus far forfeited on another level: that of acceptance. To date only 37 countries have ratified the convention—and not a single market state is among them.[326] However, the fact that state parties to the 1995 UNIDROIT Convention held a first special meeting in June 2012 to evaluate the achievements of the agreement, exchange views, and compile their practical experiences implementing the convention,[327] gives one hope for further developments that will redress this greatest deficiency of the treaty and that it will continue to contribute to the transformation of the mindset of both states and those involved in art trading.[328]

3.2 The Classical Approach: Synopsis

It was a long and difficult road to the adoption of the first international convention regulating the return of cultural objects transferred in times of peace. The process faced many challenges and setbacks including the outbreak of World War II. Finally, however, and in no small part due to the mood during the period of decolonisation, in 1970 the UNESCO Convention on the Means of Prohibiting and Preventing the Illicit Import, Export and Transfer of Ownership of Cultural Property was adopted.

Unfortunately, this treaty turned out to be quite ambiguous. On the one hand, it has to be seen as an astonishing success considering the time in which it was adopted; it came into life in a period in which many source states were only in the process of becoming independent or had just recently become so. Furthermore, it was a time in which the idea that the illicit transfer of cultural material represents a threat not only to the heritage of the states of origin, but also to the cultural heritage of all mankind, was far from being established. On the other hand, despite the changing spirit of the decolonisation era, it proved to be utterly impossible to carry through all demands of former colonies and source nations. Rather, the drafting of the convention was to say the least quite complicated, a situation that has proven common in the context of the instruments concerning the return of cultural objects.

In the end, source states had to abandon many of their demands and the adopted convention was far from what they had hoped for: The legal basis it provides is limited to certain cultural objects and it is completely devoid of the retroactive effect they had advocated. Moreover, despite the compromises they had been willing to make, many market states were still not willing to ratify the convention.

---

[326]Cf. http://www.unidroit.org/status-cp.

[327]Shyllon (2012a), p. 584.

[328]Similar Stamatoudi (2011), p. 111; cf. also Schneider (2013), p. 132.

Only in wake of the adoption of another agreement, the 1995 UNIDROIT Convention on Stolen or Illegally Exported Cultural Objects, did market states that had at that point in time already enacted regulations going beyond the requirements of the 1970 UNESCO Convention start acceding to it—likely to avoid ratifying the even further reaching new convention.

In the case of the 1995 UNIDROIT Convention the game was played anew; even though due to the foundation the 1970 UNESCO Convention had laid, the 1995 UNIDROIT Convention could be adopted with new, further reaching material regulations, such as the definition of good faith and an unconditional requirement to return stolen cultural objects, due to the positioning of market states, source countries had to make many compromises and—again—despite the compromises the source states were willing to make, in the end not even a single market state has ratified the treaty so far.

Hence, although there have been quite significant developments concerning the material regulations adopted so far, the treaty regime concerning the return of cultural objects remains somewhat ineffective on an global scale to the present day since it lacks wide acceptance; even with regard to the 1970 UNESCO Convention, which has 131 states parties by now, these state parties still see the need to adopt guidelines and establish a fund for the implementation of the treaty—40 years after its adoption.

Experience thus far has made it apparent to all parties that trying to solve the question concerning the return of cultural objects transferred in times of peace based solely on international treaties will not be successful. This realisation even found its way into the newer treaty law. Paragraphs 7 and 8 of the Preamble of the 1995 UNIDROIT Convention acknowledge that the convention will not by itself provide a solution to the problems raised by illicit trade and argue that the implementation of the convention should be accompanied by other effective measures for protecting cultural objects. This is in particular owed to the fact that despite the achievements made concerning the material regulations, the drafting and adopting process not only takes too long to address all concerns and developments in the field of cultural heritage, but new treaties and amendments generally lack sufficient acceptance to be as effective as source states need them to be in practice.

References

Asmuss K (2011) Ansprüche indigener Völker auf Rückführung rechtswidrig ausgeführten Kulturgutes: Eine Untersuchung für Ansprüche aus Art. 5 UNIDROIT-Konvention 1995 und aus allgemeinem Völkerrecht. Nomos, Baden-Baden

Beck C (2007) Die Rückgabe gestohlener und rechtswidrig ausgeführter Kulturgüter nach dem UNIDROIT-Übereinkommen 1995 und das deutsche Internationale Privatrecht. Dissertation, University of Zürich

Blake J (2015) International cultural heritage law. Oxford University Press, Oxford

Boos S (2006) Kulturgut als Gegenstand des grenzüberschreitenden Leihverkehrs. Duncker & Humblot, Berlin

Campfens E (2014) Alternative dispute resolution in restitution claims and the binding expert opinion procedure of the Dutch Restitutions Committee. In: Vadi V, Schneider HEGS (eds) Art, cultural heritage and the market: ethical and legal issues. Springer, Heidelberg, pp 61–91

Carducci N (2009) The growing complexity of international art law: conflict of laws, uniform law, mandatory rules, UNSC resolutions and EU regulations. In: Hoffman BT (ed) Art and cultural heritage: law, policy and practice. Cambridge University Press, Cambridge, pp 68–85

de Clippele MS, Lambrecht L (2015) Art law & balances: increased protection of cultural heritage law vs. private ownership: towards clash or balance? Int J Cult Prop 22:259–278

Fechner F (2005) Wohin gehören Kulturgüter? In: Grupp K, Hufeld U (eds) Recht – Kultur – Finanzen – Festschrift für Reinhard Mußgnug zum 70. Geburtstag am 26.. Oktober 2005. C.F. Müller, Heidelberg, pp 485–498

Fincham D (2008–2009) How adopting the Lex Originis rule can impede the flow of illicit cultural property. Columbia J Law Arts 32:111–150

Forrest C (2010) International law and the protection of cultural heritage. Routledge, London

Gornig GH (2011) Begründung und Rechtsgrundlagen des internationalen Kulturgüterschutzes. In: Gornig GH, Rafael AM (eds) Kulturgüter: Eine interdisziplinäre Betrachtung. Klages Verlag, Marburg, pp 117–134

Graf Vitzthum W (2013) Begriff, Geschichte und Rechtsquellen des Völkerrechts. In: Graf Vitzthum W, Proelß A (eds) Völkerrecht, 6th edn. De Gruyter, Berlin, pp 1–59

Halsdorfer A (2009) Sollte Deutschland dem UNIDROIT-Kulturgutübereinkommen 1995 beitreten? Praxis des Internationalen Privat- und Verfahrensrechts 307–311

Hartung H (2005) Kunstraub in Krieg und Verfolgung: Die Restitution von Beute- und Raubkunst im Kollisions- und Völkerrecht. De Gruyter, Berlin

Hoffman BT (2009) Introduction to parts II and III: cultural rights, cultural property, and international trade. In: Hoffman BT (ed) Art and cultural heritage: law, policy and practice. Cambridge University Press, Cambridge, pp 89–93

Kienle F, Weller M-P (2004) Die Vindikation gestohlener Kulturgüter im IPR. Praxis des Internationalen Privat- und Verfahrensrechts 290–294

Kuprecht K (2009) Die internationalrechtlichen Besonderheiten bei Kulturgüter-Restitutionsforderungen indigener Völker. Kunst und Recht 175–180

Kurpiers OR (2005) Die Lex Originis-Regel im internationalen Sachenrecht: Grenzüberschreitende privatrechtliche Ansprüche auf Herausgabe von abhanden gekommenen und unrechtmäßig ausgeführten Kulturgütern. Peter Lang, Frankfurt am Main

Lalive P (2009) A disturbing international convention: the UNIDROIT Convention on Cultural Objects. In: Prott LV (ed) Witness to history: a compendium of documents and writings on the return of cultural objects. UNESCO Publishing, Paris, pp 322–325

Meena T (2009) Nights at the museum: the value of cultural property and resolving the moral and legal problems of the illicit international art trade. Loyola Los Angel Int Comp Law Rev 31: 581–614

Nafziger JAR, Paterson RK, Renteln AD (2014) Cultural law: international, comparative, and indigenous. Cambridge University Press, Cambridge

O'Keefe PJ (2006) Using UNIDROIT to avoid cultural heritage disputes: limitation periods. Willamette J Int Law Dispute Resolution 14:227–242

Ochoa Jiménez MJ (2011) Der Schutz materieller Kulturgüter in Lateinamerika: Universelles, regionales und nationales Recht. Universitätsverlag Göttingen, Göttingen

Odendahl K (2005) Kulturgüterschutz: Entwicklung, Struktur und Dogmatik eines ebenenübergreifenden Normensystems. Mohr Siebeck, Tübingen

Pabst F (2008) Kulturgüterschutz in nicht-internationalen bewaffneten Konflikten. Duncker & Humblot, Berlin

Pallas NC (2004) Maritimer Kulturgüterschutz. Duncker & Humblot, Berlin

Prott LV (1996) UNESCO and UNIDROIT: a partnership against trafficking in cultural objects. Uniform Law Rev 1:59–71

Prott LV (1997) Commentary on the UNIDROIT Convention on Stolen and Illegally Exported Cultural Objects 1995. Institute of Art and Law, Leicester

Prott LV (2009) The UNIDROIT Convention on Stolen or Illegally Exported Cultural Objects – ten years on. Uniform Law Rev 14:215–237

Radloff J (2013) Kulturgüterrecht: Unter besonderer Berücksichtigung der Außenhandelsbeschränkungen und Mitnahmeverbote von Kunst- und Kulturgut in Privateigentum. Duncker & Humblot, Berlin

Raschèr AFG (2000) Kulturgüterschutz und Globalisierung – UNESCO-Konvention 1970 – UNIDROIT-Konvention 1995 – EG-Verordnung 3911/92 – EG-Richtlinie 93/7 – Schweizerisches Recht. Schulthess, Zürich

Reichelt G (1994) Die Vereinheitlichung des privatrechtlichen Kulturgüterschutzes nach dem UNIDROIT-Vertragsentwurf 1990. In: Dolzer R, Jayme E, Mußgnug R (eds) Rechtsfragen des internationalen Kulturgüterschutzes: Symposium vom 22./23. Juni 1990 im Internationalen Wissenschaftsforum Heidelberg. C.F. Müller, Heidelberg, pp 67–81

Renold M-A (2009) Stolen art: the ubiquitous question of good faith. In: Prott LV (ed) Witness to history: a compendium of documents and writings on the return of cultural objects. UNESCO Publishing, Paris, pp 309–313

Rietschel S (2009) Internationale Vorgaben zum Kulturgüterschutz und ihre Umsetzung in Deutschland: Das KGÜAG – Meilenstein oder fauler Kompromiss in der Geschichte des deutschen Kulturgüterschutzes? De Gruyter, Berlin

Roehrenbeck CA (2010) Repatriation of cultural property – Who owns the past? An introduction to approaches and to selected statutory instruments. Int J Leg Inf 38:185–200

Roodt C (2015) Private international law, art and cultural heritage. Edward Elgar, Cheltenham

Schaffrath C (2007) Die Rückführung unrechtmäßig nach Deutschland verbrachten Kulturguts an den Ursprungsstaat. Peter Lang, Frankfurt am Main

Schmeinck S (1994) Internationalprivatrechtliche Aspekte des Kulturgüterschutzes. Duncker & Humblot, Berlin

Schnabel G, Tatzkow M (2007) Nazi-Looted Art: Handbuch Kunstrestitution weltweit. Proprietas Verlag, Berlin

Schneider M (2010) Was hat die UNIDROIT-Konvention von 1995 zu bieten? Kunst und Recht 159–163

Schneider M (2013) Protection and return of cultural objects: the interplay of law and ethics. In: Prott LV, Redmond-Cooper R, Urice S (eds) Realising cultural heritage law: Festschrift for Patrick Joseph O'Keefe. Institute of Art and Law, Builth Wells, pp 121–132

Schönenberger B (2009) Restitution von Kulturgut: Anspruchsgrundlagen – Restiutionshindernisse – Entwicklung. Stämpfli Verlag, Bern

Sheng G (2010) International protection of cultural property: some preliminary issues and the role of international conventions. Singapore Yearb Int Law Contributors 12:57–79

Shyllon F (2012a) First special meeting of the states parties to the 1995 UNIDROIT Convention on Stolen or Illegally Exported Cultural Objects. Int J Cult Prop 19:583–584

Shyllon F (2012b) Second meeting of the states parties to the 1970 UNESCO Convention on the Means of Prohibiting and Preventing the Illicit Import, Export and Transfer of Ownership of Cultural Property. Int J Cult Prop 19:585–587

Stamatoudi IA (2011) Cultural property law and restitution: a commentary to international conventions and European Union law. Edward Elgar, Cheltenham

Streinz R (1998) Internationaler Schutz von Museumsgut: Handbuch des Museumsrechts 4. Leske + Budrich, Opladen

Thorn B (2005) Internationaler Kulturgüterschutz nach der UNIDROIT Konvention. De Gruyter, Berlin

UNIDROIT Secretariat (2001) UNIDROIT Convention on Stolen or Illegally Exported Cultural Objects: explanatory report. Uniform Law Rev 6:476–564

von Schorlemer S (1998) Stolen art. Ger Yearb Int Law 41:317–343
von Schorlemer S (2007) UNESCO dispute settlement. In: Yusuf AA (ed) Standard-setting in UNESCO: normative action in education, science and culture, vol 1. UNESCO Publishing, Paris/Martinus Nijhoff Publishers, Leiden, pp 73–103
Vrdoljak AF (2008) International law, museums and the return of cultural objects. Cambridge University Press, Cambridge
Vrdoljak AF (2012) Human rights and illicit trade in cultural objects. In: Borelli S, Francioni F (eds) Cultural heritage, cultural rights, cultural diversity: new developments in international law. Martinus Nijhoff Publishers, Leiden, pp 107–140
Weidner A (2001) Kulturgüterschutz als res extra commercium im internationalen Sachenrecht. De Gruyter, Berlin
Wessels J, Beulke W, Satzger H (2015) Strafrecht Allgemeiner Teil: Die Straftat und ihr Aufbau, 45th edn. C.F. Müller, Heidelberg

Chapter 4
The Two-Pronged Strategy: Transiting to a Cooperative and Procedural Solution

Abstract The international community realised as early as during the negotiations of the 1970 UNESCO Convention on the Means of Prohibiting and Preventing the Illicit Import, Export and Transfer of Ownership of Cultural Property that the establishment of an international treaty regime with binding obligations concerning the return of cultural objects transferred in times of peace appealing to both market and source states was difficult to achieve. Therefore, a search to complement the treaty approach began. At the same time private parties, frustrated by the uncertainty of how to face claims for the return of cultural objects created by the lack of sufficient legislation, became more proactive. These endeavours of the international community and private parties have brought to life a number of new instruments in the years following the adoption of the 1970 UNESCO Convention. This chapter is devoted to an examination of these instruments, namely UNESCO's Intergovernmental Committee for Promoting the Return of Cultural Property to its Countries of Origin or its Restitution in case of Illicit Appropriation, the ICOM Code of Ethics for Museums, the UNESCO International Code of Ethics for Dealers in Cultural Property and the Principles for Cooperation in the Mutual Protection and Transfer of Cultural Material of the International Law Association. These instruments are classified and analysed in depth, in particular in the light of their respective genesis and the interests of the actors involved in their creation as well as in comparison to one another and both the 1970 UNESCO Convention and the 1995 UNIDROIT Convention on Stolen or Illegally Exported Cultural Objects. At the same time, the general suitability of fora and soft law to contribute to the solution of controversies concerning claims for the return of cultural objects is likewise addressed.

4.1 The Need for New Approaches

Since it became evident during the negotiations of the 1970 UNESCO Convention that the establishment of an international treaty regime with binding obligations concerning the return of cultural objects transferred in times of peace which would appeal to both market and source states was difficult to achieve, the need to find

A. Taşdelen, *The Return of Cultural Artefacts*, DOI 10.1007/978-3-319-44060-6_4

further ways to solve respective disputes which would however be more acceptable to market states was apparent.

This search to find further ways to solve cultural material related disputes more promisingly has brought to life a number of new instruments in the years following the adoption of the 1970 UNESCO Convention. These new instruments range from UNESCO's Intergovernmental Committee for Promoting the Return of Cultural Property to its Countries of Origin or its Restitution in case of Illicit Appropriation to the Principles for Cooperation in the Mutual Protection and Transfer of Cultural Material of the International Law Association (ILA).

4.2 The Institutional Approach: UNESCO's Intergovernmental Committee for Promoting the Return of Cultural Property to Its Countries of Origin or Its Restitution in Case of Illicit Appropriation

4.2.1 General View

Many states, in particular those formerly colonised, but also other states victim to the illicit looting and trafficking of their cultural heritage, had hoped to create with the 1970 UNESCO Convention on the Means of Prohibiting and Preventing the Illicit Import, Export and Transfer of Ownership of Cultural Property an instrument which would not only enable them to reclaim cultural objects which would be illicitly trafficked from their territory in the future, but also a tool empowering them to claim back cultural artefacts which had already been transferred from their territory at the time of the adoption, in particular during the colonial period. However, it eventuated that the demand for a retroactive aspect to the 1970 UNESCO Convention could not prevail against the former colonial powers and market states. Hence, the 1970 UNESCO Convention was adopted without such.[1] Realising that trying to adopt international treaties imposing legally binding obligations on market states and former colonial powers to return transferred cultural objects alone was not the most promising way to solve cultural material related disputes, the source states began searching for other methods. In this context, as in the case of the 1970 UNESCO Convention, they again appealed to UNESCO.

In order to compensate for deficiencies at least to a certain degree and in particular concerning the 1970 UNESCO Convention's lack of retroactivity, in 1978 UNESCO established the Intergovernmental Committee for Promoting the Return of Cultural Property to its Countries of Origin or its Restitution in case of Illicit Appropriation. Besides promoting multilateral and bilateral cooperation with

[1] Prott (2011), p. 2.

a view to promoting the restitution or return of cultural property, fostering public information campaigns, and promoting exchanges of cultural material,[2] the ICPRCP was also established in order to deal with concrete cases,[3] in particular those which do not fall within the ambit of an international convention.[4]

Unlike a court or an arbitrational body, the committee does not issue legally binding decisions or recommendations concerning disputes.[5] Rather, it plays an advisory role by providing a framework for discussion and negotiation for the parties involved in disputes and by facilitating bilateral negotiations.[6]

The ICPRCP was initially set up for and primarily dealt with cases concerning cultural property transferred prior to the coming into force of the 1970 UNESCO Convention, i.e. chiefly transfers that had some sort of colonial connection. However, nowadays it deals with more and more cases concerning cultural objects illicitly trafficked after the entry into force of the 1970 UNESCO Convention. These cases are brought before the ICPRCP, because they do not fall within the scope of either the 1970 UNESCO Convention or the 1995 UNIDROIT Convention as at least one of the state parties involved in the dispute has or had, at the time of the transfer, not ratified the respective convention(s).[7] Another point highlighting the evolving character of the ICPRCP is the fact that in 2005 mediation and conciliation was added to its mandate and in 2010 the ICPRCP adopted the Rules of Procedure for Mediation and Conciliation based on this mandate.[8]

4.2.2 From the 1970 UNESCO Convention to the Establishment of the ICPRCP

Since the 1970 UNESCO Convention on the Means of Prohibiting and Preventing the Illicit Import, Export and Transfer of Ownership of Cultural Property lacks a clause granting it retroactive effect, cultural heritage transferred during the colonial period remained a concern for UNESCO and the source nations even after the adoption of the treaty.

---

[2]http://portal.unesco.org/culture/en/ev.php-URL_ID=35283&URL_DO=DO_TOPIC&URL_SECTION=201.html.

[3]Cf. Baufeld (2005), p. 294.

[4]Stamatoudi (2011), p. 58; Campfens (2014), p. 81.

[5]von Schorlemer (2007), p. 101.

[6]http://portal.unesco.org/culture/en/ev.php-URL_ID=35283&URL_DO=DO_TOPIC&URL_SECTION=201.html.

[7]Cf. Shyllon (2013), p. 135; cf. Stamatoudi (2011), p. 58, n 82; cf. also Odendahl (2005), p. 182; cf. also van Beurden (2014), p. 177.

[8]For further details on the ICPRCP Rules of Procedure for Mediation and Conciliation cf. pp. 181ff.

On 18 December 1973, the UN General Assembly adopted the Resolution on the Restitution of Works of Art to Countries Victims of Expropriation,[9] in which it addressed the issue of cultural artefacts transferred from colonies.[10] The UN General Assembly pointed out the special obligation of (former) colonial powers in this context[11] and that restitution would not only strengthen international cooperation, but also be just compensation for damage done.[12]

Inspired by this resolution, at the end of 1974, UNESCO adopted the Resolution on the Contribution of UNESCO to the Return of Cultural Property to Countries that have been Victims of de facto Expropriation.[13] The UNESCO Resolution not only recalled and repeated the UN Resolution[14] and invited member states to ratify the 1970 UNESCO Convention,[15] but also invited the Director-General of UNESCO to contribute towards this work of restitution by defining in general terms the most suitable methods, including exchanges on the basis of long-term loans and the promotion of bilateral arrangements to that end.[16]

Arising from this mandate, in spring 1976, UNESCO's Director-General convened a committee of experts in order to address the issue.[17] Based on the report of the committee, the former recommended the establishment of a permanent institution dealing with matters facilitating bilateral negotiations concerning the restitution and return of cultural heritage to countries that had lost it as a result of colonial or foreign occupation.[18] The General Conference of UNESCO followed the recommendation of its Director-General at its 19th session in 1976[19] and instructed him to take all necessary measures to prepare the establishment of such an institution by UNESCO's General Conference at its 20th session.[20] Consequently, in March 1978,

[9]UNGA Res 3187, 18.12.1973.

[10]UNGA Res 3187, 18.12.1973, Paragraph 8 of the Preamble: "Deploring the wholesale removal, virtually without payment, of objets d'art from one country to another, frequently as a result of colonial or foreign occupation".

[11]UNGA Res 3187, 18.12.1973, Paragraph 2: "Recognizes the special obligation in this connexion of those countries which had access to such valuable objects as a result of colonial or foreign occupation;".

[12]UNGA Res 3187, 18.12.1973, Paragraph 1: "Affirms that the prompt restitution to a country of its objets d'art, monuments, museum pieces, manuscripts and documents by another country, without charge, is calculated to strengthen international cooperation inasmuch as it constitutes just reparation for damage done;".

[13]UNESCO GC 18 C/Resolution 3.428, 23.11.1974.

[14]UNESCO GC 18 C/Resolution 3.428, 23.11.1974, Paragraphs 2 and 9 of the Preamble.

[15]UNESCO GC 18 C/Resolution 3.428, 23.11.1974, Paragraph 3.

[16]UNESCO GC 18 C/Resolution 3.428, 23.11.1974, Paragraph 5.

[17]UNESCO Doc SHC-76/CONF.615/5, 21.04.1976.

[18]UNESCO Doc 19 C/109, 30.09.1976.

[19]UNESCO GC 19 C/Resolution 4.128, 30.11.1976.

[20]UNESCO GC 19 C/Resolution 4.128, 30.11.1976, Paragraph 6: "Invites the Director-General of UNESCO:

to take all necessary measures with a view to the establishment, by the General Conference at is twentieth session, of an intergovernmental committee entrusted with the task of seeking ways and a second committee of experts was convened[21] which finalised the preliminary draft statutes for an intergovernmental committee resulting from the deliberations of the expert committee meeting of 1976, deliberations of ICOM, and the Secretariat of UNESCO.[22]

This final draft was adopted by the General Conference of UNESCO at its 20th session in 1978 as the Statutes of the Intergovernmental Committee for Promoting the Return of Cultural Property to its Countries of Origin or its Restitution in Case of Illicit Appropriation.[23] At the very same session, the General Conference of UNESCO also adopted the Recommendation for the Protection of Movable Cultural Property.[24] However, the newly founded ICPRCP took up its work with its first meeting in May 1980.[25]

4.2.3 The ICPRCP's Purpose

The mandate of the ICPRCP, which was first only postulated in general terms as seeking ways and means of facilitating bilateral negotiations for the restitution or return of cultural property to the countries having lost them as a result of colonial or foreign occupation,[26] was further elaborated on in the process of the establishment of the committee and is now described in great detail in Article 4 of the ICPRCP Statutes.

Unsurprisingly, the first responsibility of the committee is to seek ways and means of facilitating bilateral negotiations for the restitution or return of cultural property to its countries of origin.[27] A remarkable point in this context is the fact that in the final version of the statutes the phrase "countries having lost them as a result of colonial or foreign occupation" is not used. The statutes speak instead of "countries of origin". This allows the ICPRCP also to deal with cases in which the transfer of cultural property did not occur in the context of colonial or foreign occupation, but was, for instance, the result of (ordinary) theft. Thus, the committee can handle cases which may also fall within the ambit of the 1970 UNESCO

means of facilitating bilateral negotiations for the restitution or return of cultural property to the countries having lost them as a result of colonial or foreign occupation, and to convene for this purpose a committee of experts responsible for defining the terms of reference, means of action and working methods of such a committee;".

[21]UNESCO Doc CC-78/CONF.609/6, 23.03.1978.

[22]Specht (2009), p. 28.

[23]UNESCO GC 20 C/Resolution 4/7.6/5, 28.11.1978.

[24]Cf. http://portal.unesco.org/en/ev.php-URL_ID=13137&URL_DO=DO_TOPIC&URL_SECTION=201.html.

[25]http://portal.unesco.org/culture/en/ev.php-URL_ID=36205&URL_DO=DO_TOPIC&URL_SECTION=201.html.

[26]Cf., for example, UNESCO GC 19 C/Resolution 4.128, 30.11.1976, Paragraph 6.

[27]Article 4 (1) of the ICPRCP Statutes.

Convention or 1995 UNIDROIT Convention.[28] However, the ICPRCP may also submit proposals with a view to mediation or conciliation.[29]

Beyond that, the ICPRCP is also responsible for a number of other subjects related to promoting the restitution and return of cultural property. The committee is responsible for promoting multilateral and bilateral cooperation,[30] for encouraging the necessary research and studies for the establishment of coherent programmes for the constitution of representative collections in countries whose cultural heritage has been dispersed,[31] for fostering public information campaigns,[32] guiding the planning and implementation of UNESCO's programme of activities with regard to the restitution or return,[33] and for encouraging the establishment or reinforcement of museums or other institutions for the conservation of cultural property and the training of the necessary scientific and technical personnel.[34]

However, a dichotomy known from the 1970 UNESCO Convention[35] also found its way into the ICPRCP Statutes; the committee not only promotes the restitution and return of cultural property but is also responsible for promoting exchanges of cultural objects.[36] This provision has to be seen as a result of the challenge UNESCO faces: It has to balance the interests of countries trying to reclaim and protect cultural artefacts and countries pleading for the free trafficking of cultural property.

4.2.4 *The Field of Operation of the ICPRCP*

The committee was established to promote the return and restitution of cultural property. Which objects are to be considered as cultural property and thus fall within the area of responsibility of the ICPRCP is defined in Article 3 (1) of the Statutes. Hence, cultural property shall be taken to denote historical and ethnographic objects and documents including manuscripts, works of the plastic and

[28] See Vrdoljak (2008), pp. 235f for the shift in the claims brought to the attention of the committee since its establishment.

[29] Article 4 (1) of the ICPRCP Statutes.

[30] Article 4 (2) of the ICPRCP Statutes.

[31] Article 4 (3) of the ICPRCP Statutes.

[32] Article 4 (4) of the ICPRCP Statutes.

[33] Article 4 (5) of the ICPRCP Statutes.

[34] Article 4 (6) of the ICPRCP Statutes.

[35] Cf. Preamble Paragraph 2 of the 1970 UNESCO Convention: "Considering that the interchange of cultural property among nations for scientific, cultural and educational purposes increases the knowledge of the civilization of Man, enriches the cultural life of all peoples and inspires mutual respect and appreciation among nations,"

[36] Article 4 (7) of the ICPRCP Statutes.

decorative arts, paleontological and archaeological objects as well as zoological, botanical, and mineralogical specimens.

It is noteworthy that the definition provided for in the ICPRCP Statutes does not follow the pattern of the 1970 UNESCO[37] and 1995 UNIDROIT[38] Conventions which require the objects to be for certain reasons of importance and, in addition, to fall within one of the listed categories, with the 1970 UNESCO Convention demanding furthermore that the object has been specially designated. In contrast, the ICPRCP Statutes define cultural property solely by requiring it to fall within certain categories which moreover do not even match those provided for in the 1970 UNESCO and 1995 UNIDROIT Conventions.[39] This divergence is—taking into consideration that both the 1970 UNESCO Convention and the ICPRCP are instruments adopted in context of UNESCO—astonishing.

Nevertheless, abolishing the double-requirement of the agreements by solely necessitating an object to fall within the mentioned categories is, in principle,

---

[37] Article 1 of the 1970 UNESCO Convention: "For the purposes of this Convention, the term 'cultural property' means property which, on religious or secular grounds, is specifically designated by each State as being of importance for archaeology, prehistory, history, literature, art or science and which belongs to the following categories:".

[38] Article 2 of the 1995 UNIDROIT Convention: "For the purposes of this Convention, cultural objects are those which, on religious or secular grounds, are of importance for archaeology, prehistory, history, literature, art or science and belong to one of the categories listed in the Annex to this Convention.".

[39] The categories used in the 1970 UNESCO and 1995 UNIDROIT Conventions are as follows:

(a) "Rare collections and specimens of fauna, flora, minerals and anatomy, and objects of palaeontological interest;
(b) property relating to history, including the history of science and technology and military and social history, to the life of national leaders, thinkers, scientists and artist and to events of national importance;
(c) products of archaeological excavations (including regular and clandestine) or of archaeological discoveries;
(d) elements of artistic or historical monuments or archaeological sites which have been dismembered;
(e) antiquities more than one hundred years old, such as inscriptions, coins and engraved seals;
(f) objects of ethnological interest;
(g) property of artistic interest, such as:

    (i) pictures, paintings and drawings produced entirely by hand on any support and in any material (excluding industrial designs and manufactured articles decorated by hand);
    (ii) original works of statuary art and sculpture in any material;
    (iii) original engravings, prints and lithographs;
    (iv) original artistic assemblages and montages in any material;

(h) rare manuscripts and incunabula, old books, documents and publications of special interest (historical, artistic, scientific, literary, etc.) singly or in collections;
(i) postage, revenue and similar stamps, singly or in collections;
(j) archives, including sound, photographic and cinematographic archives;
(k) articles of furniture more than one hundred years old and old musical instruments."

extending the area of responsibility of the ICPRCP.[40] This extension of the scope can be ascribed to the fact that the committee does not issue legally binding decisions, but rather provides for a platform for the parties to resolve their dispute. Thus, extending the scope of the responsibility of the committee does not lead to a legally enforceable obligation of member states.

However, in practice, this general extension remains ineffective since the area of responsibility of the ICPRCP is diminished by Article 3 (2) of the Statutes. This provision narrows the right of member states to bring forth claims to cultural property which has a fundamental significance from the point of view of the spiritual values and cultural heritage and which has been lost as a result of colonial or foreign occupation or as a result of illicit appropriation. Not only does this provision re-incorporate the limitation of colonial or foreign occupation, though it allows claimants to reclaim cultural property lost as a result of illicit appropriation, it requires the cultural objects to be also of fundamental significance from the point of view of the spiritual values and cultural heritage. Thus, the committee is not meant to deal with either relatively insignificant objects or with objects which have been lost under circumstances not listed.

Article 3 (2) of the Statutes is also important from another point of view as it clarifies the entities which may make use of the committee. According to the norm, all member states and associated members of UNESCO may make a request for the restitution or return of cultural property. Moreover, Article 1 of the Statutes also stipulates that the services of the committee are available to all member states and associated members of UNESCO. Hence, all 195 current member states and 10 associated members of UNESCO[41] may avail themselves of the ICPRCP.

Furthermore, the ICPRCP Statutes extend in another area far beyond the 1970 UNESCO and 1995 UNIDROIT Conventions; even though it is not explicitly mentioned in the statutes that the ICPRCP may also deal with cases which occurred before its establishment, its history of emergence makes clear that it has also been established to handle in particular such cases. Thus, unlike the international treaties mentioned so far which lack a retroactive effect, the ICPRCP has a retroactive aspect incorporated into it.

4.2.5 The ICPRCP's Institutional Framework

Article 1 of the Statutes establishes the ICPRCP within UNESCO. Hence, the committee is a body of UNESCO,[42] which is however neither institutionally, personally nor otherwise tied to the 1970 UNESCO Convention on the Means of

---

[40]On the issue why such a double-requirement constricts the scope of a convention cf. pp. 16f.

[41]http://www.unesco.org/new/en/member-states/countries/.

[42]This is also why the committee has to report on its activities to the General Conference of UNESCO at each of its ordinary sessions (Article 4 (8) ICPRCP Statutes).

Prohibiting and Preventing the Illicit Import, Export and Transfer of Ownership of Cultural Property.[43]

The committee is comprised of 22 member states of UNESCO elected by the General Conference of UNESCO at its ordinary sessions. The election is based on various criteria; equitable geographical distribution and appropriate rotation has to be taken into consideration as well as the representative character of those states in respect of the contribution they are able to make to the restitution or return of cultural property to its countries of origin.[44] In general, member states are elected for 4 years,[45] although not all members of the committee are elected simultaneously. Half of the committee is in due course renewed every other year.[46] Nevertheless, all member states are immediately eligible for re-election[47] and free to choose their representatives who they delegate to the committee.[48] However, they ought to select specialists in cultural property[49] and have to notify the Secretariat of UNESCO of their names.[50]

More importantly, the committee is assisted by both permanent and temporary entities. While the ICPRCP Bureau and the ICPRCP Secretariat fall within the first category, ad hoc subcommittees belong to the second. The bureau is comprised of a chairman, four vice-chairmen, and a rapporteur.[51] It discharges all duties the committee lays upon it[52] and coordinates the work of the committee.[53] In addition, the bureau moderates the sessions, in particular the opening and closing the plenary meetings, ensuring the observance of the rules of procedure, and directing the discussion including the right to speak, put questions to a vote, and announce decisions.[54]

---

[43]Cf. http://www.unesco.org/new/en/culture/themes/restitution-of-cultural-property/intergovernmental-committee/historical-background/; cf. also Francioni (2013), p. 17.

[44]Article 2 (1) of the ICPRCP Statutes.

[45]This derives from Article 2 (2) in connection with Article 5 (1) of the ICPRCP Statutes. Article 2 (2) of the ICPRCP Statutes: "The term of office of members of the Committee shall extend from the end of the ordinary session of the General Conference during which they are elected until the end of its second subsequent ordinary session.".

Article 5 (1) of the ICPRCP Statutes: "The Committee shall meet in regular plenary session at least once and not more than twice every two years.".

[46]This derives from Article 2 (3) of the ICPRCP Statutes: "Notwithstanding the provisions of paragraph 2 above, the term of office of half of the members designated at the time of the first election shall cease at the end of the first ordinary session of the General Conference following that at which they were elected. The names of these members shall be chosen by lot by the President of the General Conference after the first election.".

[47]Article 5 (4) of the ICPRCP Statutes.

[48]Article 5 (5) of the ICPRCP Statutes.

[49]Rule 4.2 of the ICPRCP Rules of Procedure.

[50]Rule 1.2 of the ICPRCP Rules of Procedure.

[51]Article 7 (1) of the ICPRCP Statutes.

[52]Article 7 (2) of the ICPRCP Statutes.

[53]Rule 5.3 of the ICPRCP Rules of Procedure.

[54]Rule 5.7 of the ICPRCP Rules of Procedure.

It is elected anew by the committee every time its membership changes[55] and thus regularly every 2 years. Members of the bureau are eligible for re-election to the same posts, but the total period for which they serve may not exceed two consecutive terms of office.[56] Members of the bureau who are representatives of member states of UNESCO remain in office until a new bureau has been elected.[57, 58]

The secretariat, on the other hand, is not elected by the committee, but provided for by the Director-General of UNESCO by making available to the committee a member of the UNESCO Secretariat to act as Secretary of the Committee together with the staff and other means required for its operation.[59] The secretariat provides the necessary services for the sessions of the committee, meetings of its bureau and ad hoc subcommittees and working groups.[60] In particular, it fixes the date of the committee sessions in accordance with the bureau's instructions and takes all steps required to convene such sessions.[61]

Finally, ad hoc subcommittees can be established by the committee for the study of specific problems in the context of activities related to Article 4 (1) of the Statutes.[62] For studying specific problems related to those activities which are defined in Article 4 (2)–(7) of the Statutes, the committee can set up working groups.[63] The mandates of both are defined by the committee,[64] both meet in accordance with the decisions of the committee or its bureau, and elect themselves their chairman, vice-chairman, and if necessary, their rapporteur.[65] Both are subject to the ICPRCP Rules of Procedure.[66] However, the major difference between both entities lies in the fact that membership to ad hoc subcommittees is explicitly also open to member states of UNESCO which are not represented in the committee.[67]

---

[55] Article 7 (4) of the ICPRCP Statutes.

[56] Rule 5.2 of the ICPRCP Rules of Procedure.

[57] Article 7 (5) of the ICPRCP Statutes.

[58] Rule 5 of the ICPRCP Rules of Procedure contains additionally a number of regulations in case any member of the bureau is unable to attend (parts of) the sessions or may not be able to complete the term of his office.

[59] Article 10 (1) of the ICPRCP Statutes; Rule 11.1 of the ICPRCP Rules of Procedure.

[60] Article 10 (2) of the ICPRCP Statutes; Rule 11.2 of the ICPRCP Rules of Procedure.

[61] Article 10 (3) of the ICPRCP Statutes.

[62] Article 6 (1) of the ICPRCP Statutes.

[63] Rule 10.3 of the ICPRCP Rules of Procedure.

[64] Article 6 (2) of the ICPRCP Statutes; Rule 10.4 of the ICPRCP Rules of Procedure.

[65] Rule 10.5 of the ICPRCP Rules of Procedure.

[66] Rule 10.6 of the ICPRCP Rules of Procedure.

[67] Article 6 (1) of the ICPRCP Statutes.

4.2.6 The Modus Operandi of the ICPRCP

While the foundational cornerstones of the functioning of the ICPRCP are regulated by its statutes, Article 5 (3) of the Statutes itself mandates the committee to adopt its own rules of procedure what it has done.[68] The committee itself meets in a regular plenary session every year or every other year.[69] The dates are determined in general by each predecessor session[70] and the sessions, as a general rule, take place at the UNESCO Headquarters. However, the committee may also meet elsewhere when decided by a majority of its members.[71] For this purpose, any member state or associate member of UNESCO may invite the ICPRCP to hold a session on its territory.[72] Furthermore, the ICPRCP may also convene extraordinary sessions[73] by decision of the committee itself or at the request of at least ten of its members.[74] For both extraordinary and ordinary sessions, the secretariat is in charge of the technical execution of the convocation of the session, including notifying member states of the ICPRCP of the date, place, and provisional agenda[75] of the session. However, the secretariat is supervised by and acts in consultation with the bureau,[76] which may for this purpose or other reasons be convened at the request of the committee, its chairman or the Director-General of UNESCO also in between the sessions of the committee.[77]

Although member states are free to send as many experts and advisers as they deem necessary to the committee, each member state has only one vote.[78] However,

---

[68]The ICPRCP Rules of Procedure were adopted as UNESCO Doc CC-89/CONF-213/COL-3. Amendments to the rules of procedure or the suspension of any provision, except those reproducing provisions of the ICPRCP Statutes, may be done by a two-thirds majority of the members of the committee present and voting (Rule 12 of the ICPRCP Rules of Procedure).

[69]Article 5 (1) of the ICPRCP Statutes. However, there have been exceptions to this pattern. Between the 7th and 8th as well as between the 9th and 10th sessions a period exceeding 2 years had elapsed. For a list containing all session dates see http://www.unesco.org/new/en/culture/themes/restitution-of-cultural-property/sessions/previous-sessions/.

[70]Rule 2.8 of the ICPRCP Rules of Procedure reads on this issue: "The Committee shall determine at each session, in consultation with the Director-General, the date and place of the next session. The date and/or place may be modified, if necessary, by the Bureau, in consultation with the Director-General.".

[71]Rule 2.3 of the ICPRCP Rules of Procedure.

[72]Rule 2.5 of the ICPRCP Rules of Procedure.

[73]Article 5 (1) of the ICPRCP Statutes.

[74]Rule 2.4 of the ICPRCP Rules of Procedure.

[75]Rule 3 of the ICPRCP Rules of Procedure deals with the agenda. It contains a quite detailed list of topics which have to be included in the provisional agenda of an ordinary session. In addition, it exercises restraint in the agenda of an extraordinary session by dictating that only those items for the consideration of which the session has been convened may be included to its agenda. Nevertheless, in both cases, the agenda has to be adopted at the beginning of the session.

[76]Cf. Rules 2.2, 2.4, 2.6 and 2.7 of the ICPRCP Rules of Procedure.

[77]Article 7 (3) of the ICPRCP Statutes.

[78]Article 5 (2) of the ICPRCP Statutes.

when it comes to a case in which a member state of the ICPRCP is concerned by either an offer or request for the restitution or return of cultural material, the respective member state may continue to participate in the committee's proceedings, but has no right to vote.[79] This denial of a voting right is however mitigated by the requirement that when dealing with offers or requests for the restitution or return of cultural property, the committee shall endeavour to arrive at unanimous decisions without proceeding to a vote.[80] In other cases, decisions ought to be taken by a simple majority of the members present and voting, meaning that only affirmative or negative votes are counted.[81,82] The quorum consists of a simple majority of the state members of the ICPRCP.[83] Regarding offers or requests for the restitution or return of cultural objects, the committee has, in addition, to invite any member state or associate state of UNESCO which is concerned by the offer or request to the sessions of the ICPRCP and the meetings of the ad hoc subcommittees.[84]

Other member states or associate states of UNESCO,[85] representatives of the UN and other organisations of the UN system[86] as well as international governmental and non-governmental organisations[87,88] may participate in the sessions of the committee and those of the ad hoc subcommittees or may even be invited to them. All meetings of the committee are open unless decided otherwise.[89] When, in exceptional circumstances, private meetings are held, the committee has to determine persons who, in addition to representatives of state members of the ICPRCP, may be present.[90]

The sessions are moderated by the bureau[91] which in particular opens and closes the plenary meetings, ensures the observance of the rules of procedure, and directs

---

[79]Rule 8.2 of the ICPRCP Rules of Procedure.

[80]Rule 8.3 of the ICPRCP Rules of Procedure.

[81]Rule 8.4 of the ICPRCP Rules of Procedure.

[82]Voting is normally by show of hands. When the result of a vote by show of hands is in doubt, the Chairman of the meeting may take a second vote by roll-call. A vote by roll-call is also taken if it is requested by not less than two States members of the Committee before voting starts. The vote or abstention of each member participation in a roll-call vote shall be inserted in the report (Rule 8.5 of the ICPRCP Rules of Procedure).

Rule 8 of the ICPRCP Rules of Procedure contains further detailed regulations on voting, such as the order in which proposals have to be voted upon.

[83]Rule 6.3 of the ICPRCP Rules of Procedure.

[84]Article 8 (1) of the ICPRCP Statutes.

[85]Article 8 (2) of the ICPRCP Statutes.

[86]Article 8 (3) of the ICPRCP Statutes.

[87]ICOM and the Organization for Museums, Monuments and Sites of Africa are such international organisations explicitly enlisted in Rule 4.5 of the ICPRCP Rules of Procedure.

[88]Article 8 (4) of the ICPRCP Statutes.

[89]Rule 6.1 of the ICPRCP Rules of Procedure.

[90]Rule 6.2 of the ICPRCP Rules of Procedure.

[91]Rule 5.7 of the ICPRCP Rules of Procedure.

the discussion including the right to speak, put questions to a vote, and announce decisions. Furthermore, the chairman also decides forthwith on any point of order, which any state member of the committee may raise at any time during the discussion.[92] An appeal may be made against the ruling of the chairman. Such an appeal is put to the vote immediately and the chairman's ruling stands unless overruled by a majority of the members present and voting.[93] However, member states of the committee may, at any time, propose the suspension or adjournment of a meeting or the adjournment or closure of a debate. The motion is put to a vote immediately.[94]

Substantially, the committee has to examine offers and requests concerning the restitution or return of cultural property and the relevant documents,[95] which have to be communicated by member states or associate members of UNESCO via the Director-General of UNESCO to the committee and which have to be accompanied, in so far as is possible, by appropriate supporting documents.[96,97] The ICPRCP may adopt any decision or recommendation it deems appropriate in this context.[98] On the other hand, the committee has to prepare a summary of the proceedings[99] and submit a report on its activities at each ordinary session of UNESCO's General Conference.[100]

Other UNESCO officials and committee bodies are integrated into the work of the committee insofar as the Director-General of UNESCO or his representative as well as the secretary or his representative may make either oral or written statements to the committee, to its ad hoc subcommittees and working groups, and its bureau concerning any question under consideration.[101]

Another important provision with regard to the manner in which the ICPRCP functions is Article 11 of the Statutes, according to which each member state and associate member of UNESCO shall bear the expense of participation of its representatives in sessions of the committee and of subsidiary organs, its bureau, and its ad hoc subcommittees.

---

[92]Rule 7.2 of the ICPRCP Rules of Procedure.

[93]Rule 7.3 of the ICPRCP Rules of Procedure.

[94]Rule 7.4 of the ICPRCP Rules of Procedure.

[95]Article 9 (2) of the ICPRCP Statutes.

[96]Article 9 (1) of the ICPRCP Statutes.

[97]In 1981, the ICPRCP has adopted a Standard Form Concerning Requests for Return or Restitution.

[98]Rule 9.1 of the ICPRCP Rules of Procedure.

[99]Rule 9.2 of the ICPRCP Rules of Procedure regulates the specification of this requirement: "Following the closure of each session, a summary of the Committee's proceedings, prepared by the Rapporteur with the assistance of the Secretariat, shall be submitted for approval by the Chairman. The summary shall be transmitted to all the States members of the Committee, to the Member States and Associate Members of UNESCO which are not members of the Committee, and to the international organizations invited by the Committee to take part in the session.".

[100]Rule 9.3 of the ICPRCP Rules of Procedure.

[101]Rules 11.3 and 11.4 of the ICPRCP Rules of Procedure.

4.2.7 The ICPRCP's Work and Its Achievements

The ICPRCP has been active in a number of fields but has been particularly involved in cases concerning the return and restitution of cultural property. So far, it has assisted in the successful restitution of cultural material in 6 cases with a further 2 cases pending before the committee.

The first case was solved under the aegis of the Intergovernmental Committee in 1983, when Italy returned over 12,000 pre-Columbian objects to Ecuador following 7 years of litigation.[102] Only 3 years later, in 1986, based on a request from Jordan in 1983, the Cincinnati Art Museum (USA) and the Department of Antiquities of Amman (Jordan) came to an agreement following mediation to jointly exchange moulds of the parts of the sandstone panel of Tyche with the zodiac in their possession in order to be able to present the work in its entirety.[103]

Another country that benefited from the good offices of the ICPRCP has been Turkey. It not only regained 7000 Boğazköy cuneiform tablets from the German Democratic Republic in 1987,[104] which were also later added to the UNESCO Memory of the World List in 2001,[105] but it also got back the Boğazköy Sphinx in 2011.[106] In 1988, mediation proved again to be a successful tool for return and restitution in the case of the Phra Narai lintel, which the USA returned to Thailand.[107] Furthermore, the ICPRCP has been the framework for the discussions regarding the Makondé Mask which began in 2006 and resulted in the return of the mask from the Barbier-Mueller Museum in Geneva (Switzerland) to the United Republic of Tanzania in 2010.[108]

As previously mention, a further two cases are pending before the Intergovernmental Committee. The first case is between Iran and Belgium and concerns archaeological objects from the Necropolis of Khurvin. This case was brought to the attention of the committee in 1985, but was suspended as Iran brought the case before the courts of Belgium. The ICPRCP is currently waiting for the outcome of those proceedings.[109]

The second case still pending before the committee is also maybe the case attracting most media attention: the case of the Parthenon marbles involving Greece and the United Kingdom. These marbles, also known as Elgin Marbles, are

[102]UNESCO Doc CLT-83/CONF.216/8, 10.11.1983, p. 4; http://www.unesco.org/new/en/culture/themes/restitution-of-cultural-property/committes-successful-restitutions/.

[103]UNESCO Doc 24 C/94, 20.11.1987, p. 2.

[104]UNESCO Doc 24 C/94, 20.11.1987, pp. 4f; UNESCO Doc 25 C/91 Annex, 16.06.1989, p. 1.

[105]http://www.unesco.org/new/en/communication-and-information/flagship-project-activities/memory-of-the-world/register/full-list-of-registered-heritage/registered-heritage-page-8/the-hittite-cuneiform-tablets-from-bogazkoey/#c187076.

[106]UNESCO Doc 37 C/REP/14, 23.08.2013, p. 2.

[107]UNESCO Doc 25 C/91, 16.11.1989, p. 1.

[108]UNESCO Doc CLT-2010/CONF.203/COM.16/6REV, May 2012, p. 4.

[109]UNESCO Doc CLT-2011/CONF.208/COM.17/2REV, May 2012, p. 2.

considered by the Greeks to be an essential part of their identity.[110] They were shipped to London in the early nineteenth century from the Acropolis in Athens[111] and are exhibited in the British Museum. Greece brought the case to the attention of the Intergovernmental Committee in 1984. However, despite the more than 30 years that have passed, the case has this far not been resolved.[112,113]

Another area in which the Intergovernmental Committee has been quite successful is in the field of technical assistance. The ICPRCP endorsed and promotes Object ID, an international documentation standard for the information needed to identify cultural objects.[114] Object ID was originally the result of an initiative of the J. Paul Getty Trust and since 2004 is officially based with ICOM. The project started in 1993 and has been developed through years of research. It is the result of collaboration between various entities, such as the museum community, international police and customs agencies, the art trade, insurance industry, and valuers of art and antiques. These have all worked together in order to help combat the illegal appropriation of art objects by facilitating documentation of cultural artefacts and bringing together organisations around the world that can encourage its implementation.[115]

In this spirit, the Intergovernmental Committee also maintains close ties to other international organisations combating the illicit trafficking of cultural objects and involved in their restitution and return, including INTERPOL, UNIDROIT, and ICOM. Moreover, national specialised police forces such as the Comando Carabinieri Tutela Patrimonie Culturale (Italy) are considered to be partner institutions and report about their activities at the committee sessions.[116]

Another outcome from the work of the committee is the UNESCO International Code of Ethics for Dealers in Cultural Property which the ICPRCP requested at its 5th session in 1987[117] and after some consideration and preliminary work adopted

[110] Gillman (2010), p. 24.

[111] For further details about the circumstances of their acquisition see Cuno (2008), p. ix.

[112] UNESCO Doc CLT-85/CONF.202/2, 15.02.1985, p. 2; UNESCO Doc 37 C/REP/14, 23.08.2013, pp. 1f.

[113] This case has recently seen an interesting twist; Greece has informed the United Kingdom that it will possibly resort to the mediation and conciliation procedure provided for by the ICPRCP. The United Kingdom is currently considering the Greek proposal. UNESCO Doc ICPRCP/14/19. COM/3, September 2014, p. 2. On the ICPRCP mediation and conciliation procedure cf. pp. 181ff.

[114] UNESCO Doc CLT-98/CONF.203/INF.7, December 1998, pp. 1f; UNESCO Doc CLT-2005/CONF.202/2, January 2005, pp. 6f.

[115] http://archives.icom.museum/object-id/about.html.

[116] For a more detailed list of partners see http://www.unesco.org/new/en/culture/themes/illicit-traffic-of-cultural-property/partnerships/ and respective links on the website.

[117] UNESCO Doc 24 C/94 Annex, 20.11.1987, p. 3.

at its 10th session in 1999.[118] It was also endorsed by the 30th General Conference of UNESCO in the year of its adoption.[119]

The code of ethics builds on principles developed in the 1970 UNESCO Convention on the Means of Prohibiting and Preventing the Illicit Import, Export and Transfer of Ownership of Cultural Property as well as the 1995 UNIDROIT Convention on Stolen or Illegally Exported Cultural Objects. In addition, the experiences of countries such as France, The Netherlands, Switzerland, and the UK who implemented national dealers' codes, as well as the model rule on the Acquisitions Policies of Museums found in the Code of Professional Ethics of ICOM were taken into consideration in the drafting process of the UNESCO Code of Ethics. Last but not least, contributions and comments from dealers and dealer groups were also taken into consideration.[120]

Another achievement of the committee worthy of mention is the fund it established. As soon as the ICPRCP was founded, it was recommended, based on a study carried out by ICOM, that a fund should be created in order to facilitate the work of the committee,[121] as for certain countries of origin a lack of resources constituted an obstacle in reclaiming lost cultural property.[122] Finally, based on a recommendation of the committee adopted at its 10th session in 1999,[123] that very same year the General Conference of UNESCO established the Fund of the Intergovernmental Committee for Promoting the Return of Cultural Property to its Countries of Origin or its Restitution in case of Illicit Appropriation.[124] This fund is administered by the Director-General of UNESCO.[125] According to the Operational Guidelines of the Fund, its purpose is to finance projects related to requests in accordance with Article 3 (2) of the ICPRCP Statutes as well as projects that increase the self-reliance or strengthen national capacities for facilitating the prevention of illicit trafficking or the restitution of cultural property or exchanges of information on it.[126] Hence, priority is given to projects aimed at the preparation and implementation of the return of cultural property to its countries of origin for those countries whose cultural heritage has been extremely dispersed. The fund covers, for example, costs related to the transportation of objects including insurance, the arrangement of exhibition facilities,[127] and the financing of experts to

[118]UNESCO Doc 30 C/REP.14, 28.09.1999, p. 6.

[119]http://www.unesco.org/new/en/culture/themes/illicit-traffic-of-cultural-property/legal-and-practical-instruments/unesco-international-code-of-ethics-for-dealers-in-cultural-property/.

[120]For more details on the UNESCO International Code of Ethics for Dealers in Cultural Property cf. pp. 159ff.

[121]http://www.unesco.org/new/en/culture/themes/restitution-of-cultural-property/fund-of-the-committee/.

[122]Cf. Shyllon (2009), p. 372.

[123]UNESCO Doc 30 C/REP.14 Annex I, 28.09.1999, p. 4.

[124]UNESCO GC 30 C/Resolution 27, 17.11.1999.

[125]Rule V of the Operational Guidelines of the Fund.

[126]Rule II of the Operational Guidelines of the Fund.

[127]Rule IV a) of the Operational Guidelines of the Fund.

verify the authenticity of objects.[128] Another area given priority involves projects ensuring the establishment or improvement of museum systems or other institutions providing satisfactory conditions for the conservation of cultural material, especially in developing countries, as well as to projects that train museums professionals,[129] increase public awareness or strengthen the national and regional capacity for facilitating the restitution of cultural property.[130]

In this context, for reasons of transparency and clarity, the committee also adopted a procedure for the assessment of projects in addition to the Operational Guidelines of the Fund.[131] A base prerequisite to benefit from the fund, irrespective of details, is that the submitted project must be somehow attributed to a member state of UNESCO.[132] The fund also provides emergency assistance up to US$ 10,000 which can be accessed under easier conditions.[133]

Nevertheless, an important point in the context of the fund is its sourcing. The fund is financed by voluntary contributions of UNESCO member states, specialised agencies of the UN, intergovernmental organisations, public and private organisations as well as individuals which may contribute for either general or specific activities and in monetary form, in the form of services and in kind.[134] Despite an appeal from the Director-General of UNESCO,[135] however, the only country to contribute to the fund so far has been Greece.[136] More interestingly, despite the fund's current balance of US$ 124,202,[137] it has never been used.[138] The ICPRCP has thus, at its 19th session in October 2014, authorised the use of the Fund of the Committee for the establishment of a database on return and restitution cases operational in the short term and requested the secretariat to present to the 20th ordinary session a report on the latest developments regarding the database.[139]

A further topic that has been addressed by the committee is that of model rules defining state ownership of undiscovered artefacts. During its extraordinary session

---

[128]http://www.unesco.org/new/en/culture/themes/restitution-of-cultural-property/fund-of-the-committee/.

[129]http://www.unesco.org/new/en/culture/themes/restitution-of-cultural-property/fund-of-the-committee/.

[130]Rule IV b) of the Operational Guidelines of the Fund.

[131]http://portal.unesco.org/culture/en/files/29261/11326563663assessmente.pdf/assessmente.pdf.

[132]Rule III a) of the Operational Guidelines of the Fund; however, even though Rule III b) of the Operational Guidelines of the Fund allows "Public bodies, international governmental organizations, international non-governmental organizations, similar foundations and institutions with which UNESCO has official relations" to submit projects, this is limited by the phrase "if endorsed by a Member State".

[133]Rule III c) of the Operational Guidelines of the Fund.

[134]Rule I of the Operational Guidelines of the Fund.

[135]http://www.unesco.org/culture/laws/pdf/appealdg_march2001.pdf.

[136]Stamatoudi (2011), p. 58.

[137]UNESCO Doc ICPRCP/14/19.COM/7, August 2014, p. 2.

[138]UNESCO Doc 37 C/REP/14, 23.08.2013, p. 3.

[139]UNESCO Doc ICPRCP/14/19.COM/8, p. 3.

held in Seoul in 2008, legislation on undiscovered antiquities was one of the major issues discussed.[140] States requesting such objects encounter numerous legal obstacles. Hence, to guarantee that states have sufficient legal principles at hand to ensure their ownership, the preparation of respective model provisions was proposed. The ICPRCP invited UNESCO and UNIDROIT to establish a committee of independent experts, which was duly established and prepared the requested model rules.[141] The ICPRCP examined the finalised model rules consisting of 6 provisions[142] at its 17th session and asked the expert committee to incorporate the observations made by the committee into their explanatory guidelines and disseminate those model provisions.[143] Nevertheless, ever since their creation, the model rules have been promoted through training workshops held worldwide. Furthermore, national authorities have been made aware of the need to implement these rules within the framework of their national legislation.[144]

4.2.8 Summary

Interestingly, although the ICPRCP was first established to appease source countries which were unhappy with the 1970 UNESCO Convention, in particular its lack of retroactivity, it was established as a body independent from the 1970 UNESCO

[140] UNESCO Doc CLT-2011/CONF.208/COM.17/2REV, May 2012, p. 2.

[141] http://www.unesco.org/new/en/culture/themes/restitution-of-cultural-property/standards-for-ownership/.

[142] Model Provisions on State Ownership of Undiscovered Cultural Objects:

Provision 1—General Duty: The State shall take all necessary and appropriate measures to protect undiscovered cultural objects and to preserve them for present and future generations.

Provision 2—Definition: Undiscovered cultural objects include objects which, consistently with national law, are of importance for archaeology, prehistory, history, literature, art or science and are located in the soil or underwater.

Provision 3—State Ownership: Undiscovered cultural objects are owned by the State, provided there is no prior existing ownership.

Provision 4—Illicit excavation or retention: Cultural objects excavated contrary to the law or licitly excavated but illicitly retained are deemed to be stolen objects.

Provision 5—Inalienability: The transfer of ownership of a cultural object deemed to be stolen under Provision 4 is null and void, unless it can be established that the transferor had a valid title to the object at the time of the transfer.

Provision 6—International enforcement: For the purposes of ensuring the return or the restitution to the enacting State of cultural objects excavated contrary to the law or licitly excavated but illicitly retained, such objects shall be deemed stolen objects.

For the further information on the model rules, in particular the explanatory guidelines see: http://www.unesco.org/new/fileadmin/MULTIMEDIA/HQ/CLT/pdf/UNESCO-UNIDROIT_Model_Provisions_en.pdf.

[143] UNESCO Doc CLT-2011/CONF.208/COM.17/5, 01.07.2011, p. 3.

[144] UNESCO Doc ICPRCP/14/19.COM/3, September 2014, pp. 4f.

Convention.[145] Despite the fact that it was not authorised with the capacity to issue legally binding decisions, but rather intended to operate in a purely advisory role, the committee has become UNESCO's central institution not only to promote the return and restitution of cultural property by providing a framework for discussion and negotiation for the parties involved in disputes concerning cultural material and by promoting multilateral and bilateral cooperation, but also to combat the illicit trafficking of cultural heritage itself.[146]

The committee has continued to act in the spirit of the 1970 UNESCO and the 1995 UNIDROIT Conventions, even though in a much softer and less legally binding manner. Through its ordinary sessions, ad hoc subcommittees, and the efforts of its bureau, the committee has brought to bear what certain people consider "moral authority"[147] to the solution of a number of cases. It has furthermore conducted projects combating the illegal appropriation of art objects by facilitating their documentation, such as Object ID, fostered international cooperation, prepared an International Code of Ethics for Dealers in Cultural Property, founded a fund to facilitate the work of the committee and strengthen national capacities for facilitating the prevention of illicit trafficking as well as the restitution of cultural property and adopted the Rules of Procedure for Mediation and Conciliation. Such efforts are continuing as currently the committee is in the process of drafting model rules defining state ownership in regard to undiscovered cultural material.

4.3 The Soft Law Approach: Bringing Private Parties on Board

4.3.1 Soft Law: Prelude

The search for ways to resolve cultural object related disputes in a more promising way than relying solely on international conventions has led, in addition to the establishment of the institutional framework of the ICPRCP, to the emergence of another type of instrument—soft law.

In this context, the ICOM Code of Ethics for Museums, the UNESCO International Code of Ethics for Dealers in Cultural Property, and the ILA Principles for Cooperation in the Mutual Protection and Transfer of Cultural Material have to be

---

[145] http://www.unesco.org/new/en/culture/themes/restitution-of-cultural-property/intergovernmental-committee/historical-background/.

[146] http://www.unesco.org/new/en/culture/themes/restitution-of-cultural-property/; Stamatoudi (2011), p. 179 sees it as the institutionalisation of the diplomatic actions of UNESCO.

[147] Shyllon (2011), p. 435.

mentioned as key soft law documents concerning the return of cultural objects transferred in times of peace.[148]

Soft law is to be distinguished from international conventions for a number of reasons. First of all, its legal nature is different; while international agreements are legally binding instruments, soft law is—despite being labelled as "law"—not legally binding,[149] since it does not meet certain procedural or institutional requirements.[150] In most cases either the entity adopting the soft law is not qualified to enact legally binding rules, as in the case of the ICOM Code or the ILA Principles, or it lacks the intention to create legally binding regulations, as in the case of the UNESCO Code of Ethics.

However, this does not mean that soft law has no (legal) relevance at all. Although it is true that a breach of these self-commitments[151] may not directly lead to legal consequences, since they are not judicially enforceable,[152] as even most soft law itself does not provide for any sanctions,[153] such a breach may however have to be justified for the sake of public opinion and reputation. Furthermore, soft law in general, and in particular in the context of cultural heritage, can be consulted in court cases to determine the existence or change of a certain opinio

[148]Even though the ICOM Code of Ethics for Museums and the UNESCO International Code of Ethics for Dealers in Cultural Property are the two most relevant ethics codes at the international level concerning cultural heritage in a peacetime context, there are many other codes of ethics, both at the international and national levels addressing the issue of handling and dealing with cultural material. At the international level, the Code of Ethics of the World Association of Antique Dealer Associations and the International Association of Dealers in Art Code of Ethics and Practice should be mentioned. For further information on these see Stamatoudi (2011), pp. 175ff and O'Keefe (2007), pp. 159ff.

At the national level, the Restitution and Repatriation: Guidelines for Good Practice of the Museums and Galleries Commission of the United Kingdom, the German Code of Ethics for the International Trade in Works of Art (Thorn (2005), pp. 283ff), the Code of Ethics of the University of Pennsylvania Museum (Weidner (2001), p. 283), and the Guidelines on Due Diligence by the Department for Culture, Media and Sport of the United Kingdom (O'Keefe (2007), p. 157) are noteworthy.

However, an area in which soft law has an enormous significance in the context of cultural heritage is in the case of cultural objects looted by the Nazis. The laws enacted by the Allied Forces as well as the ones adopted by the German Government subsequent to World War II are by now precluded due to temporal aspects. After German reunification, the subject of Nazi looted cultural material once again gained attention since in East Germany the victims of the looting had not been compensated. This led to the adoption of the Principles of the Washington Conference With Respect to Nazi-Confiscated Art in 1998. For further information on soft law and its achievements in the context of Nazi confiscated art see Martinek (2011), pp. 415ff.

[149]Graf Vitzthum (2013), p. 58.

[150]Martinek (2011), pp. 417f.

[151]Müller-Karpe (2010), p. 93.

[152]Boos (2006), p. 120; Schönenberger (2009), p. 255.

[153]Martinek (2011), pp. 422f; cf. also Frigo (2009), p. 57.

juris[154] or ordre public[155] and hence be of importance in determining international customary law[156] or in specifying treaty obligations. Additionally, it facilitates the legal development in the respective area. Furthermore, in the case of cultural artefacts, soft law also has the effect of shrinking the size of the black market. When, such as in the case of the ICOM Code, museums agree to not purchase objects of a doubtful provenance, the number of potential buyers of such items diminishes which in turn decreases the incentive for persons to steal or illicitly export artefacts.[157]

However, soft law not only differs from treaty law in terms of legal character, but also with regard to originators and addressees. While international agreements are made by states or international organisations and, in general, only impose obligations on these two groups, soft law can be created by both states and private actors and address again both of them.[158] The ethics codes of ICOM and UNESCO as well as the ILA Principles are good examples of this.[159]

In the case of the ICOM Code of Ethics and the ILA Principles, furthermore, the body issuing the soft law is distinct from that which adopts international treaties. These have been adopted by ICOM and the ILA, two international non-governmental organisations and not by state-run bodies.[160] However, what unites both international treaties and soft law is the fact that they aim to regulate the behaviour of the actors involved in matters concerning cultural heritage.

4.3.2 *The ICOM Code of Ethics for Museums*

4.3.2.1 General Remarks

The first key soft law instrument to emerge concerning the return of cultural objects was the ICOM Code of Ethics for Museums. Motivated by the developments in the context of UNESCO, the international museum community, which had already studied the problem of the illicit transfer of cultural material in the 1930s,[161] again devoted itself to the issue. As a result, in 1986 the ICOM Code was adopted.[162]

---

[154]Graf Vitzthum (2013), p. 58.

[155]Weidner (2001), p. 284.

[156]Martinek (2011), p. 418.

[157]Martinek (2011), pp. 424f.

[158]For the general role private actors play in international cultural heritage law see Vrdoljak (2016), pp. 546ff.

[159]On the addressees of ICOM Code of Ethics cf. p. 191, on those of the UNESCO Code of Ethics cf. p. 206 and for the addressees of the ILA Principles cf. p. 216; cf. also Frigo (2009), p. 50.

[160]For further information on ICOM cf. p. 188; for further information on the ILA cf. p. 214.

[161]O'Keefe (2007), p. 156; for further information on the earlier involvement of the international museums community also cf. pp. 5ff.

[162]http://icom.museum/the-governance/general-assembly/resolutions-adopted-by-icoms-general-assemblies-1946-to-date/buenos-aires-1986/.

Although the ICOM Code of Ethics for Museums is soft law and as such not legally binding, its significance should not be underestimated. ICOM can boast an impressive network of 20,000 museums, 35,000 experts, 119 national committees, 30 international committees, 5 regional alliances, and 21 affiliated organisations present in 136 countries and territories.[163] This contributes to ICOM being an important partner of UNESCO in the fight against the illicit trafficking of cultural objects[164] as it represents museums, including those subject to claims for return and restitution, and their personnel at the international level. Museums on the other hand, in their role as central institutions for raising public awareness regarding both national and foreign cultural artefacts,[165] and as safeguards and trustees of cultural material,[166] play a pivotal role in the context of cultural heritage.[167]

Thus, with the ethics code, which presents a series of principles supported by guidelines for desirable professional practice in a field where legislation at the national level is diverse and far from consistent and which each member is committed to respect solely due to its membership,[168] ICOM imposes in practice minimum standards of conduct on more key actors in the field of cultural heritage than, for instance, the 1995 UNIDROIT Convention which has only been ratified by 37 states thus far.[169] This is of utmost relevance, particularly in cases where a member of ICOM is located in a state that is not a party to the relevant international

[163]http://icom.museum/icom-network/.

[164]In the fight against the illicit trafficking of cultural material ICOM has and still does undertake a number of measures. As a preventive measure, its International Committee for Museum Security is, for instance, concerned with the security of collections. The work is supported by the International Documentation Committee, which helps museums to inventory their collections, and the International Committee for the Training of Personnel. Furthermore, it maintains the so-called Red Lists which contain lists of objects subject to export restrictions. Additionally, it promotes Object ID. See also Stamatoudi (2011), pp. 180ff.

[165]Rush (2013), p. 66; cf. also Mugabowagahunde (2016), p. 146.

[166]Prott (1992), p. 160; Thorn (2005), pp. 275f; cf. also Koppar (2014), pp. 42f; see also Frigo (2009), p. 52; The idea of museums as safeguards, trustees, and stewards of cultural property is also inherent to the ICOM Code of Ethics for Museums. See Principle 2 of the ICOM Code of Ethics for Museums: "Museums that maintain collections hold them in trust for the benefit of society and its development – Principle: museums have the duty to acquire, preserve and promote their collections as a contribution to safeguarding the natural, cultural and scientific heritage. Their collections are a significant public inheritance, have a special position in law and are protected by international legislation. Inherent in this public trust is the notion of stewardship that includes rightful ownership, permanence, documentation, accessibility and responsible disposal."

[167]For the highly questionable role (certain) museums used to and occasionally still do play concerning the illicit trafficking of cultural property see Wessel (2015), pp. 92ff; on the developments in this field and the increasing willingness of museums to cooperate see however Lyons (2014), pp. 251–265.

[168]Paragraphs 1 and 2 of the Preamble and Paragraph 3 of the Introduction of the ICOM Code of Ethics for Museums.

[169]http://www.unidroit.org/status-cp.

treaties,[170] since the code in practice implements de facto the principles established by the international treaties mentioned by setting them up as minimum accepted standards of conduct in those countries.[171] At the same time, with the code of ethics, ICOM elevates its own significance as an actor in the area of cultural heritage.

Another important aspect in this context is that the ICOM Code of Ethics for Museums not only deals with matters of restitution and return, but its scope is much broader; it also covers other questions, such as the conflict of interest which may occur between a museum and its employees.[172] However, in the context of this study, only the provisions concerning the return and restitution of cultural objects shall be focused on.

4.3.2.2 The ICOM Code of Ethics' Adoption Procedure

The international museum community began to study the issue of illicitly transferred cultural artefacts as early as the 1930s.[173] However, induced to take action anew by the Recommendation on the Means of Prohibiting and Preventing the Illicit Export, Import and Transfer of Ownership of Cultural Property[174] adopted by the 13th General Conference of UNESCO on 19 November 1964, in April 1970 a group of experts met in Paris in order to study the problem of ethical rules governing museum acquisitions.[175] As an outcome of this meeting, the ICOM Ethics of Acquisition were adopted the very same year.[176]

Following up the issue in 1974, the General Assembly of ICOM adopted a resolution instructing the ICOM Executive Council to designate a group of experts particularly qualified in this field to prepare a draft code of professional ethics.[177] This draft was, after adjustments made in accordance with the comments of the national and international committees of ICOM to which it had been distributed,

[170]Weidner (2001), p. 284; O'Keefe (2007), p. 156 states that certain museums have declared that they would comply with the principles set forth in the 1970 UNESCO Convention, even though the countries in which they are situated are not state parties to the agreement.

[171]Campfens (2014), p. 71.

[172]Cf., for example, Principle 8.13 of the ICOM Code of Ethics for Museums (Outside Employment or Business Interests): "Members of the museum profession, although entitled to a measure of personal independence, must realise that no private business or professional interest can be wholly separated from their employing institution. They should not undertake other paid employment or accept outside commissions that are in conflict with, or may be viewed as being in conflict with the interests of the museum.".

[173]O'Keefe (2007), p. 156; for further information on the earlier involvement of the international museums community also cf. pp. 5ff.

[174]Printed in Yusuf (2007), pp. 377ff.

[175]Thorn (2005), p. 277; http://archives.icom.museum/acquisition.html#2.

[176]Cf. http://archives.icom.museum/acquisition.html#2.

[177]http://icom.museum/the-governance/general-assembly/resolutions-adopted-by-icoms-general-assemblies-1946-to-date/copenhagen-1974/.

adopted by the 15th General Assembly of ICOM on 4 November 1986 as the ICOM Code of Professional Ethics.[178] The code was subsequently amended by the 20th General Assembly of ICOM on 6 July 2001 and retitled the ICOM Code of Ethics for Museums. On 8 October 2004 the 21st General Assembly of ICOM revised the code of ethics a second time, resulting in its current form.[179]

4.3.2.3 The Aims and the Scope of the ICOM Code of Ethics

The ICOM Code of Ethics has been adopted with a view to the variability and inconsistency of relevant legislation at the national level. It is meant to provide general ethical guidance to museums and their staff in their service to society, the community, the public, and its various constituencies by drawing on principles generally accepted by the international museum community.[180]

The minimum standards of conduct and performance set by the code as professional self-regulation are reasonable for professional museum staff throughout the world to adhere to. At the same time they provide a statement of reasonable public expectation regarding the museum profession as a whole.[181] Thus, it is not surprising that the addressees of the eight principles and their further guidelines established by the code of ethics are not only museums, but in addition museum personnel.[182] Hence, the ethics code also directly imposes obligations on individual members of the museum profession, which is of significance in cases in which the museum they work for has not enacted any regulation to implement the code of ethics so far.

Regarding the substantive scope of the code for the return and restitution of cultural objects, it is noteworthy that the code of ethics appears to use the terms "cultural property" and "cultural heritage" quasi interchangeably. However, when the code speaks of return or restitution the word "cultural property" is used.[183] The same is true in relation to illicitness. Whenever the term "illicit" is used in the text, it is used with the term "property" or "object". Principle 4.5 for instance, speaks of "illicit trade in cultural property", while Principle 8.5 states "illicit traffic or market in [. . .] cultural property".

---

[178]http://icom.museum/the-governance/general-assembly/resolutions-adopted-by-icoms-general-assemblies-1946-to-date/buenos-aires-1986/.

[179]http://icom.museum/fileadmin/user_upload/pdf/Codes/code_ethics2013_eng.pdf.

[180]Paragraph 1 of the Preamble and Paragraphs 1–3 of the Introduction of the ICOM Code of Ethics for Museums.

[181]Paragraph 3 of the Introduction of the ICOM Code of Ethics for Museums.

[182]Cf., for example, Principle 8.7 of the ICOM Code of Ethics for Museums (Museum and Collection Security): "Information about the security of the museum or of private collections and locations visited during official duties must be held in strict confidence by museum personnel.".

[183]Cf. Principles 6.2 (Return of Cultural Property) and 6.3 (Restitution of Cultural Property) of the ICOM Code of Ethics for Museums.

When, on the other hand, a value-free activity such as dealing is addressed by the code, the term employed is "heritage".[184] The phrase "natural and cultural"—which is normally a phrase used in the context of heritage[185]—is also employed in connection with property, as in the case of Principle 8.5,[186] a fact that also supports the assumption the drafters used the terms quasi interchangeably. Finally, this presumption is further supported by the glossary of the ICOM Code of Ethics for Museums which provides a definition for "cultural heritage", but none for "cultural property". Nevertheless, the word property is always used to mean a physical object. Thus, it has to be assumed that both terms are generally employed interchangeably with the exception that heritage is the more encompassing term as it also covers the intangible aspects of culture. Hence cultural property, just as cultural heritage, is to be understood in the context of the code as any thing considered of aesthetic, historical, scientific or spiritual significance.[187]

Concerning the personal scope of the code of ethics, its addressees are museums and also directly the museum personnel. However, despite the notion of cultural heritage in the code being far broader than the definitions found in the international treaties, the ethics code is also wider in scope concerning temporal aspects. Neither the provisions on the return and restitution nor any general provision contain a time limitation. Therefore, the ICOM Code of Ethics also applies to cultural objects that have been transferred to the museum before its entry into force. In the case of restitution, however, the code requires the cultural object to have been exported or otherwise transferred in violation of the principles of international and national conventions.[188] Thus, in the context of the obligation connected to restitution,[189] which is further-reaching than the duty imposed by the code in the context of return, there must have been at least a breach of national legislation by the transfer of the cultural artefact. Although this is not a direct time limitation, in practice it operates as one since legislation protecting cultural heritage is a relatively new development dating back to only the late nineteenth century.[190]

---

[184] Cf., for instance, Principle 8.14 of the ICOM Code of Ethics for Museums (Dealing in Natural or Cultural Heritage).

[185] The best example of which is the 1972 Convention Concerning the Protection of the World Cultural and Natural Heritage (World Heritage Convention).

[186] Principle 8.5 of the ICOM Code of Ethics for Museums (The Illicit Market): "Members of the museum profession should not support the illicit traffic or market in natural and cultural property, directly or indirectly.".

[187] Definition of "Cultural Heritage" in the Glossary of the ICOM Code of Ethics for Museums: "Any thing or concept considered of aesthetic, historical, scientific or spiritual significance.".

[188] Cf. Principle 6.3 of the ICOM Code of Ethics for Museums (Restitution of Cultural Property).

[189] In the case of return, the ICOM Ethics Code only requires museums to initiate dialogues (Principle 6.2 of the ICOM Code of Ethics for Museums); in the case of restitution, museums should take prompt and responsible steps to cooperate in its return (Principle 6.3 of the ICOM Code of Ethics for Museums).

[190] Cf. Stamatoudi (2011), p. 31.

4.3.2.4 The ICOM Code of Ethics' Principles on Return and Restitution

The ICOM Code of Ethics for Museums contains both a principle concerned with the return of cultural artefacts[191] and one with regard to the restitution of cultural material.[192] The distinction between return and restitution is based on the manner of the transfer of the object[193] and, depending on whether or not the cultural object has been transferred in violation of principles of international and national conventions, places different obligations on museums. Irrespective of this, in both cases the ICOM Code of Ethics takes into account the fact that cultural property has a character beyond that of ordinary property which also includes strong affiliations with national, regional, local, ethnic, religious or political identity.[194]

Where a country or people of origin reclaiming an object or specimen shown to be part of that country's or people's cultural or natural heritage can demonstrate that the very same has been exported or otherwise transferred in violation of the principles of international and national conventions, the museum concerned should, if legally free to do so, take prompt and responsible steps to cooperate in its return.[195] In all other cases, museums should only be prepared to initiate dialogues for the return of cultural property to a country or people of origin. This should be undertaken in an impartial manner, based on scientific, professional, and humanitarian principles as well as applicable local, national, and international legislation, in preference to action at a governmental or political level.[196]

Therefore, with regard to transfers in violation of the principles of international and national conventions, the museums concerned ought to take prompt and responsible steps to cooperate in the return of the respective cultural object. This obligation is only limited by the requirement that the country or people of origin has to prove that the respective object is part of its cultural or natural heritage and by any possible legal constraints that may exist.

In all other cases, the museum concerned has only to initiate dialogues and, moreover, these dialogues are subject to scientific, professional, and humanitarian

---

[191] Principle 6.2 of the ICOM Code of Ethics for Museums (Return of Cultural Property).

[192] Principle 6.3 of the ICOM Code of Ethics for Museums (Restitution of Cultural Property).

[193] Cf. in this context also Frigo (2009), p. 53.

[194] Cf. Principle 6 of the ICOM Code of Ethics for Museums.

[195] Principle 6.3 of the ICOM Code of Ethics for Museums (Restitution of Cultural Property): "When a country or people of origin seeks the restitution of an object or specimen that can be demonstrated to have been exported or otherwise transferred in violation of the principles of international and national conventions, and shown to be part of that country's or people's cultural or natural heritage, the museum concerned should, if legally free to do so, take prompt and responsible steps to co-operate in its return.".

[196] Principle 6.2 of the ICOM Code of Ethics for Museums (Return of Cultural Property): "Museums should be prepared to initiate dialogues for the return of cultural property to a country or people of origin. This should be undertaken in an impartial manner, based on scientific, professional and humanitarian principles as well as applicable local, national and international legislation, in preference to action at a governmental or political level.".

principles as well as applicable local, national, and international legislation. Therefore, in the case of illicitly transferred objects, the obligation of the museum is further-reaching and at the same time the duty is less limited. However, the obligation imposed in the case of an illicit transfer is only trumped by that which concerns human remains or material of sacred significance. For these cases, the ICOM Code of Ethics dictates that requests for their return must be addressed expeditiously with respect and sensitivity.[197]

Further to this, not only does the code of ethics itself draw an internal distinction between the obligations imposed, depending on the legality of the transfer of the artefact, but the obligations imposed on museums by the ethics code also differ in general from those in the international treaties. On the one hand, they are more favourable from the claimant's point of view as they do not condition the return or restitution to the payment of any sort of compensation.[198] On the other hand, corresponding with the nature of the code of ethics, the principles do not provide a clear legal basis. Moreover, they only oblige museums to initiate dialogues or cooperate in the return of an object in dispute and thus only impose a duty to cooperate rather than a compulsory obligation to return or restitute. This duty, as previously mentioned, can be additionally subject to legal constraints.

Hence, museums can exploit this to effectively block any claims for return or restitution by referring to their statutes which might prohibit them from disposing of any item in their collection.[199] However, it is to be expected that over the course of time the existence of such self-regulation will apply inexorable force to museums to change their attitude as well as statutes and be more sensitive to claims.

4.3.2.5 The ICOM Code of Ethics' Principles Fighting Illicit Trafficking and Encouraging Return and Restitution

The ICOM Code of Ethics for Museums also contains a number of principles concerning subjects closely related to the question of return and restitution of cultural material. The first of these principles, for which regulations can be found in the ethics code, is acquisition. This matter is primarily dealt with under Principle

[197] Principle 4.4 of the ICOM Code of Ethics for Museums (Removal from Public Display).

[198] Cf., for example, Article 7 (b) (ii) of the 1970 UNESCO Convention: "States Parties to this Convention undertake: [...] at the request of the State Party of origin, to take appropriate steps to recover and return any such cultural property imported after the entry into force of this Convention in both States concerned, provided, however, that the requesting State shall pay just compensation to an innocent purchaser or to a person who has valid title to that property.".

Cf. also Article 4 (1) of the 1995 UNIDROIT Convention: "The possessor of a stolen cultural object required to return it shall be entitled, at the time of its restitution, to payment of fair and reasonable compensation provided that the possessor neither knew nor ought reasonably to have known that the object was stolen and can prove that it exercised due diligence when acquiring the object.".

[199] Stamatoudi (2011), p. 173; see in this context also O'Keefe (2007), pp. 157f for examples of uncooperative museums.

2, which stresses that the notion of stewardship also includes rightful ownership. The first subheading of Principle 2 deals consequently with "Acquiring Collections".

The acquisition policy of a museum is connected to the highest degree to the issue of restitution and return. If museums pursue a policy of not purchasing cultural objects of a questionable provenance,[200] effectively, there will be no cultural material anyone could possibly reclaim from them. Hence, it is not surprising that Principle 2.2 of the ICOM Code of Ethics for Museums dictates that no object or specimen should be acquired by purchase, gift, loan, bequest or exchange unless the acquiring museum is satisfied that a valid title is held. Interestingly, the ethics code distinguishes between "valid title" and "legal title"; the former being the indisputable right to ownership of property, supported by the full provenance of the item from discovery or production,[201] while the latter is defined as the legal right to ownership of property in the country concerned, which, in certain countries, may be a conferred right.[202] Thus, the ICOM Code of Ethics clearly states that evidence of lawful ownership in a country alone does not necessarily constitute a valid title.[203] Hence, in cases in which the owner has obtained the title of a cultural object that has been illicitly exported, for instance, by good faith or acquisitive prescription, the museum is still restricted from acquiring the object even if, according to national legislation, this would not constitute a problem.

In order to clarify whether or not a valid title is present, every effort must be made before acquisition to ensure that any object or specimen offered for purchase, gift, loan, bequest or exchange has not been illegally obtained in or exported from its country of origin or any intermediate country in which it might have been owned legally, including the museum's own country. Due diligence in this regard should establish the full history of the item from discovery or production to the present day by making every endeavour to establish the facts of a case before deciding a course of action, particularly in identifying the source and history of an item offered for acquisition or use before it is acquired.[204,205] Thus, the onus to determine the lawfulness of the title of the owner is on the museum,[206] for which it has to conduct active investigations.

Museums should in particular refrain from acquiring objects where there is reasonable cause to believe their recovery involved the unauthorised, unscientific

[200]The ICOM Code of Ethics for Museums defines provenance in its glossary as the full history and ownership of an item from the time of its discovery or creation to the present day, from which authenticity and ownership is determined.

[201]Glossary of the ICOM Code of Ethics for Museums.

[202]Glossary of the ICOM Code of Ethics for Museums.

[203]Principle 2.2 of ICOM Code of Ethics for Museums (Valid Title).

[204]Principle 2.3 (Provenance and Due Diligence); Glossary of ICOM Code of Ethics for Museums.

[205]Among others, the provenance of a cultural object being part of a museum collection is also one of the points which have to be included in the documentation of the collection in accordance with Principle 2.20 of ICOM Code of Ethics for Museums (Documentation of Collections).

[206]Stamatoudi (2011), pp. 169f; DeAngelis (2009), p. 405.

or intentional destruction or damage of monuments, archaeological or geological sites or species and natural habitats. In the same way, acquisition should not occur if there has been a failure to disclose the findings to the owner or occupier of the land or to the proper legal or governmental authorities.[207] Another restriction concerning the acquisition of cultural material is to be found in Principle 6.4 of the ICOM Code of Ethics for Museums. According with this, museums should abstain from purchasing or acquiring cultural objects from any occupied territory.[208]

Although these regulations appear quite strict at first glance, particularly considering the requirement to investigate the full provenance of an item from discovery or production to the present day, which in the case of certain ancient artefacts is in practice impossible,[209] they are softened by the usage of the word "should". Hence, these obligations are not strictly binding and may be waived under certain circumstances, a matter for which the ethics code itself does not provide even general guidance on.[210] It only provides for two exceptions to the regulations which are to be found in Principle 2.9 on acquisitions outside of the collections policy and Principle 3.4 on the exceptional collecting of primary evidence. Nonetheless, these exceptions can be used as a guide to establish criteria to determine circumstances in which normal obligations and procedures can be waived.

According to Principle 2.9, museums may acquire objects or specimens outside the museum's stated policy in exceptional circumstances. However, before doing so, the governing body should consider the professional opinions available to it and the views of all interested parties. Consideration will include the significance of the object or specimen including its context in the cultural or natural heritage and the special interests of other museums collecting such material. However, even in these circumstances, objects without a valid title should not be acquired.[211]

Furthermore, according to Principle 3.4, which provides the second exception, in exceptional cases an item without provenance may be of such an inherently outstanding contribution to knowledge that it would be in the public interest to preserve it. However, the acceptance of such an item into a museum collection

---

[207]Principle 2.4 of ICOM Code of Ethics for Museums (Objects and Specimens from Unauthorised or Unscientific Fieldwork).

[208]Additionally, Principles 2.5 (Culturally Sensitive Material), 2.6 (Protected Biological or Geological Specimens), 2.7 (Living Collections), and 2.8 (Working Collections) of the ICOM Code of Ethics for Museums contain special rules for the acquisition of specimens of a particular highly sensitive character.

Another important aspect is to be found in Principle 2.10 of the ICOM Code of Ethics for Museums (Acquisition by Members of the Governing Body and Museum Personnel). According to the principle "(s)pecial care is required in considering any item, either for sale, as a donation or as a tax-benefit gift, from members of governing bodies, museum personnel, or the families and close associates of these persons.".

[209]Similar Stamatoudi (2011), pp. 170f.

[210]Cf. Flora (2013), p. 233 argues that American museums seem to include the idea of bringing an object into the public domain to their ethical considerations.

[211]Principle 2.9 of ICOM Code of Ethics for Museums (Acquisition Outside Collections Policy).

should be nevertheless the subject of a decision by specialists in the discipline concerned and without national or international prejudice.[212]

Although certain authors appear to ascribe both provisions nearly the same scope,[213] they cover distinctly differing circumstances. In the first case, the museum may purchase an object or specimens contrary to its own stated policy in exceptional circumstances. However, it has to take certain factors into consideration when doing so, such as the significance of the object or specimen including its context in the cultural or natural heritage and the special interests of other museums collecting such material. Furthermore, the museum still should not acquire objects without a valid title.

The second case however deals with primary evidence. Here the code of ethics speaks of the acceptance of an item with such an inherently outstanding contribution to knowledge that it would be in the public interest to preserve it, but without provenance. In this case, the museum may accept cultural objects in exceptional cases and subject to a decision of a specialist in the discipline concerned. The two important phrases in this context are "without provenance" and "in the public interest to preserve it". Hence, Principle 3.4 of the ICOM Code of Ethics for Museums covers cases in which the provenance of an object cannot be determined. Thus, it may be available as a result of an illegal action. The code of ethics nonetheless allows the museum to accept it, if it is worth being preserved. The wording e contrario though means that the object must be at least in danger of loss or destruction. Therefore, unlike Principle 2.9, Principle 3.4 allows museums to accept even cultural material without provenance in light of its possible loss as long as it is of an inherently outstanding contribution to knowledge and the decision is made by an unbiased specialist.

As mentioned earlier, both provisions, Principle 2.9 and Principle 3.4, can also be used to determine how the margin of appreciation concerning the phrasing "should" used in the context of the obligations mentioned above has to be exercised. Accordingly, the more valuable the cultural material is for its contribution to knowledge and the more likely it is that the non-acquisition will lead to its loss, the more museums may depart from the obligation imposed by the acquisition guidelines set forth by the ICOM Code of Ethics.

However, in the case where a museum should somehow have acquired or otherwise be in the possession of unprovenanced material, it should at least avoid displaying or otherwise using material of questionable origin or lacking provenance as such, if the display or usage can be seen to condone and contribute to the illicit trade in cultural heritage.[214,215] A key point to note here is that nothing in the ethics

---

[212]Principle 3.4 of ICOM Code of Ethics for Museums (Exceptional Collecting of Primary Evidence).

[213]Cf. Stamatoudi (2011), pp. 171f.

[214]Principle 4.5 of ICOM Code of Ethics for Museums (Display of Unprovenanced Material).

[215]The ICOM Code of Ethics for Museums also contains a special provision concerning the removal of human remains and material of sacred significance from public display. According to Principle 4.4 of the ICOM Code of Ethics for Museums (Removal from Public Display), requests for removal from public display of human remains or material of sacred significance from the originating communities must be addressed expeditiously with respect and sensitivity.

code prevents a museum from acting as an authorised repository for unprovenanced, illicitly collected or recovered specimens and objects from the territory over which it has lawful responsibility.[216] On the other hand, where museums provide an identification service, they should not act in any way that could be regarded as benefiting from such activity, directly or indirectly. Furthermore, the identification and authentication of objects that are believed or suspected to have been illegally or illicitly acquired, transferred, imported or exported should not be made public until the appropriate authorities have been notified.[217]

Another subject closely related to the question of return and restitution is the disposal of a collection. This is why Principle 2 has also a subheading attributed to this matter. Even though one might think that return and restitution are to be distinct from disposal as only the sale or donation of objects is covered by the term "disposal", Principle 2.15 of the Code of Ethics for Museums acknowledges repatriation as one form of removing an object from a collection.[218] Thus, the term "disposal" also includes return and restitution and therefore the guidelines established by the code of ethics concerning disposal apply to them also. Hence, where the museum has legal powers permitting disposals or has acquired objects subject to conditions of disposal, the legal or other requirements and procedures must be complied with fully when disposing of the object.[219] Moreover, the removal of an object or specimen from a museum collection must only be undertaken with a full understanding of the significance of the item, its character, whether it is renewable or not, legal standing, and any loss of public trust that might result from such action.[220,221]

---

[216]Principle 2.11 of ICOM Code of Ethics for Museums (Repositories of Last Resort).

[217]Principle 5.1 of ICOM Code of Ethics for Museums (Identification of Illegally or Illicitly Acquired Objects).

[218]Principle 2.15 of the ICOM Code of Ethics for Museums (Disposal of Objects Removed from the Collections): "Each museum should have a policy defining authorised methods for permanently removing an object from the collections through donation, transfer, exchange, sale, repatriation, or destruction, and that allows the transfer of unrestricted title to the receiving agency. Complete records must be kept of all deaccessioning decisions, the objects involved, and the disposition of the object. There will be a strong presumption that a deaccessioned item should first be offered to another museum.".

[219]Principle 2.12 of ICOM Code of Ethics for Museums (Legal or Other Powers of Disposal).

[220]Principle 2.13 of ICOM Code of Ethics for Museums (Deaccessioning from Museum Collections).

[221]Again, the ICOM Code of Ethics establishes a restriction concerning museum personnel, the governing body, and their families or close associates. According to Principle 2.17 of the ICOM Code of Ethics for Museums (Purchase of Deaccessioned Collections), they should not be permitted to purchase objects that have been deaccessioned from a collection for which they are responsible.

Furthermore, Principle 2.16 of the ICOM Code of Ethics for Museums (Income from Disposal of Collections) dictates that museum collections are held in public trust and may not be treated as a realisable asset. Money or compensation received from the deaccessioning and disposal of objects and specimens from a museum collection should be used solely for the benefit of the collection and usually for acquisitions to that same collection.

In addition to acquisition and disposal, the ICOM Code of Ethics also includes regulations concerning the involvement of museum personnel with the art market. Accordingly, members of the museum profession should not participate directly or indirectly in dealing[222] in natural or cultural heritage.[223] This also includes that they should not accept any gift, hospitality or any form of reward from a dealer, auctioneer or other person as an inducement to purchase or dispose of museum items or to take or refrain from taking official action. Moreover, museum professionals should not recommend a particular dealer, auctioneer or appraiser to a member of the public.[224]

Members of the museum profession should in particular not directly or indirectly support the illicit traffic or market in natural and cultural property,[225] but rather be conversant with relevant international, national, and local legislation and the conditions of their employment. They should avoid situations that could be construed as improper conduct[226] and assist the police or other proper authorities in investigating possible stolen, illicitly acquired or illegally transferred material.[227]

However, the ethics code not only expects individual personnel to conduct themselves in a legal manner, but the museum as an institution is under the same expectation. Museums should conform to all national and local laws, respect the legislation of other states as they affect their operation,[228] and acknowledge relevant international legislation.[229]

---

[222]"Dealing" is defined in the Glossary of the ICOM Code of Ethics for Museums as "buying and selling items for personal or institutional gain".

[223]Principle 8.14 of ICOM Code of Ethics for Museums (Dealing in Natural or Cultural Heritage).

[224]Principle 8.15 of ICOM Code of Ethics for Museums (Interaction with Dealers).

[225]Principle 8.5 of ICOM Code of Ethics for Museums (The Illicit Market).

[226]Principle 8.1 of ICOM Code of Ethics for Museums (Familiarity with Relevant Legislation).

[227]Principle 8.8 of ICOM Code of Ethics for Museums (Exception to the Obligation for Confidentiality).

[228]Principle 7.1 of ICOM Code of Ethics for Museums (National and Local Legislation).

[229]Principle 7.2 of the ICOM Code of Ethics for Museums (International Legislation):

"Museum policy should acknowledge the following international legislation which is taken as a standard in interpreting the *ICOM Code of Ethics*:

- UNESCO Convention for the Protection of Cultural Property in the Event of Armed Conflict (The Hague Convention, First Protocol, 1954 and Second Protocol, 1999);
- UNESCO Convention on the Means of Prohibiting and Preventing the Illicit Import, Export and Transfer of Ownership of Cultural Property (1970);
- Convention on International Trade in Endangered Species of Wild Fauna and Flora (1973);
- UN Convention on Biological Diversity (1992);
- UNIDROIT Convention on Stolen and Illegally Exported Cultural Objects (1995);
- UNESCO Convention on the protection of the Underwater Cultural Heritage (2001);
- UNESCO Convention for the Safeguarding of the Intangible Cultural Heritage (2003).".

4.3.2.6 Final Remarks

At first glance, the significance of the ICOM Code of Ethics for Museums may appear ambiguous. Unlike in the case of the 1970 UNESCO Convention and the 1995 UNIDROIT Convention, the obligations established for museums by the ICOM Code with regard to return and restitution are not limited by requirements concerning the payment of compensation or time constraints. In particular, the section on the acquisition of new objects imposes far-reaching obligations on museums. On the other hand, the obligation in the context of return and restitution is basically limited to the duty to cooperate, whereas the conventions impose much stricter obligations for cases that fall within their ambit. The 1995 UNIDROIT Convention, for instance, requires in Article 3 that the possessor of a cultural object which has been stolen returns it. Furthermore, in the ICOM Code's heavily regulated area of acquisition, the use of the phrase "should" unburdens museums to a degree of the duties imposed by the very same chapter. The relevance of the ICOM Code of Ethics is further diminished by its legally non-binding nature. Even having said all that, probably the point giving the greatest cause to question the effectiveness of the ICOM Code of Ethics is the fact that it is self-regulated by the museums, the very institutions that consistently face claims for the return of cultural heritage in their possession and accusations that they would own and even purchase cultural objects of dubious or illegal provenance.[230] Thus, the ICOM Code basically trusts the fox in the henhouse.

Nevertheless, the ICOM Code constitutes an important achievement and is of great significance. Regarding the return of transferred cultural objects, the principles of the ICOM Code of Ethics play a key role. They prevent museums from simply ignoring demands for the return of cultural material in their collections. Such behaviour can no longer be justified in the face of public opinion without reputational damage, especially since museums have set themselves the standards embodied in the code. Thus, the fear that by following their own agenda and pursuing their own interests with the ICOM Code museums might actually hinder claims for return is more than balanced by the pressure they have exposed themselves to by adopting the code of ethics.

Another positive aspect of the ICOM Code of Ethics is that since museums are major players in the art market,[231] the code of ethics has a significant impact on the illicit trade in cultural objects and its black market; as museums drop out as possible buyers, the number of possible purchasers of artefacts with a dubious provenance significantly decreases and with such a decline in demand, the value of illicitly trafficked objects declines also. This, in turn, diminishes the incentive for conducting illicit excavations and for illicit trafficking.[232]

In addition, the ICOM Code of Ethics also indirectly affects the black market since private collectors wishing to donate or loan cultural objects to museums, for

[230] Cf. Grant (2014).

[231] Cf. Blake (2015), p. 34.

[232] Cf. O'Keefe (2007), p. 157; cf. also Polk (2013), p. 120.

tax relief for example, have to prove their provenance[233] which again decreases the demand for and thus the value of illicit cultural material. These effects can already be seen as museums have changed their policies and it has become harder to ignore the provenance of cultural material—so have the consequences of avoiding it.[234]

Thus, as with most soft law,[235] the ICOM Code of Ethics has already sensitised the public concerning the issue of contested cultural heritage. It is to be expected that the code, which already can be consulted in court cases to determine the existence or change of a certain ordre public[236] as well as for the interpretation of certain legal provisions and obligations, will further pave the way for a change in mentality which in turn may eventually lead to a change in (binding) legislation.

Last but not least, a final aspect should not be lost sight of: the ICOM Code of Ethics also creates legal certainty for the museums themselves.[237] They know which acquisitions are unproblematic and those that may see them held accountable for and face a future return or restitution claim.

Ultimately, it can be noted that the ICOM Code rose from and embodies the spirit of the 1970 UNESCO and 1995 UNIDROIT Conventions as well as the ICPRCP, in particular the aspect of cooperation. Furthermore, it advances the principles established by these instruments, despite diminishing the obligation of the conventions to return to a duty to cooperate, by further elaborating on them and setting up more detailed and new principles relevant to the return of cultural artefacts as well as by including private parties to the process and addressing them directly.

4.3.3 The UNESCO International Code of Ethics for Dealers in Cultural Property

4.3.3.1 Introduction

After some time, UNESCO also realised that non-governmental actors play a key role when it comes to the illicit transfer of cultural objects as well as disputes concerning such artefacts.[238] Hence, it became aware of the fact that any solution

---

[233] Thorn (2005), p. 277.

[234] Brodie (2009), p. 54; cf. also O'Keefe (2007), p. 158 who reports for example of Dr. Dietrich von Bothmer whose nomination as an Honorary Fellow of the prestigious Society of Antiquaries of London had been withdrawn following concerns expressed about his acquisition policies while at the Metropolitan Museum of Article; cf. also Campfens (2014), pp. 73f.

[235] For further information on soft law and its achievements in the context of Nazi confiscated art see Martinek (2011), pp. 415ff.

[236] Weidner (2001), p. 284.

[237] Cf. Weidner (2001), pp. 282f; cf. also Nafziger et al. (2014), p. 735.

[238] Cf. http://www.unesco.org/new/en/culture/themes/illicit-traffic-of-cultural-property/legal-and-practical-instruments/unesco-international-code-of-ethics-for-dealers-in-cultural-property/; cf. also Zimmerman (2015), p. 15; cf. further Brodie (2015), p. 328.

must take these actors into consideration rather than solely focusing on the inter-governmental level.[239,240] In 1999[241] this realisation led to the adoption of the second key soft law instrument concerning the return of cultural objects: the UNESCO International Code of Ethics for Dealers in Cultural Property.

The UNESCO Code is soft law like the ICOM Code of Ethics, and compliance with it voluntary. Dealers in cultural property may submit themselves to the code on a voluntary basis, but are not directly forced to do so. However, the major difference with the ICOM Code is that it has not been adopted by the respective international non-governmental association of the dealers in cultural objects; rather, it has been passed by the ICPRCP and endorsed by UNESCO.[242]

The UNESCO Code of Ethics was adopted because the member states of the ICPRCP realised particularly the key role traders in cultural material play to combat the illicit trafficking of cultural property.[243] They passed the code of ethics due to concern over the traffic in stolen, illegally alienated, clandestinely excavated, and illegally exported cultural property. Their goal was to eliminate the illicit trafficking of such objects[244] by providing a harmonised version of the numerous national dealers' codes relating to illicit traffic, by avoiding problems which some existing provisions in such codes had revealed, and by giving international recognition to dealers who adopted the code.[245]

At the same time, the UNESCO Code of Ethics is interlinked with the international treaties. For a start, Article 5 (e) of the 1970 UNESCO Convention imposes on state parties the obligation to ensure that their national services establish for the benefit of dealers[246] in cultural property, rules in conformity with the ethical principles set forth in the convention and take steps to ensure the observance of these rules. By adopting and implementing the UNESCO Code of Ethics, state parties not only fulfil this requirement, but due to a global uniformity of the regulations created by the code, they also ensure that their national dealers in

---

[239]Another good example of this realisation is UNESCO's 2003 Convention for the Safeguarding of the Intangible Cultural Heritage. In contrast to the 1972 World Heritage Convention, it adds in its Article 15 the requirement for states to ensure, within the framework of their safeguarding activities of the intangible cultural heritage, the widest possible participation of communities, groups and, where appropriate, individuals that create, maintain and transmit such heritage, and to involve them actively in its management. See further on this issue Cameron (2016), pp. 327f.

[240]For a general overview on the role and viewpoint of private actors concerning cultural heritage see Nafziger et al. (2014), pp. 208ff.

[241]UNESCO Doc CLT/CH/INS-06/25 rev, 1999, p. 3.

[242]UNESCO Doc CLT/CH/INS-06/25 rev, 1999, p. 3.

[243]For the highly questionable role of (certain) dealers in the illicit trafficking of cultural property see Wessel (2015), pp. 107ff.

[244]http://www.unesco.org/new/en/culture/themes/illicit-traffic-of-cultural-property/legal-and-practical-instruments/unesco-international-code-of-ethics-for-dealers-in-cultural-property/.

[245]UNESCO Doc CLT-98/CONF.203/1, December 1998, p. 1.

[246]Article 5 (e) of the 1970 UNESCO Convention actually speaks of "those concerned" and lists curators, collectors, and antique dealers as examples.

cultural objects do not face competitive disadvantages compared to dealers situated in other state parties.

Furthermore, the question of whether the dealer a person has purchased a cultural object from has committed himself to obey the UNESCO Code of Ethics may also be of importance concerning the matter of whether or not the purchaser has exercised due diligence when purchasing the item. For a customer of a dealer obeying the UNESCO Code of Ethics it will be much easier to meet the due diligence requirement of Article 4 (4) of the 1995 UNIDROIT Convention, since the purchaser may rely on the presumption of legality of the transaction created by the dealer's submission to the UNESCO Code of Ethics and only has to doubt the legality of the transaction and hence take further action in the case of suspicious circumstances. Thus, such a purchaser will more likely be entitled to compensation.[247]

4.3.3.2 From a Study to the Adoption of the UNESCO Code of Ethics

Based on a study[248] examining the illicit trade in cultural heritage, contemporary legislation, administrative measures, and practices as well as national and international codes of ethics conducted due to a request from UNESCO in 1994,[249] the ICPRCP invited at its 8th session in 1994 UNESCO's Director-General to include an item on an international code of ethics for dealers in the agenda of its 9th session,[250] which he did.

During the session a contentious debate developed in which some doubted the effectiveness of such a code and others emphasised its impacts, for instance, on the determination of good faith in the context of the 1995 UNIDROIT Convention.[251] Progress was made however and the members of the ICPRCP finally agreed on recommending the Director-General of UNESCO to invite member states of UNESCO and the states parties to the 1970 UNESCO Convention to express their views on the Draft International Code of Ethics for Dealers in Cultural Property[252] which was prepared based on the CINOA Ethics Code, various national codes of ethics, and the ICOM Code of Ethics for Museums.[253]

At its 10th session in 1999, the committee finally adopted the UNESCO International Code of Ethics for Dealers in Cultural Property and invited UNESCO's Director-General to bring this to the attention of the General Conference of UNESCO with a view to its adoption by that body as an international standard of

[247] UNESCO Doc CLT-98/CONF.203/1, December 1998, p. 1.

[248] O'Keefe (1994).

[249] UNESCO Doc 30 C/REP.14, 28.09.1999, p. 5.

[250] UNESCO Doc 28 C/101 Annex I, 16.11.1995, p. 4.

[251] UNESCO Doc 29 C/REP.12, 12.11.1997, p. 8.

[252] UNESCO Doc 29 C/REP.12 Annex I, 12.11.1997, p. 4.

[253] Stamatoudi (2011), p. 168.

UNESCO,[254] which occurred at the 30th General Conference of UNESCO meeting in November 1999.[255]

4.3.3.3 The Purpose and the Ambit of the UNESCO Code of Ethics

The code was adopted in the face of worldwide concern over the traffic in stolen, illegally alienated, clandestinely excavated, and illegally exported cultural property. It was issued to establish a number of principles of professional practice for dealers in cultural property in order to eliminate the illicit trading of cultural objects from their professional activities.[256]

This was to be achieved by distinguishing cultural material being illicitly traded from that in licit trade[257] by providing a harmonised version of numerous national dealer codes relating to illicit trafficking, by avoiding problems which some existing provisions in such codes had revealed, and by giving international recognition to dealers who adopted the code.[258] At the same time, the international recognition given to the dealers by permitting them to use a special logo is used as leverage in order to encourage them to take over the burden of verifying the legal provenance of artefacts.

However, although the title of the code of ethics uses the phrase "Dealers in Cultural Property", the provisions of the ethics code later on speak of "Traders in Cultural Property",[259] covering both dealers and auctioneers.[260] Thus, addressees to the code are not only dealers in cultural property, but also auctioneers.

However, concerning the substantive scope of the code with regard to return and restitution, it is surprising that the UNESCO International Code of Ethics for Dealers in Cultural Property itself does not provide any definition of "cultural property". Thus, to answer the question of whether or not an object has to be classified as "cultural property" and thus falls within the scope of the code, one has to have recourse to other sources. Since the code of ethics has been adopted to harmonise various national codes,[261] national legislation or other sources at the national level are inapplicable in determining its scope as this might lead to a distinct application of the code of ethics in various jurisdictions and would thus

[254] UNESCO Doc 30 C/REP.14 Annex I, 28.09.1999, p. 2.

[255] UNESCO Doc CLT/CH/INS-06/25 rev, 1999, p. 3.

[256] http://www.unesco.org/new/en/culture/themes/illicit-traffic-of-cultural-property/legal-and-practical-instruments/unesco-international-code-of-ethics-for-dealers-in-cultural-property/.

[257] http://www.unesco.org/new/en/culture/themes/illicit-traffic-of-cultural-property/legal-and-practical-instruments/unesco-international-code-of-ethics-for-dealers-in-cultural-property/.

[258] UNESCO Doc CLT-98/CONF.203/1, December 1998, p. 1.

[259] Cf., for example, Article 1 of the UNESCO International Code of Ethics for Dealers in Cultural Property: "Professional traders in cultural property will not import, export or transfer the ownership of this property when they have reasonable cause to believe it has been stolen, illegally alienated, clandestinely excavated or illegally exported.".

[260] Stamatoudi (2011), p. 165.

[261] UNESCO Doc CLT-98/CONF.203/1, December 1998, p. 1.

counteract the harmonisation effort. Therefore, the source for determining "cultural property" in the context of the code must rather be sought at the international level. Here, one might think of two documents that provide for definitions of "cultural property". Since the code has been adopted to complement the 1970 Convention on the Means of Prohibiting and Preventing the Illicit Import, Export and Transfer of Ownership of Cultural Property,[262] one may argue that the convention's definition of "cultural property" has to apply to the code as well.

However, it has to be kept in mind that the UNESCO International Code of Ethics for Dealers in Cultural Property was enacted by the ICPRCP. According to its statutes, this committee is responsible for historical and ethnographic objects and documents including manuscripts, works of the plastic and decorative arts, palaeontological and archaeological objects and zoological, botanical, and mineralogical specimens.[263] Hence, it may also only adopt documents covering these objects. Enacting any documents including other or further objects into their list would automatically mean that the committee has acted outside of its scope. Therefore, "cultural property" in the context of the UNESCO International Code of Ethics for Dealers in Cultural Property has to be defined in parallel to the definition found in the Statute of the ICPRCP.

Concerning the temporal scope of the code of ethics, it can be determined that it is wider than the scopes of the related international treaties. Neither the provisions on return and restitution nor any general provisions contain a time limitation. Therefore, the UNESCO Code of Ethics also applies to cases in which dealers face claims for cultural material that has been illicitly transferred before the entry into force of the code. However, in the case of a claim for return, the code requires the object to be the product of a clandestine excavation, be acquired illegally or dishonestly from an official excavation site or monument[264] or to have been illegally exported.[265] Hence, in both cases, somehow there must be a violation of legislation specifically protecting cultural property or excavation sites. Again, although this is not a direct time limitation, in practice it operates as one since legislation protecting cultural heritage and excavation sites is a relatively recent development only dating back to the late nineteenth century.[266]

4.3.3.4 The UNESCO Code of Ethics' Principles Concerning Return

Although both UNESCO instruments, the 1970 UNESCO Convention and the ICPRCP, draw a terminological distinction between "return" and "restitution",[267]

---

[262] O'Keefe (2007), p. 161.

[263] Article 3 (1) of the ICPRCP Statutes.

[264] Cf. Article 3 of the UNESCO International Code of Ethics for Dealers in Cultural Property.

[265] Cf. Article 4 of the UNESCO International Code of Ethics for Dealers in Cultural Property.

[266] Cf. Stamatoudi (2011), p. 31.

[267] Cf., for instance, Articles 7 (b) (ii) and 13 (b) of the 1970 UNESCO Convention as well as Article 2 (1) of the ICPRCP Statutes.

surprisingly, the UNESCO Code of Ethics only applies the term "return"[268]; the term "restitution" is completely absent. Nevertheless, in substance the code of ethics draws a distinction between two different cases. Article 3 of the Code covers those cases of objects being the product of a clandestine excavation or having been acquired illegally or dishonestly from an official excavation site or monument, whereas Article 4 of the Code deals with cases in which an item of cultural property has been illegally exported.

The distinction, however, appears somehow redundant[269] as except for the difference just mentioned, both provisions are identical; the other requirements to activate the duties imposed by the norms as well as the obligations inflicted on traders are the same.

According to Articles 3 and 4 of the Code of Ethics, a trader who is in possession of an object where there is reasonable cause to believe that it has been the product of a clandestine excavation, has been acquired illegally or dishonestly from an official excavation site or monument or has been illegally exported and where that country seeks its return within a reasonable period of time, will take all legally permissible steps to cooperate in the return of that object to the country of origin or respectively export.

Thus, two requirements must be fulfilled for the obligation imposed by the provisions to be triggered. Firstly, there must be reasonable cause to believe that the cultural object is the product of a clandestine excavation, has been acquired illegally or dishonestly from an official excavation site or monument or has been illegally exported. Secondly, the country of origin or export must seek its return within a reasonable period of time.

However, neither the meaning of "reasonable cause to believe", nor of "within a reasonable period of time" is further clarified by the code of ethics itself. The term "reasonable cause to believe" has to be read in a manner which requires the trader to actively investigate the provenance of the artefact by examining the background of the object, querying the persons involved and in particular paying attention to any circumstances likely arousing suspicion, such as being offered well below market price, a large payment in cash or missing documentation regarding the provenance of the object.[270] Hence, simply assuming the object being offered to be of licit origin is insufficient. However, if the inquiry does not bring to light any suspicious

[268]Cf. Article 3 and 4 of the UNESCO International Code of Ethics for Dealers in Cultural Property.

[269]Particularly since the UNESCO Code of Ethics itself lists all alternatives in the very same provision without distinguishing like in Article 3 and 4 of the UNESCO International Code of Ethics for Dealers in Cultural Property. Article 1 of the UNESCO International Code of Ethics for Dealers in Cultural Property reads: "Professional traders in cultural property will not import, export or transfer the ownership of this property when they have reasonable cause to believe it has been stolen, illegally alienated, clandestinely excavated or illegally exported.".

[270]Stamatoudi (2011), p. 165.

circumstances there is no reasonable cause to believe that the object is of illicit nature.[271]

A very interesting point in this context is the fact that the ICOM Code of Ethics establishes a duty to cooperate even for cases in which the object has been legally transferred,[272] whereas the UNESCO Code of Ethics only imposes such a duty on traders in cases where there is somehow an illicit aspect adherent to the cultural material. This could be explained by the fact that the addressees of the ICOM Code are museums which in general actually own the cultural property in dispute, whereas the UNESCO Code addresses traders who regularly just handle the disputed object rather than having the actual title.

In determining whether or not a demand for return has been made in a reasonable time, all circumstances of the case have to be taken into account. On the one hand, the costs the seller and the trader have to carry, such as storage costs or those for the conservation of the object, must be considered. On the other hand, the country seeking the cultural property must have sufficient time to prepare its case and examine the value and the authenticity of the object. In principle, it can be assumed that the demand for return has been made in a reasonable time when the country reclaiming it has not caused a culpable dalliance.

If these two requirements are met, the trader has to actively become involved with the country seeking the object. However, the obligation imposed by the provisions is again restricted twofold. Firstly, the trader must only take all legally permissible steps. On the surface this appears just, since everyone is bound by law and the code of ethics is only a soft law instrument complementing (national) legislation.[273] However, this provides a loophole for traders unwilling to cooperate as they may, for instance in jurisdictions where a good faith purchaser acquires the legal title of ownership over an object, refer to the legislation in order to justify their unwillingness to urge the owner to return an artefact.

However, a second restriction to the duty imposed on the traders concerns its content. Just as in the case of the ICOM Code of Ethics,[274] traders are only obligated to cooperate. Although one might argue that they have to cooperate with the aim of returning the artefact,[275] the UNESCO Code of Ethics does not oblige them to actually do so. The cooperation might very well end with a rejection of the request.

[271] O'Keefe (2007), p. 162.

[272] Cf. Principle 6.2 of the ICOM Code of Ethics for Museums (Return of Cultural Property): "Museums should be prepared to initiate dialogues for the return of cultural property to a country or people of origin. This should be undertaken in an impartial manner, based on scientific, professional and humanitarian principles as well as applicable local, national and international legislation, in preference to action at a governmental or political level.".

[273] Stamatoudi (2011), p. 168.

[274] Cf. Principles 6.2 and 6.3 of the ICOM Code of Ethics for Museums.

[275] Odendahl (2005), p. 180.

4.3.3.5 The UNESCO Code of Ethics' Principles Facilitating Return by Targeting Illicit Trafficking

The UNESCO International Code of Ethics for Dealers in Cultural Property has been adopted with the view of eliminating the illicit trade in cultural property from the professional activities of traders in such objects.[276] Thus, the code of ethics contains a number of return related rules which through neutralising the illicit trade conducted by traders in cultural property will eventually eliminate the conditions under which the return of cultural objects is necessary in the first place.

First of all, the code of ethics dictates that professional traders in cultural property will not import, export or transfer the ownership of this property when they have reasonable cause to believe it has been stolen, illegally alienated, clandestinely excavated or illegally exported.[277] While this provision may be seen as the quintessence of the code,[278] other provisions substantiate the obligations derived from this clause.

A substantiation of the prohibition to import or export the mentioned cultural objects is constituted by Articles 3 and 4 of the UNESCO Code of Ethics. According to these norms, where there is reasonable cause to believe that cultural property is related to an listed illicit act, no trader ought to assist in any further transaction with that object, except with the agreement of the country of origin or export. Thus, the country of origin or export may permit the trader to further transact and hence import or export the cultural material at issue.

Moreover, regarding the transfer of ownership, Article 2 of the UNESCO Code of Ethics makes clear that a trader who is acting as an agent for the seller and not selling on his own account is not deemed to guarantee title to the property, provided that he makes known to the buyer the full name and address of the seller. Nevertheless, this may not be understood in a manner that would provide the trader with the opportunity to circumvent his obligations imposed by Article 1 of the Code. Hence, the trader may only proceed with the transaction by refraining from guaranteeing the title if there is no reasonable cause to believe the cultural artefact has been stolen, illegally alienated, clandestinely excavated or illegally exported. Where there is such cause, he does not benefit of Article 2 the UNESCO Code of Ethics.[279]

Traders are furthermore not permitted to exhibit, describe, attribute, appraise or retain any item of cultural property with the intention of promoting or failing to prevent its illicit transfer or export. In addition, they will not refer the seller or other person offering the item to those who may perform such services.[280] Interestingly, it

[276] http://www.unesco.org/new/en/culture/themes/illicit-traffic-of-cultural-property/legal-and-practical-instruments/unesco-international-code-of-ethics-for-dealers-in-cultural-property/.

[277] Article 1 of the UNESCO International Code of Ethics for Dealers in Cultural Property.

[278] See, for example, O'Keefe (2007), p. 161.

[279] Stamatoudi (2011), p. 166.

[280] Article 5 of the UNESCO International Code of Ethics for Dealers in Cultural Property.

is not only prohibited for traders to act with the intention of promoting illicit transfer, but their obligation goes far beyond: they also may not as much as fail to prevent the illicit transfer or export. Thus, they have to actively assess their behaviour when dealing with cultural material considering whether or not this might lead to its illicit transfer or export and actively prevent it.[281]

Since smaller pieces are easier to hide and thus more suitable for illicit trafficking, but also due to the scientific value of intact pieces and collections, traders in cultural property are also not permitted to dismember or sell separately parts of one complete item of cultural property.[282] They rather have to undertake, to the best of their ability, to keep together items of cultural heritage that were originally meant to be kept together.[283]

Last but not least, violations of the code of ethics are investigated by a body to be nominated by participating dealers with the body itself establishing the required procedure. A person aggrieved by the failure of a trader to adhere to the principles of the code of ethics may lay a complaint before that body, which then investigates the complaint. Results of the complaint and the principles applied will be made public.[284] Hence, unlike the ICOM Code of Ethics, the UNESCO Code of Ethics also provides some form of control mechanism which steps in in case of misconduct.

4.3.3.6 Assessment

In light of the non-binding legal nature of the UNESCO International Code of Ethics for Dealers in Cultural Property, its relevance may, especially in comparison to the legally binding 1970 UNESCO and 1995 UNIDROIT Conventions, appear doubtful. However, even when compared to the ICOM Code of Ethics for Museums the UNESCO Code seems somehow unformed. The ICOM Code goes beyond solely establishing principles by elaborating them further with guidelines and including a glossary that defines central terms. The UNESCO Code of Ethics appears, in contrast, like a slimmed down version of the former which does not even provide for the definition of the most central terms such as the constantly employed phrase "reasonable cause to believe".

The fact that it imposes, just as the ICOM Code of Ethics for Museums but in contrast to the 1970 UNESCO and 1995 UNIDROIT Conventions, solely an obligation on traders to cooperate concerning the return of illicitly transferred cultural property raises concerns over its effectiveness in achieving its stated aims. Additionally, the fact that it completely neglects cases in which, despite the legality of transaction, the country of origin may still have a valid interest in

[281]Stamatoudi (2011), p. 167.

[282]Article 6 of the UNESCO International Code of Ethics for Dealers in Cultural Property.

[283]Article 7 of the UNESCO International Code of Ethics for Dealers in Cultural Property.

[284]Article 8 of the UNESCO International Code of Ethics for Dealers in Cultural Property.

reclaiming an object further calls into question the relevance of the UNESCO Code of Ethics.[285] Nevertheless, as in the case of the ICOM Code of Ethics, one should not simply dismiss the code. Traders in cultural property play a key role in combating the illicit trafficking of cultural property since they occupy, as those who transfer objects from those who conduct the (illicit) appropriation to the final buyers, a key position in the trafficking network.

Regarding the return of transferred cultural heritage, the very existence of the UNESCO Code in practice makes it very problematic for traders to ignore demands for the return of cultural property in their custody, since this behaviour can no longer be justified in the face of public opinion as it deviates from the ethical principles established by the code. Traders will all the more be pressured to comply with the professional provisions of conduct set by the ethics code and at least respond to the claims for return since customers will likely prefer to deal with traders that are publicly known to respect the ethical standards. This is a simple cause and effect situation as the customers themselves will be more easily accepted to have been in good faith at the time of the purchase when buying from such traders and thus be entitled to compensation in case a purchased item turns out to be of illicit nature and hence has to be restituted.[286] Another incentive for traders in cultural property to comply with the principles established by the code is the fact that they are under scrutiny from their fellow dealers.[287]

However, the adherence to higher standards by traders in cultural property not only weakens illicit trading since key links in the trafficking chain are broken, in the long run it also paves the way for a change in mentality which eventually may lead to a change of legislation. As already seen, the code of ethics can be consulted in court cases to determine the existence or change of a certain ordre public[288] and thus for the interpretation of certain legal provisions and obligations.

Last but not least, another aspect should not be lost sight of: the code also creates legal certainty for the traders themselves.[289] They know which actions are unproblematic, in which cases they should abstain from further transactions with certain objects, and what they should do rather than just selling the artefact for the client.

Hence, the UNESCO Code, like the ICOM Code, follows the spirit of the 1970 UNESCO and 1995 UNIDROIT Conventions as well as the ICPRCP, in particular the aspect of cooperation, and enhances these instruments by expanding their spirit

---

[285]The ICOM Code of Ethics for Museums provides for these cases with Principle 6.2 (Return of Cultural Property), a regulation which reads "Museums should be prepared to initiate dialogues for the return of cultural property to a country or people of origin. This should be undertaken in an impartial manner, based on scientific, professional and humanitarian principles as well as applicable local, national and international legislation, in preference to action at a governmental or political level.".

[286]Stamatoudi (2011), p. 168.

[287]Stamatoudi (2011), p. 168 with the same view.

[288]Weidner (2001), p. 284.

[289]Cf. Weidner (2001), pp. 282f.

and principles directly on another private party most relevant to the return of cultural artefacts: traders.

4.3.4 The ILA Principles for Cooperation in the Mutual Protection and Transfer of Cultural Material

4.3.4.1 General Overview

The newest soft law instrument of relevance in the field of the return of cultural objects is the Principles for Cooperation in the Mutual Protection and Transfer of Cultural Material adopted by the International Law Association. The ILA is an international non-governmental organisation founded in 1873[290] for the study, clarification, and development of international law, both public and private, and the furtherance of international understanding and respect for international law.[291] To further its purpose, in 1988 the ILA established its Cultural Heritage Law Committee.[292]

Faced with the growing number of demands for the return of cultural objects by various entities ranging from states, ethnic and indigenous groups through to individuals, and in light of the fact that many national legislations do not take into consideration neither the unique nature nor the symbolic, religious, historical, and aesthetic dimension of cultural objects,[293] the ILA's Cultural Heritage Law Committee saw the need to develop a non-mandatory set of principles which would function as a minimum standard with regard to disputes arising out of requests for the return of cultural objects and lessen the embitterment surrounding these disputes by promoting non-confrontational approaches and outcomes.[294]

The committee began its work by preparing background reports[295] which resulted, at the 71st Biennial ILA Conference in 2004, in the first Draft Principles for Cooperation in the Mutual Protection and Transfer of Cultural Material being presented.[296] This draft was however later amended and, at a second session in 2005, reviewed and substantially modified.[297] After further review and some minor changes, the Principles for Cooperation in the Mutual Protection and Transfer of

[290] http://www.ila-hq.org/en/about_us/index.cfm.

[291] Article 3.1 of the ILA Constitution.

[292] Cf. Nafziger (2006), p. 320.

[293] Cf. Paterson (2006), pp. 327f.

[294] Cf. Paterson (2006), p. 328.

[295] Cf. Nafziger (2007–2008), p. 147.

[296] See ILA (2004), pp. 2ff.

[297] A list of major modifications can be found in Nafziger (2007–2008), p. 157.

Cultural Material were finally adopted at the 72nd Biennial ILA Conference in 2006.[298]

4.3.4.2 The Goals and Scope of Application of the ILA Principles

As previously stated, the principles were adopted in light of the increasing number of claims for the return of cultural objects.[299] They are intended to develop a more voluntary collaborative framework which can function as a minimum standard for avoiding and settling these disputes.[300] The principles build on the realisation that disputing parties normally prefer negotiation to litigation.[301] Therefore, based on current practice and aware of the significant moral, legal, and practical issues concerning requests for the international transfer of cultural objects, but also their significance for cultural identity and diversity and as part of the world heritage,[302] the principles aim at avoiding confrontation. Instead, they try to engender a collaborative, non-confrontational approach to requests for the transfer of cultural material in order to establish a more productive relationship between and among parties, in particular claimants and possessors. To this end, they emphasise the need for a spirit of partnership among private and public actors through international cooperation.[303] Moreover, another goal of the principles is to eliminate significant practical and legal problems, such as the legal advantage parties have that are situated in the same state as the ruling court over non-domestic parties in cases where claimant, recipient, and object are not located in the same state.[304] However, the principles themselves clarify that nothing in the principles should be interpreted to affect rights enjoyed by the parties or obligations otherwise binding on them.[305]

With all of this in mind it is not surprising that the principles begin by defining the terms "requesting party" and "recipient". The former are persons, groups of persons, museums, and other institutions, however legally constitutioned, as well as governments and other public authorities that request the transfer of cultural material.[306] In this context, Principle 4 is noteworthy as it clarifies that the recipient's obligations also apply in cases of a request for the transfer of cultural material

[298] ILA (2006), p. 1.

[299] Cf. Paterson (2006), p. 327.

[300] Cf. Paterson (2006), p. 328.

[301] Cf. ILA (2006), p. 6.

[302] Paragraphs 1, 2, 4, and 10 of the Preamble of the ILA Principles for Cooperation in the Mutual Protection and Transfer of Cultural Material.

[303] Paragraphs 5, 6, and 8 of the Preamble of the ILA Principles for Cooperation in the Mutual Protection and Transfer of Cultural Material.

[304] Cf. ILA (2006), p. 6.

[305] Principle 10 of the ILA Principles for Cooperation in the Mutual Protection and Transfer of Cultural Material.

[306] Principle 1.1 of the ILA Principles for Cooperation in the Mutual Protection and Transfer of Cultural Material.

originating with indigenous peoples and cultural minorities even when such a request is not supported by the government of the state in whose territory the museum or institution is principally domiciled or organised. Thus, the principles recognise indigenous peoples and cultural minorities as valid requesting parties.

The term "recipient", on the other hand, refers to states, museums or any other institutions receiving a request for the transfer of cultural material.[307] Hence, the principles are designed not only to be employed when dispute arises between states, but also in cases in which a dispute exists among private parties or between a private party on the one side and a foreign or even its own government on the other.

However, just as in the UNESCO Code of Ethics, the ILA Principles abstain from providing a definition of "cultural material". Rather, the question of whether or not an object has to be classified as cultural material and thus falls within the scope of the principles has to be answered by recourse to other sources with the resulting implications, again this is just as in case of the UNESCO Code.[308]

When it comes to the temporal scope of the principles, as in the case of the previously discussed codes of ethics, no provision in the ILA Principles contains a time limitation. Hence, the Principles for Cooperation in the Mutual Protection and Transfer of Cultural Material also apply to cases concerning cultural objects that were transferred before their entry into force.

4.3.4.3 The ILA's Principle on Return

The central provision of the ILA Principles for Cooperation in the Mutual Protection and Transfer of Cultural Material addressing the return of cultural objects is Principle 2. Interestingly, the clause does not start with imposing an obligation on the recipient of a request for the return of an object, but rather by calling the requesting party to make its request in writing, addressed to the recipient and with a detailed description of the material whose transfer is requested, including detailed information and reasons sufficient to substantiate the request.[309] However, once the requesting party has done so, the recipient has to respond in good faith and in writing to the request within a reasonable time, either agreeing with it or setting out reasons for disagreement with it and, in any event, proposing a timeframe for implementation or negotiations.[310] Thus, as with the ICOM and the UNESCO Codes of Ethics, the ILA Principles do not establish any unconditional obligation to return an object in dispute. Instead, the principles only require the recipient to

[307] Principle 1.2 of the ILA Principles for Cooperation in the Mutual Protection and Transfer of Cultural Material.

[308] On the problems arising due to the missing definition of cultural property in the context of the UNESCO Code of Ethics cf. p. 206.

[309] Principle 2.1 of the ILA Principles for Cooperation in the Mutual Protection and Transfer of Cultural Material.

[310] Principle 2.2 of the ILA Principles for Cooperation in the Mutual Protection and Transfer of Cultural Material.

respond in good faith. However, doing so requires the recipient to understand the concerns and perceptions of the requesting party, in particular the spiritual, ceremonial, and other uniquely cultural aspects of the requested cultural object, since this will likely promote a successful solution to the issue. The recipient should furthermore make sure that the party requesting the return has been accurately identified, which can be problematic in cases where the request has been made on behalf of a community. Moreover, responding in good faith requires the recipient to consider future problems, to think of the costs associated with the return, and to communicate specific legal as well as non-legal constraints the recipient faces with regard to the return of the object.[311] Should a disagreement arise, the recipient has to give reasons for disagreeing and both parties ought to enter into good faith negotiations concerning the cultural material at issue.[312]

In this context, it is noteworthy that the principles themselves provide guidance with regard to the negotiations. Principle 8 of the ILA Principles contains an exemplary list of considerations which reflect recognition of the special significance of cultural objects to societies and a changing public policy in this field.[313] Hence, good faith negotiations concerning requests for the transfer of cultural material should consider, inter alia, the significance of the requested object for the requesting party, the reunification of dispersed cultural material, the accessibility to the cultural material in the requesting state, as well as its protection.[314]

As the last factor indicates, the principles do not advocate a return in all cases. The negotiations should result in a mutually agreeable solution.[315] This does not necessarily mean that the object ought to be returned, which becomes particularly apparent when considering Principle 3. According to this principle, museums and other institutions have to develop guidelines consistent with those of ICOM for responding to requests for the transfer of cultural material which may include alternatives to outright transfer, such as partnership agreements ensuring appropriate access, display, conservation, storage, future collaboration on research, loans, dividing collections, production of copies, shared management and control as well as assistance in establishing institutional facilities and training programmes.[316]

[311]Cf. Notes on Principle 2 of the ILA Principles for Cooperation in the Mutual Protection and Transfer of Cultural Material.

[312]Principle 2.3 of the ILA Principles for Cooperation in the Mutual Protection and Transfer of Cultural Material.

[313]Cf. Notes on Principle 8 of the ILA Principles for Cooperation in the Mutual Protection and Transfer of Cultural Material.

[314]Principle 8 of the ILA Principles for Cooperation in the Mutual Protection and Transfer of Cultural Material.

[315]Cf. Nafziger (2007–2008), p. 148.

[316]Principle 3.1 of the ILA Principles for Cooperation in the Mutual Protection and Transfer of Cultural Material and Notes on Principle 3 of the ILA Principles for Cooperation in the Mutual Protection and Transfer of Cultural Material; see further for the possibilities offered by the concept of co-ownership to solve claims concerning cultural property Renold (2015), pp. 163–176; on how to use MOUs for the purpose of implementing these solutions see Lyons (2014), pp. 251–265.

However, whenever a substantial portion of the collection of an institution is seldom or never on public display or is otherwise inaccessible, that institution should agree to lend or otherwise make available cultural material not on display to a requesting party, particularly a party at the place of origin. This is tempered by the fact that it should only do so as long as no compelling reason to the contrary exists.[317]

Notably there is one exception to this approach of the ILA Principles of abstaining from imposing any obligation to return cultural objects. With regard to human remains, in conformity with most legislation, the principles require museums and other institutions possessing such remains to affirm the recognition of their sanctity and to agree to transfer it upon request to any requesting party who provides evidence of a close or, among multiple requesting parties, the closest demonstrable affiliation with the remains.[318] Hence, in the case of human remains the principles clearly favour and require the return of such material.

4.3.4.4 The ILA Principles on Information: The Key Factor Fostering Return

The ILA Principles for Cooperation in the Mutual Protection and Transfer of Cultural Material also include a number of provisions that promote conditions benefitting claims for return and their mutual solution. Without knowing exactly where a specific cultural object is located or even if it exists at all, it is impossible to request its return. Thus, reliable inventories can be seen as a minimum precondition for the successful resolution of requests for the return of cultural objects.[319] Therefore, information concerning the location of cultural material is of the utmost importance. For this reason, Principle 3.2 of the ILA Principles requires museums and other institutions to prepare and publish detailed inventories of their collections. If they lack sufficient resources of their own to do so, the provision refers these museums to the assistance of ICOM and other sources. Principle 6.1 repeats this obligation for all state museums and other institutions that hold or control holdings or collections of cultural material; they shall take steps to prepare inventories and a register of such material. However, the principles suggest that the register may take the form of a database of information that is available to interested parties, preferably in accordance with modern practice by electronic means.[320] Moreover, museums and other institutions should submit annual reports of the

[317]Principle 3.3 of the ILA Principles for Cooperation in the Mutual Protection and Transfer of Cultural Material.

[318]Principle 5 of the ILA Principles for Cooperation in the Mutual Protection and Transfer of Cultural Material and the relevant notes.

[319]Cf. Notes on Principle 6 of the ILA Principles for Cooperation in the Mutual Protection and Transfer of Cultural Material.

[320]Cf. also Notes on Principle 6 of the ILA Principles for Cooperation in the Mutual Protection and Transfer of Cultural Material.

information recorded in these registers for general publication to any national services that are established to manage and protect cultural material.[321] Here is a point of intersection between the ILA Principles and the 1970 UNESCO Convention, since state parties to the latter can employ the national services they have to establish in accordance with Article 5 of the 1970 UNESCO Convention for the purposes of Principle 6 of the ILA Principles.

However, the national service responsible for the maintenance of a state register should, on the other hand, in a separate section of such register, record all inquiries by identifying the name of the party making the inquiry, the cultural material involved, and the response of the museum or institution concerned. Having these registers, such services are obligated to submit every 3 years up to date copies of registered items to UNESCO in order to facilitate accessibility.[322]

These registers were also introduced with an eye to claims for the return of cultural material, since Principle 6.4 of the ILA Principles explicitly states that each register shall be made available to any requesting party that is interested in the transfer of cultural material, so as to help identify the location and provenance of such items and to facilitate claims, again, preferably by electronic means.[323]

Providing knowledge on the location or even existence of cultural property is also the aim of Principle 7. According to this provision, persons, groups of persons, museums, and other institutions possessing significant, newly-found cultural material should promptly notify appropriate government authorities, communities, and international institutions of their finds, together with as complete as possible a description of the material, including its provenance.

In contrast to the ICOM and UNESCO Codes of Ethics though, the ILA Principles do not stop at simply imposing obligations to conduct good faith negotiations with regard to the transfer of cultural material. They go further by also making arrangements for the worst case scenario, i.e. the failure of negotiations. The principles provide that if the parties are unable to reach a mutually satisfactory settlement of a dispute related to a request within a period of 4 years from the time of the request, upon a request of either party, both parties shall submit the dispute to good offices, consultation, mediation, conciliation, ad hoc arbitration or institutional arbitration.[324] Hence, even though the principles do not aim at replacing litigation,[325] they clearly favour alternative dispute resolution in the context of

[321]Principle 6.2 of the ILA Principles for Cooperation in the Mutual Protection and Transfer of Cultural Material.

[322]Principle 6.3 of the ILA Principles for Cooperation in the Mutual Protection and Transfer of Cultural Material.

[323]Cf. also Notes on Principle 6 of the ILA Principles for Cooperation in the Mutual Protection and Transfer of Cultural Material.

[324]Principle 9 of the ILA Principles for Cooperation in the Mutual Protection and Transfer of Cultural Material.

[325]Paterson (2006), p. 329.

which suitable bodies, such as UNESCO, could be asked to provide assistance be it either monetary or professional in nature.[326]

4.3.4.5 Evaluation

The ILA Principles for Cooperation in the Mutual Protection and Transfer of Cultural Material are a further development of the soft law in the field of claims for the return of cultural objects. They share much communality with the ICOM and UNESCO Codes of Ethics. They do not impose an unconditional obligation on recipients to return, but rather require them to enter into good faith negotiations, and as with other soft law sources are not legally binding.

However, in a number of ways the principles go beyond the codes of ethics; first of all, they do not aim at a limited number of addressees, but are meant to be used in any kind of dispute concerning claims for the return of cultural objects. They are applicable to disputes involving a variety of actors, from governments and museums to individuals and indigenous groups, as well as minorities. More importantly, with regard to the return of cultural objects, they provide guidance concerning those aspects which should be taken into account when facing a claim for return. Moreover, they even make arrangements in the case that negotiations fail.

Hence, despite their soft law nature, the ILA Principles are of great significance. Adopted by the International Law Association currently with some 3500 members,[327] all of which are lawyers in the field of international law, the principles enjoy the backing of a significant and relevant legal community.

Based on existing practice, they further promote the spirit of the 1970 UNESCO and 1995 UNIDROIT Conventions, the ICPRCP, as well as the ICOM and UNESCO Codes of Ethics, in particular the aspect of cooperation, and advance the principles established by these instruments by including and addressing every conceivable party to a cultural property related dispute and providing a substantive framework to initially avoid and then resolve disputes arising from claims for the return of cultural objects in a non-confrontational manner[328] allowing the parties to remain good relations. Furthermore, since the principles are to be applied to all cases, regardless of whether they are international in nature or simply national, it can be expected that they will eliminate significant practical and legal problems that regularly arise in the context of cross-border claims.[329]

---

[326]Cf. Notes on Principle 9 of the ILA Principles for Cooperation in the Mutual Protection and Transfer of Cultural Material.

[327]http://www.ila-hq.org/en/about_us/index.cfm.

[328]Cf. Paragraph 9 of the Preamble of the ILA Principles for Cooperation in the Mutual Protection and Transfer of Cultural Material.

[329]Cf. ILA (2006), p. 6.

4.4 The Two-Pronged Strategy: Resume

When in the context of the 1970 UNESCO Convention it became apparent that a system of binding rules of general application imposing an obligation to return stolen or illicitly transferred cultural objects, not to mention those artefacts transferred in colonial times, on former colonial powers and market states would not lead to a solution acceptable to all parties involved, a two-pronged strategy evolved. While continuing to promote and support the international treaties, a search began for other ways to resolve the cultural property related disputes which would prove to be more acceptable to the recipients of claims.

This development brought to life a number of new instruments in the years following the adoption of the 1970 UNESCO Convention. At first glance, all these instruments may seem unrelated and without any coherent form of structure, since they have been brought about by different institutions, have different addressees, and to a greater or lesser degree function in different ways and spheres. On closer examination however a measure of coherence becomes apparent. The first instrument to be adopted after the 1970 UNESCO Convention, the ICPRCP, remained true to both the spirit of the time and the convention by trying to solve the issue solely at a governmental level. Thus, it was designed for intergovernmental interaction only.

Remaining unsure of how to face claims for the return of cultural objects due to a lack of sufficient legislation and frustrated by this situation, private parties brought themselves into the solution process, making clear to all concerned that any solution would have to take them into consideration. The subsequent instruments, the ICOM and the UNESCO Codes of Ethics, consequently address the role and obligations of private parties. This development took another step forward with the ILA Principles which unite the earlier governmental approach with the later strategy to address private parties by introducing comprehensive rules meant to be used in any kind of dispute concerning claims for the return of cultural objects. They are meant to be applied to intergovernmental disputes as well as disputes between private parties or even a private party on the one side and a government on the other.

In addition to this first development regarding the addressees of the regulations, another development concerning the regulations themselves can be observed. Since it became evident that any binding obligation of general application to return cultural property (illicitly) transferred in times of peace would not be acceptable to market states and former colonial powers, this approach was abandoned in favour of a more procedural and non-confrontational one; in soft law instruments, but also in the context of the ICPRCP, the obligation to return imposed by the 1970 UNESCO and 1995 UNIDROIT Conventions has been replaced by an obligation to cooperate. Moreover, this obligation took consistently clearer meaning with each soft law instrument.

Hence, the approach to find ways to supplement the adoption of international conventions to solve cultural object related disputes has led to a shift in strategy. While initially the goal was to issue substantive laws in international treaties establishing mandatory obligations to return, later the actors began employing softer instruments by establishing fora where such disputes can be addressed and focusing on rules governing the interaction, in particular the cooperation of the parties involved in the dispute, including non-governmental actors.

As promising as these new instruments are, since the recipients of claims are more willing to accept them and participate in the cooperative approach, the classical practice of adopting and promoting legally binding conventions has not been abandoned, but rather has been further pursued for a number of reasons. Firstly, the 1970 UNESCO and the 1995 UNIDROIT Conventions on the one hand, and the ICPRCP and the soft law instruments on the other hand, mutually support each other. More importantly, even though it is much harder to negotiate and adopt international conventions and persuade states to become parties, once such conventions have been adopted and relevant states have become party to them, their effect is much greater. For instance, for those cases which fall within their ambit, the 1970 UNESCO and 1995 UNIDROIT Conventions provide clear regulations and legally binding duties on state parties to return cultural artefacts rather than enter into solely a process of cooperation. Finally, again despite the difficulties in negotiating and adopting an international convention, it remains easier to promote an already existing treaty than bring into life a new soft law instrument.

References

Baufeld S (2005) Kulturgutbeschlagnahmen in bewaffneten Konflikten, ihre Rückabwicklung und der deutsch-russische Streit um die so genannte Beutekunst. Peter Lang, Frankfurt am Main

Blake J (2015) International cultural heritage law. Oxford University Press, Oxford

Boos S (2006) Kulturgut als Gegenstand des grenzüberschreitenden Leihverkehrs. Duncker & Humblot, Berlin

Brodie N (2009) An archaeologist's view of the trade in unprovenanced antiquities. In: Hoffman BT (ed) Art and cultural heritage: law, policy and practice. Cambridge University Press, Cambridge, pp 52–63

Brodie N (2015) Syria and its regional neighbors: a case of cultural property protection policy failure? Int J Cult Prop 22:317–335

Cameron C (2016) UNESCO and cultural heritage: unexpected consequences. In: Logan W, Craith MN, Kockel U (eds) A companion to heritage studies. Wiley Blackwell, Chichester, pp 322–336

Campfens E (2014) Alternative dispute resolution in restitution claims and the binding expert opinion procedure of the Dutch Restitutions Committee. In: Vadi V, Schneider HEGS (eds) Art, cultural heritage and the market: ethical and legal issues. Springer, Heidelberg, pp 61–91

Cuno J (2008) Who owns antiquity? Museums and the battle over our ancient heritage. Princeton University Press, Princeton

DeAngelis IP (2009) How much provenance is enough? Guidelines for the acquisition of archaeological materials. In: Hoffman BT (ed) Art and cultural heritage: law, policy and practice. Cambridge University Press, Cambridge, pp 398–408

Flora H (2013) The quest for the masterpiece – traditional practices of collecting in American museums. In: Francioni F, Gordley J (eds) Enforcing international cultural heritage law. Oxford University Press, Oxford, pp 228–239

Francioni F (2013) Plurality and interaction of legal orders in the enforcement of cultural heritage law. In: Francioni F, Gordley J (eds) Enforcing international cultural heritage law. Oxford University Press, Oxford, pp 9–21
Frigo M (2009) Ethical rules and codes of honour related to museum activities: a complementary support to the private international law approach concerning the circulation of cultural property. Int J Cult Prop 16:49–66
Gillman D (2010) The idea of cultural heritage, revth edn. Cambridge University Press, Cambridge
Graf Vitzthum W (2013) Begriff, Geschichte und Rechtsquellen des Völkerrechts. In: Graf Vitzthum W, Proelß A (eds) Völkerrecht, 6th edn. De Gruyter, Berlin, pp 1–59
Grant D (2014) What happens when museums return antiquities? In: Hyperallergic – sensitive to art & its discontents. http://hyperallergic.com/115015/what-happens-when-museums-return-antiquities/. Accessed 25 April 2016
International Law Association (2004) Cultural Heritage Law Committee Berlin conference report., http://www.ila-hq.org/en/committees/index.cfm/cid/13. Accessed 25 April 2016
International Law Association (2006) Cultural Heritage Law Committee Toronto conference report., http://www.ila-hq.org/en/committees/index.cfm/cid/13. Accessed 25 April 2016
Koppar DH (2014) Role of museums in preservation and propagation of tribal culture. In: Vyas NN (ed) Tribal heritage and museum development. Himanshu Publications, Udaipur, pp 40–48
Lyons CL (2014) Thinking about antiquities: museums and internationalism. Int J Cult Prop 21:251–265
Martinek M (2011) Die Wiedergutmachung NS-bedingter Kulturgutverluste als Soft Law-Problem. In: Wittinger M, Wendt R, Ress G (eds) Verfassung – Völkerrecht – Kulturgüterschutz: Festschrift für Wilfried Fiedler zum 70. Geburtstag. Duncker & Humblot, Berlin, pp 415–446
Mugabowagahunde M (2016) African indigenous heritage in colonial and postcolonial museums: the case of the Batwa of Africa's Great Lakes Region. In: Logan W, Craith MN, Kockel U (eds) A companion to heritage studies. Wiley Blackwell, Chichester, pp 146–159
Müller-Karpe M (2010) Antikenhandel ./. Kulturgüterschutz. Zur Missachtung des bestehenden Handelsverbots für archäologisches Kulturgut ungeklärter Provenienz an einem Beispiel. Kunst und Recht 91–94
Nafziger JAR (2006) The development of international cultural law. Am Soc Int Law Proc 100:317–322
Nafziger JAR (2007–2008) The principles for cooperation in the mutual protection and transfer of cultural material. Chicago J Int Law 8:147–167
Nafziger JAR, Paterson RK, Renteln AD (2014) Cultural law: international, comparative, and indigenous. Cambridge University Press, Cambridge
O'Keefe PJ (1994) Feasibility of an international code of ethics for dealers in cultural property for the purpose of more effective control of illicit traffic in cultural property. In: UNESCO Doc CLT-94/WS/11
O'Keefe PJ (2007) Commentary on the 1970 UNESCO Convention, 2nd edn. Institute of Art and Law, Leicester
Odendahl K (2005) Kulturgüterschutz: Entwicklung, Struktur und Dogmatik eines ebenenübergreifenden Normensystems. Mohr Siebeck, Tübingen
Paterson RK (2006) New Principles for Cooperation in the Mutual Protection and Transfer of Cultural Material. Am Soc Int Law Proc 100:327–329
Polk K (2013) The trade in antiquities: is it time for additional approaches to reducing destruction and theft? In: Prott LV, Redmond-Cooper R, Urice S (eds) Realising cultural heritage law: Festschrift for Patrick Joseph O'Keefe. Institute of Art and Law, Builth Wells, pp 111–120
Prott LV (1992) Restitutionspolitik der UNESCO in Zusammenarbeit mit Museen. In: Reichelt G (ed) Internationaler Kulturgüterschutz: Wiener Symposium 18./19 Oktober 1990. Manz, Wien, pp 157–162

Prott LV (2011) Strengths and weaknesses of the 1970 Convention: an evaluation 40 years after its adoption. In: UNESCO Doc CLT/2011/CONF.207/7, p 3
Renold MA (2015) Cultural co-ownership: preventing and solving cultural property claims. Int J Cult Prop 22:163–176
Rush LW (2013) Illicit trade in antiquities – a view 'From the Ground'. In: Francioni F, Gordley J (eds) Enforcing international cultural heritage law. Oxford University Press, Oxford, pp 65–76
Schönenberger B (2009) Restitution von Kulturgut: Anspruchsgrundlagen – Restiutionshindernisse – Entwicklung. Stämpfli Verlag, Bern
Shyllon F (2009) The recovery of cultural objects by African states through the UNESCO and UNIDROIT conventions and the role of arbitration. In: Prott LV (ed) Witness to history: a compendium of documents and writings on the return of cultural objects. UNESCO Publishing, Paris, pp 369–382
Shyllon F (2011) The 16th session of the UNESCO Intergovernmental Committee for Promoting the Return of Cultural Property to its Countries of Origin or its Restitution in case of Illicit Appropriation, 21–23 September 2010. Int J Cult Prop 18:429–435
Shyllon F (2013) Museums and universal heritage: right of return and right of access for Africans. In: Prott LV, Redmond-Cooper R, Urice S (eds) Realising cultural heritage law: Festschrift for Patrick Joseph O'Keefe. Institute of Art and Law, Builth Wells, pp 133–144
Specht J (2009) Comments on the establishment of the committee. In: Prott LV (ed) Witness to history: a compendium of documents and writings on the return of cultural objects. UNESCO Publishing, Paris, pp 28–29
Stamatoudi IA (2011) Cultural property law and restitution: a commentary to international conventions and European Union law. Edward Elgar, Cheltenham
Thorn B (2005) Internationaler Kulturgüterschutz nach der UNIDROIT Konvention. De Gruyter, Berlin
van Beurden J (2014) How to break the deadlock in the debate about colonial acquisitions? In: Vadi V, Schneider HEGS (eds) Art, cultural heritage and the market: ethical and legal issues. Springer, Heidelberg, pp 165–181
von Schorlemer S (2007) UNESCO dispute settlement. In: Yusuf AA (ed) Standard-setting in UNESCO: normative action in education, science and culture, vol 1. UNESCO Publishing, Paris/Martinus Nijhoff Publishers, Leiden, pp 73–103
Vrdoljak AF (2008) International law, museums and the return of cultural objects. Cambridge University Press, Cambridge
Vrdoljak AF (2016) Challenges for international cultural heritage law. In: Logan W, Craith MN, Kockel U (eds) A companion to heritage studies. Wiley Blackwell, Chichester, pp 541–556
Weidner A (2001) Kulturgüterschutz als res extra commercium im internationalen Sachenrecht. De Gruyter, Berlin
Wessel G (2015) Das schmutzige Geschäft mit der Antike: Der globale Handel mit illegalen Kulturgütern. Ch. Links Verlag, Berlin
Yusuf A (2007) Standard-setting in UNESCO: conventions, recommendations, declarations and charters adopted by UNESCO (1948 – 2006), vol 2. UNESCO Publishing, Paris/Martinus Nijhoff Publishers, Leiden
Zimmerman O (2015) Die Zerstörung, der Raub und der illegal Handel mit Kulturgut: Besitz von Raubkunst muss gesellschaftlich und rechtlich geächtet werden. Politik und Kultur 15

Chapter 5
The Alternative Dispute Resolution Approach: Formalisation and Juridification of the Dispute Resolution Procedure

Abstract The seeds of the idea to employ alternative dispute resolution as a way to solve cultural object related disputes can be traced back to the 1970 UNESCO Convention on the Means of Prohibiting and Preventing the Illicit Import, Export and Transfer of Ownership of Cultural Property and the 1995 UNIDROIT Convention on Stolen or Illegally Exported Cultural Objects. For example, Article 17 (5) of the 1970 UNESCO Convention provides the possibility for UNESCO to extend, upon request, its good offices to reach a settlement between two state parties which are engaged in a dispute over the implementation of the convention. The 1995 UNIDROIT Convention even contains an arbitration clause. However, it has only been in recent years, when the treaty approach had been complemented by a more cooperative and procedural approach, that alternative dispute resolution entered the limelight and rules of procedure for alternative dispute resolution tailored specifically for cultural object related disputes came into being. Both UNESCO's Intergovernmental Committee for Promoting the Return of Cultural Property to its Countries of Origin or its Restitution in case of Illicit Appropriation and ICOM in cooperation with WIPO have adopted rules of procedure for mediation (and conciliation). This chapter assesses the benefits and limitations of alternative dispute resolution as a means to solve cultural heritage related disputes in general before analysing both instruments, the ICPRCP Rules of Procedure for Mediation and Conciliation and the ICOM-WIPO Mediation Rules, in detail and highlighting their linkages with the instruments covered in the previous chapters.

5.1 Alternative Dispute Resolution: Assessment

Once, due to the two-pronged strategy, a shift from trying to find solutions based on substantive law obligations to return cultural objects to a more cooperative and procedural approach had taken place, the question of which form such a cooperative and procedural solution could take had to be further investigated. This was all the

A. Taşdelen, *The Return of Cultural Artefacts*, DOI 10.1007/978-3-319-44060-6_5

more urgent since as even to this very day there is no single specialised forum with regard to disputes concerning cultural material.[1]

Hence, although the seeds of the idea of alternative dispute resolution as a way to solve cultural objects related disputes can be traced back to the 1970 UNESCO and the 1995 UNIDROIT Conventions, it was only in recent years that in compliance with the idea to follow the path of cooperation, rules of procedure for alternative dispute resolution tailored specifically for cultural object related disputes came into being. Progress in this field is evidenced by the fact that both the ICPRCP and ICOM, in cooperation with the World Intellectual Property Organization (WIPO), have adopted rules of procedure for mediation (and conciliation).

These rules of procedure constitute a major development with regard to cultural property related disputes. Although at first one might think of litigation as an appropriate procedure to solve these disputes,[2] for a number of reasons, cultural diplomacy and alternative dispute resolution, in particular mediation and conciliation,[3] are at least as suitable in the context of cultural heritage.[4] First of all, litigation is generally time consuming as the parties rely on the justice system which may, due to a lack of capacity or workload, need long periods to conduct court hearings and interrogations and thus lengthen the whole process.[5] This stands in stark contrast to alternative dispute resolution mechanisms as the parties can generally start the process as soon as they agree on a date[6] and an intermediary/third party in charge of the dispute settlement. The duration of litigation is in general further prolonged by the fact that litigation is embedded in a strict formalistic process which may require the court to observe certain procedures. In alternative dispute resolution, however, the parties are free to determine the applicable rules, including the procedural rules—a flexibility giving further advantage to alternative dispute resolution.[7]

This possibility for the parties, to be able to mutually determine the applicable rules, allows them furthermore to permit the intermediary to include in addition or instead of the law ethical, moral or other aspects to address sensitive, non-legal elements of a cultural, emotional, ethical, historical, moral, political, religious or spiritual nature in finding a solution to the dispute.[8] This allows parties to resolve

[1] Cf. Francioni (2013), p. 17.

[2] Stamatoudi (2011), pp. 189ff, 208.

[3] Cf. Nafziger et al. (2014), p. 604; for the role of MOUs in this context see also Lyons (2014), pp. 251–265.

[4] Many authors seem to favour alternative dispute resolution over litigation in cultural property related disputes. This appears however to be a general trend in the international law on culture. Cf., for instance, Campfens (2014), p. 79; cf. also von Schorlemer (2007), p. 84. Kuprecht and Siehr (2012), pp. 265ff all emphasise the benefits alternative dispute resolution may have for cultural material related disputes concerning indigenous groups. For the role of the Permanent Court of Arbitration in this context see Daly (2009), pp. 465ff.

[5] Cf. Stamatoudi (2011), p. 193.

[6] Varner (2011–2012) p. 482.

[7] Cf. Beckmann (2008), p. 118.

[8] Urbinati (2014), p. 94; Theurich (2010), p. 575.

disputes regarding cultural objects which have been transferred before any law concerning the protection of cultural heritage had been passed and which thus could otherwise not be resolved for reasons of time limitation. Moreover, in some cases, particularly those in which the transfer occurred long ago, finding hard evidence is often very troublesome.[9] Alternative dispute resolution allows parties to overcome these obstacles by adopting more suitable (procedural) rules.[10]

Moreover, this also automatically solves another problem; in the case of litigation, the claimant can bring the claim under the jurisdiction most favourable to him. However, even then the claimant cannot be sure which rules the court will ultimately apply to the case because of the rules on the conflict of laws.[11] Besides this, litigation may give rise to multiple contradicting judgments,[12] since the claimant can bring action in different jurisdictions. Despite the fact that actions have been brought in multiple jurisdictions, even if a sound outcome has been achieved, the enforcement of foreign national courts' judgements can prove to be an issue due to the different legal traditions and mentalities involved.[13] By allowing the disputing parties to determine the rules, alternative dispute resolution not only permits the parties to create a more neutral playing field as it were,[14] it also serves the predictability and enforceability of the decision.[15]

However, the possibility of determining the (procedural) rules applicable to the dispute in question may not only furthermore reduce the time necessary to conduct the procedure, but also further contribute to another benefit of alternative dispute resolution—cost-effectiveness.[16]

In addition, alternative dispute resolution has yet another advantage: the benefit of expertise. While in litigation the courts generally lack specific expertise in cultural heritage law, in alternative dispute resolution, parties are free to choose specialised experts as intermediaries. Thus, in alternative dispute resolution the person charged with finding a solution is likely to actually have considerable knowledge concerning the subject matter, whereas in litigation the court generally only superficially grasps the matter through expert witnesses.[17]

Furthermore, alternative dispute resolution is a cooperative procedure. It can only be conducted when all parties agree. This not only results in less reluctance of parties to become involved, since they are not forced to be subject to a procedure the principle rules of which they are not able to shape,[18] the absence or at least the

[9]Stamatoudi (2009), p. 118; cf. also Palmer (2013), p. 100; cf. also Nafziger et al. (2014), p. 604.

[10]Stamatoudi (2011), p. 191. Nevertheless, the legal rules generally shape the discourse of the dispute resolution; cf. Strother (2014), p. 375.

[11]Bandle and Theurich (2011), p. 29; cf. also Stamatoudi (2011), pp. 190f.

[12]Theurich (2010), p. 576.

[13]Barker (2009), p. 485; Stamatoudi (2009), p. 118.

[14]Wichard and Wendland (2009), p. 477.

[15]Similar Varner (2011–2012), p. 483.

[16]Chechi (2013), p. 190.

[17]Similar Varner (2011–2012), p. 483.

[18]Cf. Chechi (2013), p. 193.

minimisation of hostility also makes it possible for the involved parties to maintain good relations after the procedure.[19]

The opportunity for the parties to keep the procedure confidential is another positive aspect of alternative dispute resolution.[20] This contributes to the good faith participation of the parties in the process. Additionally, it permits them in certain cases to make further concessions[21] without having to fear that in other cases, which they may not consider to be similar, they have to face demands for the same concessions.

Last but not least, possibly the most important advantage of alternative dispute resolution is the influence parties have to shape the outcome. Unlike litigation, where an all or nothing approach is more likely—where one party or the other is awarded the object in dispute[22]—in cases of alternative dispute resolution the outcome may be much more flexible.[23] Parties may agree, for example, on a conditional return, a return accompanied by cultural cooperation measures, a loan, a donation, special ownership regimes, production of replicas or even a formal recognition of the importance of the object in dispute to the cultural identity of the claimant.[24]

Thus, it is not surprising that both the 1970 UNESCO Convention and the 1995 UNIDROIT Convention include provisions on alternative dispute resolution. Article 17 (5) of the 1970 UNESCO Convention allows UNESCO to extend, at the request of at least two states parties which are engaged in a dispute over its implementation, its good offices to reach a settlement between them. Furthermore, Article 8 (2) of the 1995 UNIDROIT Convention states that parties may agree to submit the dispute to any court or other competent authority or to arbitration.

However, alternative dispute resolution is not a miracle cure for all the problems in this field. It also has its negative aspects, not the least of which is that it relies on cooperation. Thus, in cases where one party to the dispute is reluctant to participate in alternative dispute resolution, it may not be possible to conduct any such procedure. Unlike in litigation, no party can be forced to participate.[25]

Secondly, only the outcome of arbitration is enforceable[26]; the results of softer forms of alternative dispute resolution, such as mediation and conciliation, are not.[27] Thirdly, confidentiality may cut both ways. It may lead to results which may be in the interest of the participating parties, but, due to a lack of publicity, not in the public interest.[28] Furthermore, confidentiality can lead to unjust results, particularly

[19]Cf. Palmer (2009), p. 359.

[20]Wichard and Wendland (2009), p. 479.

[21]Stamatoudi (2009), p. 118.

[22]Renold (2015), p. 163; Chechi (2013), p. 194.

[23]Cf. Nafziger et al. (2014), p. 605.

[24]See Cornu and Renold (2010), pp. 19ff.

[25]Merrills (2011), p. 29; Palmer (2009), p. 358.

[26]Shyllon (2009), pp. 375f; Merrills (2011), p. 111.

[27]Beckmann (2008), p. 117.

[28]Cf. also Varner (2011–2012), pp. 487, 488.

in cases of an imbalance of power between parties.[29] Fourthly, parties have no possibility to legally redress the outcome of arbitration.[30] Finally, in litigation, normally more evidence is gathered which may be useful in ongoing similar or future cases.[31]

Nevertheless, the rules of procedures tailored specifically to instrumentalise alternative dispute resolution for cultural objects related disputes adopted by the ICPRCP and ICOM in cooperation with WIPO are a major development in this area. However, both, the ICPRCP Rules of Procedure for Mediation and Conciliation and the ICOM-WIPO Mediation Rules concentrate on softer forms of alternative dispute resolution; they leave out arbitration.

5.2 The ICPRCP Rules of Procedure for Mediation and Conciliation

5.2.1 Overview

The first alternative dispute resolution rules of procedure tailored specifically for disputes over cultural heritage were adopted by the Intergovernmental Committee for Promoting the Return of Cultural Property to its Countries of Origin or its Restitution in case of Illicit Appropriation. This is not surprising taking into account that the committee is UNESCO's central instrument to promote the return and restitution of cultural property and combat its illicit trafficking,[32] in which function it has already served as an intermediary in cultural material related disputes.[33]

This development is however somewhat interesting considering the fact that, at the time the ICPRCP was first founded, the idea it could achieve any form of judiciary character was strongly opposed by many state members. When the chairperson stated that when the committee felt that the position of the holding country was unjustified, it could extend its good offices or perhaps even arbitrate, many state parties objected to this.[34] This opposition was so severe that he felt the need to clarify in the following session that he had used the word "arbitration" in a general way and that whatever opinions he expressed should be corrected in light of the statutes. He emphasised that the committee could only bring together people of

[29]Campfens (2014), pp. 80f.

[30]Beckmann (2008), p. 118.

[31]Stamatoudi (2011), p. 190.

[32]Stamatoudi (2011), p. 179 sees it as the institutionalisation of the diplomatic actions of UNESCO.

[33]For an overview of cases in which the ICPRCP was involved cf. pp. 139f.

[34]Shyllon (2009), pp. 374f.

goodwill eager to find workable solutions and that its path was that of mediation and moral pressure.[35]

However, times have changed and so did the attitude of member states. They felt the need to strengthen the role of the ICPRCP as an intermediary in cultural property related disputes.[36] Hence, even though the member states have not gone as far as bestowing judiciary capacity on the committee, they have enacted the ICPRCP Rules of Procedure for Mediation and Conciliation in order to permit the committee to play a (more) active role in mediation and conciliation and thus solidify its role as an intermediary in cultural objects related disputes by providing it with an alternative dispute resolution mechanism.

5.2.2 The Issuing of the ICPRCP Rules of Procedure for Mediation and Conciliation

While initially member states objected to the idea of the ICPRCP achieving any form of judiciary character, by 2003 this attitude had changed to such an extent that at its 32nd session the UNESCO General Conference invited its Director-General to present a strategy to facilitate the restitution of stolen and illicitly exported cultural property by strengthening the mandate of the ICPRCP in terms of proposals of mediation and conciliation for member states.[37] When the proposition was also seconded by the Intergovernmental Committee at its 13th session in 2005,[38] the General Conference of UNESCO expanded the mandate of the committee at its 33rd session in 2005 by amending Article 4 (1) of the ICPRCP Statutes. Accordingly, now the committee may also submit proposals with a view to mediation or conciliation to the member states concerned, being understood that mediation implies the intervention of an outside party to bring the concerned parties to a dispute together and assist them in reaching a solution, while under conciliation, the concerned parties agree to submit their dispute to a constituted organ for investigation and efforts to effect a settlement. Furthermore, for the exercise of the mediation and conciliation functions, the committee has also been authorised to establish appropriate rules of procedure.[39]

However, these rules of procedure were not adopted immediately. At its 14th session the ICPRCP first presented a draft.[40] At the 15th session a working group was established to negotiate further on the draft. However, it was superseded by an ad hoc subcommittee which was created between the 15th and 16th sessions and

[35]UNESCO Doc CLT-83/CONF.216/8, 10.11.1983, p. 5.

[36]Cf. UNESCO GC 32 C/Resolution 38, 16.10.2003, Paragraph 9 (a).

[37]UNESCO GC 32 C/Resolution 38, 16.10.2003, Paragraph 9 (a).

[38]UNESCO Doc 33 C/REP/15 Annex II, 21.10.2005, pp. 2f.

[39]UNESCO GC 33 C/Resolution 44, 21.10.2005.

[40]UNESCO Doc CLT-2007/CONF.211/COM.14/2, 31.05.2007, p. 2.

which elaborated further on the draft.[41] The draft was then adopted at the 16th session of the ICPRCP in 2010 as the Rules of Procedure for Mediation and Conciliation.[42,43]

5.2.3 The Application Field of the ICPRCP Rules of Procedure

Article 1 (1) of the Rules of Procedure clarifies that any request for the restitution or return of cultural property as defined under Article 3 of the ICPRCP Statutes, which is submitted to the committee, may also be dealt with under a mediation or a conciliation procedure if the parties to the dispute so agree. Hence, the scope of the ICPRCP Rules of Procedure for Mediation and Conciliation runs in parallel with that of the committee itself. Thus, it is also subject to the same limitations established by Article 3 (2) of the Statutes. Hence, a mediation and conciliation procedure may only be initialised for cultural artefacts which have a fundamental significance from the point of view of the spiritual values and cultural heritage and which has been lost as a result of colonial or foreign occupation or as a result of illicit appropriation.

However, the question concerning the personal scope of application was one of the most controversially discussed issues in the context of the rules of procedure. While some favoured the idea that private parties should also be enabled to initiate and participate in the procedure, others objected it arguing that due to the complementary nature of the procedure to the general work of the committee and for practical reasons the personal scope of the application of the procedures should be in parallel to that of the ICPRCP.[44] In the end, the later view prevailed. Hence, only member states and associate members of UNESCO may activate such a proce-

---

[41]UNESCO Doc CLT-2010/CONF.203/COM.16/2 Rev, July 2010, p. 2; Urbinati (2014), p. 95, n 12.

[42]UNESCO Doc CLT-2010/CONF.203/COM.16/5, September 2010, p. 4.

[43]In the meanwhile, both the Athens International Conference on Return of Cultural Property to its Country of Origin in March 2008 and the extraordinary session in honour of the 30th Anniversary of the ICPRCP stressed the importance of mediation and conciliation.

Conclusions of the Athens Conference Paragraph 6: "The role of the Intergovernmental Committee for Promoting the Return of Cultural Property to its Countries of Origin or its Restitution in case of Illicit Appropriation must be strengthened through the necessary means, resources and infrastructure. Effort should be made to encourage mediation either through the Committee or by other means of alternative dispute resolution;".

Recommendations of the extraordinary session Paragraph 13: "Considers that adoption of rules of procedure on mediation and conciliation will be a significant step to strengthen the role of the Committee;".

[44]Urbinati (2014), p. 100.

dure,[45] a stance which is explicitly repeated in Article 4 (1) of the Rules of Procedure. However, states also represent the interests of public or private institutions located in their territory or the interests of their nationals.[46] But, as an exception to this general rule, a request to initiate a mediation or conciliation procedure may be submitted by a member state or associate member of UNESCO with regard to a public or private institution, if the latter is in possession of the cultural artefact concerned and if the state domicile to the institution has been immediately informed of the request by the initiating member state or associated member of UNESCO and does not object.[47]

On the other hand, the parallel structure of the scope of the rules of procedure with the ambit of the Intergovernmental Committee also means that there is no time restraint. Thus, procedures may also deal with requests concerning objects which have been transferred even before the establishment of the ICPRCP.[48]

5.2.4 The ICPRCP Rules of Procedure's Definitions of "Mediation" and "Conciliation"

Mediation is defined as a process whereby, with prior consent of the parties concerned, an outside party intervenes to bring them together and to assist them in reaching an amicable solution to their dispute with respect to the restitution or return of cultural material.[49] Conciliation, on the other hand, means a process whereby, subject to their prior consent, the parties concerned submit their dispute with respect to the restitution or return of cultural objects to a constituted organ for investigation and for efforts to effect an amicable settlement of their dispute.[50]

Although both procedures are forms of alternative dispute resolution[51] with a number of similarities, they must be distinguished from one another. But both procedures also have certain things in common. They include a third party to the dispute in order to reach an amicable solution. Furthermore, in both cases, being subject to the procedure requires the prior consent of the parties, and the result of

---

[45] Cf. Article 3 (2) of the ICPRCP Statutes: "A request for the restitution or return by a Member State or Associate Member of UNESCO may be made concerning any cultural property which has a fundamental significance from the point of view of the spiritual values and cultural heritage of the people of a Member State or Associate Member of UNESCO and which has been lost as a result of colonial or foreign occupation or as a result of illicit appropriation.".

[46] Article 4 (2) of the Rules of Procedure for Mediation and Conciliation.

[47] Article 4 (3) of the Rules of Procedure for Mediation and Conciliation.

[48] Cf. Vrdoljak (2008), p. 235; for further and more detailed information on the scope of the Intergovernmental Committee and thus the Rules of Procedure for Mediation and Conciliation cf. also p. 132f.

[49] Article 2 (1) of the Rules of Procedure for Mediation and Conciliation.

[50] Article 2 (3) of the Rules of Procedure for Mediation and Conciliation.

[51] Cf. Stamatoudi (2011), pp. 198, 201.

the procedure is not binding.[52] Finally, both procedures give priority to other procedures[53] since neither prejudice the application and the effects of any other procedure or means of dispute settlement. Moreover, the procedures do not prevent or delay any legal proceedings in pursuance of applicable national legislation.[54,55] However, what distinguishes both procedures is the particular role of the third party involved.

On a sliding scale from good offices to arbitration, mediation is located much closer to the former. Hence, the mediator is a facilitator of the negotiations. He ought to both introduce new proposals which do not have to be based on strict legal doctrine[56] as well as interpret and transmit existing proposals to the parties. The mediator acts in confidence and usually on information provided by the parties rather than independent investigation,[57] although he is not prevented from conducting his own investigations.[58]

Conciliation, on the other hand, is situated much closer on the sliding scale to arbitration and hence involves a much more institutionalised procedure.[59] The conciliator proposes solutions based on impartial investigations of the facts and, generally, taking into account rules of law as well as state practice.[60]

5.2.5 The Constitution of the ICPRCP Rules of Procedure's Mediation and Conciliation Bodies

The voluntary character of the procedures is also reflected in the constitution of the mediation and conciliation entities. The individuals acting as mediators are freely chosen by the parties for which they have 60 days from the day initiating the procedure.[61] If state parties fail to do so, UNESCO's Director-General appoints

---

[52]Merrills (2011), p. 58; in case of conciliation Paragraph 6 of the Annex to the Vienna Convention on the Law of Treaties explicitly states: "The report of the Commission, including any conclusions stated therein regarding the facts or questions of law, shall not be binding upon the parties and it shall have no other character than that of recommendations submitted for the consideration of the parties in order to facilitate an amicable settlement of the dispute.".

[53]Urbinati (2014), p. 105.

[54]Article 6 (4) and (5) of the Rules of Procedure for Mediation and Conciliation.

[55]This is also why the literature seems to use both terms interchangeably.

[56]Article 3 (4) of the Rules of Procedure for Mediation and Conciliation nevertheless requires the parties, mediators, and conciliators to give due regard to international law and recognised principles.

[57]Stamatoudi (2011), pp. 198, 201.

[58]Cf. Article 8 (3) of the Rules of Procedure for Mediation and Conciliation.

[59]Merrills (2011), p. 58.

[60]Stamatoudi (2011), p. 201; Article 3 (4) of the Rules of Procedure for Mediation and Conciliation also requires parties, mediators, and conciliators to give due regard to international law and recognised principles.

[61]Article 7 (1) of the Rules of Procedure for Mediation and Conciliation.

them after consultation with the parties as soon as possible.[62] Unlike in the case of the general mediation scheme, where authoritative representatives of states or intergovernmental organisations are appointed to give weight and authority to their proposals,[63] in the context of UNESCO, mediators are intended to be independent experts on the return of cultural heritage[64] and may not act as representatives or counsels of either party in any proceedings concerning the dispute at issue.[65]

The same is true for the conciliation procedure. Each party to the dispute appoints one or two conciliators to the conciliation commission whereby the same procedure and limitations mentioned with regard to the mediators apply.[66] Furthermore, the number of conciliators is mutually agreed upon by the parties concerned. In addition, the president of the commission, an additional conciliator who has to have a nationality different from that of the parties involved, is chosen jointly by the parties.[67] If the parties cannot agree on that person within 60 days, the Director-General of UNESCO appoints one after consultation with the parties concerned as soon as possible.[68]

For this purpose, and in order to provide information and assistance to the parties in appointing mediators or conciliators, a list of potential mediators and conciliators is drawn up and maintained by the UNESCO Secretariat. The parties are however free to appoint mediators or conciliators not included in this list. Nevertheless, the secretariat invites each member state of UNESCO to nominate two individuals who could fulfil the role of mediator or conciliator in international cultural material related disputes. The list is reviewed at 2-year intervals when member states may confirm existing nominations or submit new ones.[69]

At any stage of the procedure, after consultation with the other party, any party may request the replacement of a mediator or conciliator based on a breach of confidentiality or the general principles of fairness, impartiality and good faith. The grounds must be set out clearly and the new mediator or conciliator has to be

---

[62] Article 7 (2) of the Rules of Procedure for Mediation and Conciliation.

[63] Urbinati (2014), p. 98.

[64] Article 2 (2) of the Rules of Procedure for Mediation and Conciliation; Article 7 (3) of the Rules of Procedure for Mediation and Conciliation states further: "Mediator(s) [...] shall be selected taking into consideration their expertise in the field of restitution and/or their knowledge with regard to the nature of the dispute or the specificity of the cultural property at stake.".

[65] Article 5 (b) of the Rules of Procedure for Mediation and Conciliation.

[66] In particular, they ought to be experts in the field of return and restitution of cultural property and may not act as a representative or counsel of either party in any proceedings concerning the dispute at issue. Furthermore, they have to be appointed within 60 days of the written request to initiate the procedure. Otherwise, the Director-General has to appoint them after consultation with the parties as soon as possible.

[67] Articles 2 (4), (5) and 5 (b) of the Rules of Procedure for Mediation and Conciliation.

[68] Articles 2 (5) and 7 (2) of the Rules of Procedure for Mediation and Conciliation.

[69] Article 2 (6) of the Rules of Procedure for Mediation and Conciliation.

appointed according to the same procedure originally used,[70] which is also true in the case of any other vacancy that arises.[71]

5.2.6 *The Mediation and Conciliation Procedure of the ICPRCP Rules of Procedure*

First of all, it is important to realise that the Rules of Procedure for Mediation and Conciliation are not strictly binding, which is, in light of the voluntary character of the procedures, not surprising. Hence, the parties themselves may amend them before commencing the procedure[72] or the conciliator may do so, unless the parties to the dispute otherwise agree.[73]

Nonetheless, any mediation and conciliation procedure under the current rules of procedure is subject to certain basic principles. First of all, the initiation of any such procedure requires the written consent of the parties.[74] Furthermore, the procedure must be conducted in conditions of confidentiality and in accordance with the general principles of fairness, impartiality, and good faith.[75] The requirement of impartiality is primarily directed towards the mediator and conciliators, whereas the principle of good faith addresses above all the parties involved.[76] Thus, parties must in particular participate in a responsible manner and cooperate in order to proceed as expeditiously as possible.[77] Last but not least, the parties as well as the mediator or conciliator have to furthermore participate with a view to facilitate an amicable and just solution or settlement of the dispute having due regard to international law and recognised principles.[78] However, this can also be viewed as an additional expression of the good faith requirement.

Concerning the procedures, these may either be initiated by the parties themselves or recommended by the ICPRCP to parties having a case pending before it.[79] However, when parties initiate a mediation or conciliation procedure, upon mutual consent, either party has to submit in writing a request containing the names and contact information of the parties, the subject of the dispute, and relevant supporting documents to UNESCO's Director-General who must acknowledge the receipt and inform the chairman of the ICPRCP.[80]

---

[70]Article 7 (4) of the Rules of Procedure for Mediation and Conciliation.

[71]Article 7 (5) of the Rules of Procedure for Mediation and Conciliation.

[72]Article 1 (2) of the Rules of Procedure for Mediation and Conciliation.

[73]Article 8 (8) of the Rules of Procedure for Mediation and Conciliation.

[74]Article 3 (1) of the Rules of Procedure for Mediation and Conciliation.

[75]Article 3 (2) of the Rules of Procedure for Mediation and Conciliation.

[76]Same Urbinati (2014), p. 110.

[77]Article 3 (3) of the Rules of Procedure for Mediation and Conciliation.

[78]Article 3 (4) of the Rules of Procedure for Mediation and Conciliation.

[79]Article 6 (1) and (2) of the Rules of Procedure for Mediation and Conciliation.

[80]Article 6 (1) and (3) of the Rules of Procedure for Mediation and Conciliation.

After the parties submit to the mediator(s) or conciliators the issue which is the subject of the dispute, their position thereon and all relevant documentation, which are transmitted to the other party,[81] the mediator(s) or the conciliation commission sets in consultation with the parties the times, places and dates of their meetings and specifies in which language(s) documentation and evidence shall be submitted.[82] New documents, as well as arguments, may be submitted by each party in writing at any time before the procedure is concluded.[83] Parties have also the right to request the mediators and the conciliation commission to allow witnesses, experts, and third parties to provide documentation and evidence.[84] Nonetheless, the mediators or conciliators may conduct their own inquiries and research to determine the facts of the dispute.[85]

At any time given, consultations are confidential, in particular when the mediator or the conciliators meet and communicate separately with each party. Therefore, no recordings are to be made and information or documents obtained are not to be disclosed, unless the parties or the party concerned agrees otherwise.[86]

The mediator or conciliator shall endeavour to bring the parties to reach an amicable settlement of the dispute within 1 year from the date of his appointment.[87] However, the parties may also set an extendable time limit for the conclusion of the procedure, beyond which, if no settlement has been reached, the procedure shall be deemed to have been concluded.[88] In addition to the elapsing of the time limit and the reaching of an amicable settlement of the dispute, the procedure is also deemed to have been concluded when all parties concerned consent in writing that this is so or when one of the parties has notified in writing its withdrawal from the procedure.[89]

Irrespective of the details concluding a procedure, the parties have to inform the chairman of the ICPRCP, who in turn informs UNESCO's Director-General and the members of the committee at the next session of the results.[90,91] When the procedure has been concluded without a settlement, the issue which is the subject of the dispute remains before the committee as any other unsolved question which has

[81] Article 8 (1) of the Rules of Procedure for Mediation and Conciliation.

[82] Article 8 (2) of the Rules of Procedure for Mediation and Conciliation.

[83] Article 8 (5) of the Rules of Procedure for Mediation and Conciliation.

[84] Article 8 (4) of the Rules of Procedure for Mediation and Conciliation.

[85] Article 8 (3) of the Rules of Procedure for Mediation and Conciliation.

[86] Article 8 (6) and (7) of the Rules of Procedure for Mediation and Conciliation.

[87] Article 8 (9) of the Rules of Procedure for Mediation and Conciliation.

[88] Article 8 (10) of the Rules of Procedure for Mediation and Conciliation.

[89] Article 10 (1) of the Rules of Procedure for Mediation and Conciliation.

[90] Article 10 (2) of the Rules of Procedure for Mediation and Conciliation.

[91] The parties also have the obligation to inform the committee jointly on the state of progress of the procedure at the sessions (Article 9 of the Rules of Procedure for Mediation and Conciliation).

been submitted to it.[92] If, however, an outcome has been reached, this is only binding on the parties if they reach a binding agreement on it.[93,94]

Finally, the rules of procedure also provide for regulations regarding the costs of the procedure. Hence, the parties must bear in equal share the costs of the mediation or conciliation procedure unless another arrangement has been made. This flexibility redresses the imbalance in financial means of the parties generally involved in claims for return—often in the constellation of developing countries requesting from developed countries[95]—since it allows countries otherwise lacking sufficient financial means to pursue their goal and use the costs of the procedure as a bargaining chip. A financially limited requesting state may, for instance, accept the cultural material in dispute as a permanent loan rather than having it returned with its title, when in return the other party bears the costs of the procedure.

However, in the event of a withdrawal of one party, this will not have an effect on the obligation of that party in question to pay the expenses incurred up to the date of the notification of the withdrawal.[96] Furthermore, expenses incurred for witnesses, experts or legal assistance when requested by only one party, is borne by that party, unless another arrangement has been made.[97]

5.2.7 *Synopsis*

The amendment of the ICPRCP Statute and the adoption of the Rules of Procedure for Mediation and Conciliation have to be considered as the most significant systematic development in the context of the ICPRCP so far. This permits the committee to have more effect on cultural property related disputes than it ever had before.

However, in correspondence with the general nature of alternative dispute resolution mechanisms, parties to the dispute ultimately remain in charge of the procedure. They may amend or even change the rules of procedures to suit their special needs.[98] The committee plays only an ancillary role by, for instance, providing a list of potential mediators and conciliators.[99]

However, at least there are certain things it can do. Furthermore, despite mediation and conciliation being procedures which do not mandatorily result in

---

[92] Article 10 (3) of the Rules of Procedure for Mediation and Conciliation.

[93] Article 10 (4) of the Rules of Procedure for Mediation and Conciliation.

[94] Interestingly, Article 4 (4) of the Rules of Procedure for Mediation and Conciliation explicitly states that the representatives of the parties have the requisite authority to prepare the terms and conditions of a settlement.

[95] Urbinati (2014), p. 106.

[96] Article 11 (1) of the Rules of Procedure for Mediation and Conciliation.

[97] Article 11 (2) of the Rules of Procedure for Mediation and Conciliation.

[98] Cf. Article 1 (2) of the Rules of Procedure for Mediation and Conciliation.

[99] Article 2 (6) of the Rules of Procedure for Mediation and Conciliation.

legally binding outcomes,[100] both have to be conducted in conditions of confidentiality and in accordance with the general principles of fairness, impartiality, and good faith.[101] Thus, the rules of procedure make the committee leave the realm of being merely a diplomatic forum and gain a character—at least to a certain degree—closer to a judicial body. More importantly, the rules also contribute to the juridification of the procedure concerning disputes over cultural heritage and are conducive to resolving these disputes, as they establish the principle of employing independent experts on the return and restitution of cultural material[102] as mediators and conciliators. Besides this, the ICPRCP Rules of Procedure are in the spirit of prior instruments and serve to enhance their principles (and effectiveness) particularly by establishing a formalised procedure in which state parties involved to a cultural property related dispute can interact and fulfil their obligation to cooperate as required by not only the ILA Principles but also present in both the 1970 UNESCO and 1995 UNIDROIT Conventions and promoted by the ICPRCP.

5.3 The ICOM-WIPO Mediation Rules

5.3.1 General Remarks

Approximately 1 year after the adoption of the ICPRCP Rules of Procedure for Mediation and Conciliation, another set of alternative dispute resolution rules of procedure tailored specifically for cultural object related disputes came into being. These new rules of procedure were the outcome of cooperation between ICOM and WIPO.

As already shown in the context of the ICOM Code of Ethics, ICOM has been and still is encouraging its members facing claims for restitution and return to enter into dialogue with a view to resolving the issue by seeking a negotiated settlement where possible.[103] To further this purpose, ICOM began developing a mediation programme with regard to disputes involving museums. This has resulted in a cooperative effort with WIPO,[104] a specialised agency of the United Nations with currently 189 member states which was founded in 1967.[105] WIPO promotes the protection of intellectual property throughout the world through cooperation among states and, where appropriate, in collaboration with other international

[100]Merrills (2011), p. 58.

[101]Article 3 (2) of the Rules of Procedure for Mediation and Conciliation.

[102]Cf. Article 2 (2) of the Rules of Procedure for Mediation and Conciliation; Article 7 (3) of the Rules of Procedure for Mediation and Conciliation.

[103]ICOM Doc 2005/LEG.06, April 2005, p. 1; http://icom.museum/the-governance/general-assembly/resolutions-adopted-by-icoms-general-assemblies-1946-to-date/shanghai-2010/.

[104]http://icom.museum/programmes/art-and-cultural-heritage-mediation/icom-wipo-mediation-rules/.

[105]http://www.wipo.int/about-wipo/en/.

organisations[106] and hence may seem a strange partner for ICOM. However, WIPO with its Arbitration and Mediation Center[107] not only contributes expertise in matters of alternative dispute resolution (mechanisms), it also has certain expertise in the field of cultural heritage due in particular to its Intergovernmental Committee on Intellectual Property (IP) and Genetic Resources (GR), Traditional Knowledge (TK) and Folklore.[108,109]

The cooperation has borne fruit and led to the adoption of the ICOM-WIPO Mediation Rules, which are jointly administrated by both organisations. The rules are meant to provide a neutral and confidential forum that provides the flexibility as well as the required legal and technical expertise to resolve disputes in a manner satisfactory to the parties involved.[110] The ICOM-WIPO Mediation Rules are a specifically tailored dispute resolution option with specific model mediation clauses that take account of the particular dispute resolution needs regarding claims for the return of cultural property.[111] They make allowance for the fact that such disputes regularly involve complex legal as well as sensitive non-legal issues of a cultural, economic, ethical, historical, moral, political, religious or spiritual nature, combine tangible and intangible matters in a single case and present challenges in terms of evidence and statutes of limitations.[112]

Certain aspects of these rules even go beyond those of the ICPRCP as they contain, for instance, much more detailed regulations and are thus more extended. In addition, they open the mediation procedure to private parties.[113]

5.3.2 The Path Leading to the Adoption of the ICOM-WIPO Mediation Rules

In 2005, ICOM's Legal Affairs and Properties Committee presented a recommendation concerning an International Mediation Process for the Resolution of Disputes over the Ownership of Objects in Museum Collections.[114] Based on this recommendation, the Executive Council of ICOM began to actively promote

---

[106]Article 3 WIPO Convention.

[107]See for further information on the Arbitration and Mediation Center http://www.wipo.int/amc/en/center/background.html.

[108]See for further information on the intergovernmental committee http://www.wipo.int/tk/en/igc/. See also Groth et al. (2015), pp. 17–29.

[109]See for the suitability of intellectual property law to protect and promote cultural heritage Shyllon (2016), pp. 55–68.

[110]Cf. http://icom.museum/programmes/art-and-cultural-heritage-mediation/icom-wipo-mediation-rules/.

[111]http://www.wipo.int/amc/en/center/specific-sectors/art/icom/rules/.

[112]http://icom.museum/programmes/art-and-cultural-heritage-mediation/icom-wipo-mediation-rules/.

[113]Same Urbinati (2014), pp. 112ff.

[114]Cf. ICOM Doc 2005/LEG.06, April 2005.

mediation in preference to legal action. Furthermore, it established an ICOM panel of suitable, qualified, experienced, trained, and independent mediators, available to assist the parties in dispute resolution.[115] However, 2 years later, in 2007, the General Assembly of ICOM adopted Resolution No. 4 on Preventing Illicit Traffic and Promoting the Physical Return, Repatriation and Restitution of Cultural Property. In this resolution the assembly recommended the development of new and innovative methods to promote and facilitate return, repatriation, and restitution and urged ICOM members to support and initiate actions leading to physical repatriation wherever applicable. It furthermore recommended the use of the mediation process as a first recourse in this context.[116] In 2010, in its Resolution 15 on Heritage Restitution, ICOM's General Assembly again encouraged all the parties concerned who were in dispute concerning documents and objects which have in the past been confiscated from colonised countries to enter into dialogue with a view to resolving the issues of restitution. Moreover, it drew attention to the ICOM Code of Ethics for Museums and to ICOM's adherence to international conventions governing such matters.[117]

WIPO's Programme on IP and GR, TK and Traditional Cultural Expression (TCE), on the other hand, started operating as early as 1998.[118] At its 26th session in 2000, the WIPO General Assembly then established the Intergovernmental Committee on IP and GR, TK and Folklore[119] which has held regular sessions since 2001.[120] Furthermore, the potential role of alternative dispute resolution in the context of GR, TK, and Folklore has been discussed ever since.[121]

This naturally placed WIPO in a position to be able to contribute to the cooperation with ICOM, not only through its knowledge on substantive matters, but also with its expertise on alternative dispute resolution (mechanisms). This expertise originates in particular from WIPO's Arbitration and Mediation Center which was established in 1994. The centre not only adopted in the very year of its foundation the WIPO Mediation, Arbitration and Expedited Arbitration Rules, but also updated these in 2002, and issued Expert Determination Rules in 2007. Eventually, it revised and merged both of these documents into the WIPO Mediation, (Expedited) Arbitration and Expert Determination Rules in 2014.[122] Moreover, the centre also develops, in collaboration with relevant international organisations, dispute resolution schemes which are tailored for the special needs

[115]Cf. http://icom.museum/the-governance/general-assembly/resolutions-adopted-by-icoms-general-assemblies-1946-to-date/vienna-2007/.

[116]Cf. http://icom.museum/the-governance/general-assembly/resolutions-adopted-by-icoms-general-assemblies-1946-to-date/vienna-2007/.

[117]Cf. http://icom.museum/the-governance/general-assembly/resolutions-adopted-by-icoms-general-assemblies-1946-to-date/shanghai-2010/.

[118]WIPO Doc WIPO/GA/26/6, 25.08.2000, p. 3.

[119]WIPO Doc WIPO/GA/26/10, 03.10.2000, p. 23.

[120]Theurich (2010), pp. 582f.

[121]Theurich (2010), pp. 582ff with further references.

[122]Cf. http://www.wipo.int/amc/en/rules/.

of particular sectors.[123] This has allowed WIPO to gain considerable expertise in the area of alternative dispute resolution.[124]

These factors allowed the collaboration between ICOM and WIPO to bear fruit and led to the adoption of the ICOM-WIPO Mediation Rules. The Art and Cultural Heritage Mediation programme was launched in July 2011[125] after formalising the collaboration of both institutions with a memorandum of understanding on 3 May 2011.[126]

5.3.3 The Field of Operation of the ICOM-WIPO Mediation Rules

According to Article 2 (a) of the Mediation Rules, the scope of the mediation procedure is intended to cover disputes relating to art and cultural heritage, including but not limited to return and restitution, loan and deposit, acquisition, and intellectual property. The phrase "including but not limited to" denotes that the enumeration is only of exemplary nature and thus the mediation procedure is not limited to disputes concerning solely the return and restitution of cultural objects, as is the case with the ICPRCP Rules of Procedure for Mediation and Conciliation. Rather, it is applicable in all disputes concerning any area of activity of ICOM. Hence, the ICOM-WIPO Mediation Rules have a much broader substantive scope than the ICPRCP Rules of Procedure.[127]

The same is true for the personal scope of the ICOM-WIPO Mediation Rules. While the ICPRCP mediation procedure is, in accordance with Article 4 (1) of the ICPRCP Rules of Procedure, in principle[128] only open to member states and associate members of UNESCO, Article 2 (a) of the ICOM-WIPO Mediation Rules declares its mediation procedure applicable to disputes involving public or private parties including but not limited to states, museums, indigenous communities, and individuals. Again, due to the phrase "including but not limited to", the listing is only of exemplary nature. Hence, the ICOM-WIPO mediation procedure is open to anyone and not only states.

---

[123]It has for example elaborated special alternative dispute resolution rules for disputes in the film and media sector (cf. http://www.wipo.int/amc/en/film/) and concerning domain name disputes (cf. http://www.wipo.int/amc/en/domains/).

[124]Bandle and Theurich (2011), p. 32.

[125]ICOM Minutes of the 27th Session of the General Assembly – ICOM International Museums Meetings – Paris, France, 6 June, 2012, p. 1.

[126]WIPO Doc WO/GA/40/9, 26.07.2011, p. 2, n 6; ICOM Minutes of the 26th Session of the General Assembly – ICOM June Meetings – Paris, France, 8 June, 2011, p. 9.

[127]Same Urbinati (2014), p. 99.

[128]As an exception, however, a request to initiate a mediation or conciliation procedure may be submitted by a member state or associate member of UNESCO with regard to a public or private institution, if the latter are in possession of the cultural property concerned, and if the respective state has been immediately informed of the request by the initiating member state or associated member of UNESCO and does not object (Article 4 (3) of the ICPRCP Rules of Procedure).

However, just as with the ICPRCP Rules of Procedure, the ICOM-WIPO Mediation Rules do not provide any provision concerning the temporal scope of the mediation procedure. Thus, as is the case with the ICPRPC procedure, the ICOM-WIPO procedure does not face any time limitation[129] and hence is even applicable to disputes concerning items which have been transferred before the establishment of the procedure.

5.3.4 The ICOM-WIPO Mediation Rules' Notion of "Mediation"

The first prominent distinction between the ICPRCP Rules of Procedure for Mediation and Conciliation and the ICOM-WIPO Mediation Rules that strikes the reader is the fact that, unlike the ICPRCP Rules of Procedure, the ICOM-WIPO Rules only cover mediation. Thus, conciliation is not an available alternative dispute resolution mechanism under the ICOM-WIPO Rules.

Furthermore, unlike the ICPRCP Rules of Procedure, the ICOM-WIPO Rules do not provide for a definition of the term "mediation".[130] However, certain provisions of the ICOM-WIPO Mediation Rules address issues associated with mediation and thus provide an impression on how the drafters of the ICOM-WIPO Mediation Rules understood the term "mediation".

Article 16 (a) of the ICOM-WIPO Mediation Rules states that the mediator shall promote the settlement of the issues in dispute between the parties in any manner that the mediator believes to be appropriate. However, he shall have no authority to impose a settlement on the parties. Thus, the result of the procedure is not binding, unless both parties agree so, in which case the agreement may be enforceable under general contract law.[131]

Furthermore, according to Article 22 (iii) of the Mediation Rules, the mediation can be ended by a written declaration of any party at any time. From this provision it can be derived that the mediation procedure is a consensual process which requires the consent of the parties at every stage, including its initiation.

In addition, Article 15 (a) of the Rules states that as soon as possible after being appointed, the mediator shall, in consultation with the parties, establish a timetable for the submission by each party to the mediator and to the other party of a statement summarising the background of the dispute, the party's interests and contentions in relation to the dispute, and the present status of the dispute, together with such other information and materials as the party considers necessary for the purposes of the mediation and, in particular, to enable the issues in dispute to be identified. Thus, the mediator acts based on information provided by the parties

[129]Same Urbinati (2014), p. 101.

[130]Urbinati (2014), p. 97.

[131]Same Urbinati (2014), p. 98.

rather than conducting independent investigations. Article 9 of the Mediation Rules furthermore requires the mediator to be impartial whilst Articles 17–21 show that the mediation procedure is of a confidential nature.

Overall, these provisions reveal that the understanding of "mediation" in the context of the ICOM-WIPO Mediation Rules correlates with the general understanding of mediation and the understanding of the ICPRCP Rules of Procedure for Mediation and Conciliation. Hence, mediation is a procedure based on mutual consent and close to negotiations or good offices. It is meant to reach an amicable solution and includes an impartial third party, the mediator, who plays an active role and is both authorised and expected to put forward productive proposals to advance the process in a confidential and more informal manner based on information provided for by the parties.[132] Nevertheless, the Introduction to the Mediation Rules state that parties in mediation under the ICOM-WIPO Mediation Rules also have the possibility to combine the mediation procedure with other dispute resolution mechanisms, such as the WIPO Arbitration, Expedited Arbitration, or Expert Determination.[133]

Interestingly, the ICOM-WIPO Mediation Rules provide a provision which states that neither the mediator, WIPO, the Arbitration Center, ICOM, nor the ICOM Secretariat are liable to any party for any act or omission in connection with the mediation conducted, except in respect of deliberate wrongdoing.[134] In addition, the parties and, by accepting appointment, the mediator agree that any statements or comments, whether written or oral, made or used by them or their representatives in preparation for or in the course of the mediation are not to be relied upon to found or maintain any action for defamation, libel, slander or any related complaint.[135]

Another interesting point not provided for by the ICPRCP Rules is Article 31 of the Mediation Rules. This provision explicitly clarifies that the parties agree that, to the extent permitted by the applicable law, the running of the limitation period under the statute of limitations or an equivalent law shall be suspended in relation to the dispute that is the subject of the mediation from the date of the commencement of the mediation until the date of the termination of the mediation.

---

[132] Merrills (2011), p. 26; Article 2 (1) of the ICPRCP Rules of Procedure for Mediation and Conciliation.

[133] http://www.wipo.int/amc/en/center/specific-sectors/art/icom/rules/.

[134] Article 29 of the ICOM-WIPO Mediation Rules.

[135] Article 30 of the ICOM-WIPO Mediation Rules.

5.3.5 The ICOM-WIPO Mediation Rules' Appointment Procedure for the Mediator

The voluntary character of the mediation procedure is also reflected in the appointment process of the mediator. The parties have 7 days starting from the commencement of the mediation to agree on the person of the mediator or on another appointment procedure, which is much less time than the 60 days allowed in ICPRCP mediation.[136] However, the WIPO Arbitration and Mediation Center has to appoint any mediator so selected.[137] If the parties fail to do so, the Arbitration Center sends as soon as possible to each party an identical list of candidates. Where possible, the list comprises the names of at least three candidates in alphabetical order and includes or is accompanied by a statement of each candidate's qualifications. However, if the parties have agreed on any particular qualifications, the list has to contain the names of candidates that satisfy those qualifications.[138]

The parties then have the right to delete the name of any candidate or candidates to whose appointment they object. They have to number any remaining candidates in order of preference[139] and return the list to the WIPO Arbitration Center within 7 days after the date on which the list was received by them. If any party fails to do so, it is deemed that it has assented to all candidates appearing on the list.[140]

After receiving the list from the parties, the centre appoints a person from the list as mediator, taking into account the preferences and objections expressed by the parties.[141] However, if the lists which have been returned do not show a person who is acceptable as mediator to both parties, a nominated person is not able or does not wish to accept the centre's invitation or if there appear to be other reasons precluding that person from being the mediator and there does not remain on the lists a person who is acceptable as mediator to both parties, the WIPO Center is authorised to appoint the mediator.[142] As an exception, the centre is also authorised to appoint the mediator in cases in which the procedure described is not appropriate.[143]

Hence, in the ICOM-WIPO mediation procedure there could well be cases in which the parties have not chosen or somehow influenced the appointment of the mediator, whereas in the ICPRCP mediation procedure, even if the parties consensually fail to appoint a mediator, the Director-General of UNESCO only is permitted to appoint one after consultation with the parties concerned.[144] However,

[136] Cf. Article 7 (1) of the ICPRCP Rules of Procedure for Mediation and Conciliation.

[137] Article 7 (a) of the ICOM-WIPO Mediation Rules.

[138] Article 7 (b) (i) of the ICOM-WIPO Mediation Rules.

[139] Article 7 (b) (ii) of the ICOM-WIPO Mediation Rules.

[140] Article 7 (b) (iii) of the ICOM-WIPO Mediation Rules.

[141] Article 7 (b) (iv) of the ICOM-WIPO Mediation Rules.

[142] Article 7 (b) (v) of the ICOM-WIPO Mediation Rules.

[143] Article 7 (c) of the ICOM-WIPO Mediation Rules.

[144] Article 7 (2) of the ICPRCP Rules of Procedure for Mediation and Conciliation.

according to the ICOM-WIPO Rules, an agreement of the parties concerning the nationality of the mediator has to be respected.[145] But if the parties have not agreed on the nationality of the mediator, the mediator has to be, in the absence of special circumstances such as the need to appoint a person having particular qualifications, a national of a country other than the countries of the parties.[146] Interestingly, unlike the ICPRCP Rules,[147] the ICOM-WIPO Rules do not explicitly declare the same procedures applicable for cases of vacancy or replacement of the mediator.

Here it must be noted that as in the case of the ICPRCP Rules, the ICOM-WIPO Rules depart from the general mediation scheme; instead of preferring authoritative representatives of states or intergovernmental organisations to give weight and authority to their proposals, the ICOM-WIPO Rules favour independent experts in the field of the return and restitution of cultural heritage as mediators whose proposals carry weight and importance based on their expertise rather than their institutional position.[148]

In order to provide disputing parties with adequate mediators, similar to the case of the ICPRCP Mediation Rules,[149] a selection commission composed of members from ICOM and the WIPO Center maintains in its discretion a list of mediators with specific expertise in art, cultural heritage, and related areas.[150]

In any case, the mediator has to be impartial and independent.[151] Therefore, before accepting appointment, which has to be done in writing and communicated to the Arbitration Center[152] and where he is deemed to have undertaken to make available sufficient time to enable the mediation to be conducted and completed expeditiously,[153] the mediator has to disclose to the parties and the WIPO Center any circumstances that might give rise to justifiable doubt as to his impartiality or independence or confirm in writing that no such circumstances exist[154] or disclose them promptly when new circumstances arise at any stage during the mediation.[155] Even so, the ICOM-WIPO Mediation Rules do not regulate the consequences of a breach of this or any other obligation, such as the replacement of the mediator.

Following his or her appointment, the Arbitration Center has to notify the parties of the appointment of the mediator[156] and, unless required by a court of law or

---

145 Article 8 (a) of the ICOM-WIPO Mediation Rules.

146 Article 8 (b) of the ICOM-WIPO Mediation Rules.

147 Cf. Article 7 (4) and (5) of the ICPRCP Rules of Procedure for Mediation and Conciliation.

148 Same Urbinati (2014), p. 98.

149 Cf. Article 2 (6) of the ICPRCP Rules of Procedure for Mediation and Conciliation.

150 Article 6 of the ICOM-WIPO Mediation Rules; cf. also Article 7 (b) (i) (2) of the ICOM-WIPO Mediation Rules.

151 Article 9 (a) of the ICOM-WIPO Mediation Rules.

152 Article 10 (b) of the ICOM-WIPO Mediation Rules.

153 Article 10 (a) of the ICOM-WIPO Mediation Rules.

154 Article 9 (b) of the ICOM-WIPO Mediation Rules.

155 Article 9 (c) of the ICOM-WIPO Mediation Rules.

156 Article 10 (c) of the ICOM-WIPO Mediation Rules.

authorised in writing by the parties, the mediator must not act in any other capacity whatsoever in any pending or future proceedings, whether judicial, arbitral or otherwise, relating to the subject matter of the dispute.[157]

5.3.6 The Mediation Procedure of the ICOM-WIPO Mediation Rules

All procedures are in general subject to the ICOM-WIPO Mediation Rules as in effect on the date of the commencement of the mediation. However, corresponding with the voluntary character of the mediation procedure, it is not surprising that this is only the case where a mediation agreement provides for mediation under the ICOM-WIPO Mediation Rules, which then form part of that mediation agreement.[158]

However, as in the case of the ICPRCP Rules,[159] parties may amend or modify the ICOM-WIPO Mediation Rules to fit their special needs. This is also emphasised by the fact that the mediation has to be conducted in the manner agreed by the parties and by the fact that the Introduction to the Rules refers to them as specific model mediation clauses.[160]

Nevertheless, any mediation under the current rules is subject to certain guiding principles. The confidentiality of the procedure is crucial in the context of the ICOM-WIPO mediation. This is owed to the fact that reputation and long-standing relationships are of inestimable importance in the (museum) business.[161] Where the ICPRCP Rules content themselves with saying that the mediation procedure is to be conducted in conditions of confidentiality[162] and that consultations are confidential,[163] the ICOM-WIPO Mediation Rules not only devote an entire chapter to confidentiality,[164] they additionally address the issue in three provisions outside of the chapter on confidentiality.[165]

---

[157] Article 24 of the ICOM-WIPO Mediation Rules.

[158] Cf. Article 2 (b) of the ICOM-WIPO Mediation Rules.

[159] Cf. Article 1 (2) of the ICPRCP Rules of Procedure for Mediation and Conciliation.

[160] Cf. Article 12 of the ICOM-WIPO Mediation Rules; http://www.wipo.int/amc/en/center/specific-sectors/art/icom/rules/.

[161] Cf. http://icom.museum/programmes/art-and-cultural-heritage-mediation/icom-wipo-mediation-rules/.

[162] Article 3 (2) of the ICPRCP Rules of Procedure for Mediation and Conciliation.

[163] Article 8 (6) of the ICPRCP Rules of Procedure for Mediation and Conciliation.

[164] Articles 17–21 of the ICOM-WIPO Mediation Rules.

[165] Articles 15 and 23 of the ICOM-WIPO Mediation Rules.

The ICOM-WIPO Rules dictate that no recordings of any kind are to be made of any meeting of the parties with the mediator.[166] Furthermore, each person[167] involved in the mediation has to sign an appropriate confidentiality undertaking prior to taking part in the mediation, must respect the confidentiality of the mediation, and may not use or disclose to any outside party any information concerning or obtained in the course of the mediation.[168] In addition, any such person has to, on the termination of the mediation, return to the party providing it, any brief, document, or other materials supplied by that party, without retaining any copy thereof. Moreover, notes taken by a person concerning the meetings of the parties with the mediator have to be destroyed on the termination of the mediation.[169]

The mediator, the WIPO Center and the ICOM Secretariat have to maintain the confidentiality of the mediation, any settlement agreement, and, to the extent that they describe information that is not in the public domain, any information that is disclosed during the mediation.[170] Moreover, the ICOM-WIPO Meditation Rules dictate that parties must not even introduce as evidence or in any manner whatsoever in any judicial or arbitration proceeding information concerning the mediation.[171] This prohibition is so comprehensive that they may not even disclose the very existence of the mediation.[172]

The parties are only relieved of the latter duties when such information falls in the public domain or disclosure is necessary to comply with a legal requirement imposed on a party, in order to establish or protect a party's legal rights against a third party or to the extent necessary in connection with a court action or as otherwise required by law.[173] Additionally, most confidentiality provisions are subject to the limiting phrasing "unless otherwise agreed by the parties".[174] Hence, the parties may consensually agree to waive the confidentiality requirement as a whole, to a certain extent or concerning only a certain issue[175]—which occurs on occasion.[176]

Concerning the general principles the mediation procedure is subject to, mediators have furthermore to be impartial and independent.[177] In addition, they, but

[166]Article 17 of the ICOM-WIPO Mediation Rules.

[167]Article 18 of the ICOM-WIPO Mediation Rules contains a quite extensive, but not exhaustive, list of such persons. Thus, "any person" includes the mediator, the parties and their representatives and advisors, any independent experts, and any other persons present during the meetings.

[168]Article 18 of the ICOM-WIPO Mediation Rules.

[169]Article 19 of the ICOM-WIPO Mediation Rules.

[170]Article 21 (a) of the ICOM-WIPO Mediation Rules.

[171]Article 20 of the ICOM-WIPO Mediation Rules.

[172]Cf. Article 20 (a) (i) of the ICOM-WIPO Mediation Rules.

[173]Articles 20 (b) (i), (ii) and 21 (a) of the ICOM-WIPO Mediation Rules.

[174]Cf., for example, Articles 19 and 21 (a) of the ICOM-WIPO Mediation Rules.

[175]Another exception is the utilisation of the information in a statistical manner or for statistical purposes as long as the identity of the parties is not revealed or the particular circumstances are not to be identified, unless again the information is in the public domain (Article 21 (c) of the ICOM-WIPO Mediation Rules).

[176]Cf. Cornu and Renold (2010), p. 12.

[177]Article 9 (a) of the ICOM-WIPO Mediation Rules.

also the parties, ought to bear in mind the ICOM Code of Ethics for Museums.[178] Last but not least, all parties have to cooperate in good faith with the mediator to advance the mediation as expeditiously as possible.[179] Hence, the overall ICOM-WIPO mediation procedure is subject to the same basic principles as ICPRCP mediation procedures.[180]

With regard to the procedure itself, it is initiated by a party to a mediation agreement[181] that wishes to commence mediation.[182] Thus, unlike in the case of the ICPRCP procedure,[183] the ICOM-WIPO procedure requires a pre-existing mediation agreement between the parties in dispute. However, an agreement reached when one party desires mediation is sufficient.[184] The Introduction to the Rules explicitly states that in disputes where no mediation agreement, clause or submission agreement exists, WIPO and ICOM are available to carry out their good offices, aiming to facilitate the submission of disputes to mediation by providing procedural advice to the parties. Hence, an interested party who wishes to submit an existing dispute to mediation may, free-of-charge and on a confidential basis, request either ICOM or the WIPO Center to contact the other party and explore if the latter would be willing to consider agreeing to such submission.[185]

Unlike in the case of the ICPRCP Rules, where each party must submit such a document,[186] in the case of the ICOM-WIPO Rules only the party requesting mediation must submit a request for mediation in writing[187] to the centre and at the same time a copy of this writing to the other party. This document has to contain or be accompanied by the names, addresses, and telephone, telefax, email or other communication references of the parties to the dispute as well as of the representative of the party filing the request, a copy of the mediation agreement, and a brief statement of the nature of the dispute.[188]

---

[178] Article 13 (a) of the ICOM-WIPO Mediation Rules.

[179] Article 13 (b) of the ICOM-WIPO Mediation Rules.

[180] For the general principles the ICPRCP mediations and conciliations are subject to cf. p. 241.

[181] See the Recommended ICOM-WIPO Mediation Clause for Future Disputes at http://www.wipo.int/amc/en/center/specific-sectors/art/icom/clauses/.

[182] Article 3 (a) of the ICOM-WIPO Mediation Rules.

[183] Cf. Article 6 (1) and (2) of the ICPRCP Rules of Procedure for Mediation and Conciliation.

[184] Cf. the Recommended ICOM-WIPO Mediation Submission Agreement for Existing Dispute at http://www.wipo.int/amc/en/center/specific-sectors/art/icom/clauses/.

[185] http://www.wipo.int/amc/en/center/specific-sectors/art/icom/rules/.

[186] Cf. Article 6 (3) of the ICPRCP Rules of Procedure for Mediation and Conciliation.

[187] In compliance with Article 3 (c) of the ICOM-WIPO Mediation Rules "writing" in the context of the Mediation Rules means any form that provides a record of the communication, including email or other online options. Consequently, WIPO also provides the WIPO Electronic Case Facility which allows parties and all other actors in a case to file submissions electronically in order to facilitate communication.

[188] Article 3 (a) and (b) of the ICOM-WIPO Mediation Rules.

The date of the receipt of the request by the WIPO Center is deemed to be the date of the commencement of the mediation.[189] This is why the WIPO Center has to inform the parties in writing of both the receipt and the date of the commencement of the mediation.[190]

Finally, the mediation procedure starts. If and to the extent that the parties have agreed on a certain manner, the procedure is conducted according to that manner. Otherwise or to the extent that the parties have not made such agreement, the mediator determines in accordance with the ICOM-WIPO Mediation Rules the manner in which the mediation is to be conducted.[191]

The mediator in particular is free to meet and to communicate separately with each party.[192] Again, confidentiality plays a key role. Therefore, the information given at such meetings and in such communications must not be disclosed to the other party without the express authorisation of the party supplying the information.

This does not preclude the parties from being represented or assisted in their meetings with the mediator.[193] In such a case, the names and addresses of persons authorised to represent a party as well as the names and positions of the persons who will be attending the meetings of the parties with the mediator on behalf of that party have to be communicated by that party to the other party, the mediator, and the WIPO Center immediately after the appointment of the mediator.[194]

Furthermore, as soon as possible after being appointed, the mediator must establish in consultation with the parties a timetable for the submission by each party to him and to the other party of a statement summarising the background of the dispute, the party's interests, and contentions in relation to the dispute as well as the present status of the dispute, together with any other information and materials the party considers necessary for the purposes of the mediation and, in particular, to enable the issues in dispute to be identified.[195] Moreover, the mediator may at any time during the mediation suggest that a party provides additional information or materials the mediator deems useful.[196]

Similar to ICPRCP mediation,[197] parties may on their own initiative submit to the mediator written information or materials. Again, this information is considered to be confidential and the mediator must not disclose such information or materials to the other party without the written authorisation of the supplying party.[198]

---

[189] Article 4 of the ICOM-WIPO Mediation Rules.

[190] Article 5 of the ICOM-WIPO Mediation Rules.

[191] Article 12 of the ICOM-WIPO Mediation Rules.

[192] Article 14 of the ICOM-WIPO Mediation Rules.

[193] Article 11 (a) of the ICOM-WIPO Mediation Rules.

[194] Article 11 (b) of the ICOM-WIPO Mediation Rules.

[195] Article 15 (a) of the ICOM-WIPO Mediation Rules.

[196] Article 15 (b) of the ICOM-WIPO Mediation Rules.

[197] Cf. Article 8 (5) of the ICPRCP Rules of Procedure for Mediation and Conciliation.

[198] Article 15 (c) of the ICOM-WIPO Mediation Rules.

The mediation procedure ends when the parties sign a settlement agreement covering any or all of the issues in dispute between them or by the decision of the mediator if in his judgment further efforts at mediation are unlikely to lead to a resolution of the dispute.[199] In this case, the mediator may propose procedures or means for resolving any remaining issues which he considers are most likely to lead to the most efficient, least costly, and most productive settlement of those issues. While doing so, he must have regard to the circumstances of the dispute and any business relationship between the parties. The mediator may propose in particular an expert determination of one or more particular issues, (expedited) arbitration or the submission of last offers of settlement by each party and, in the absence of a settlement through mediation, arbitration conducted on the basis of those last offers pursuant to an arbitral procedure in which the mission of the arbitral tribunal is confined to determining which of the last offers shall prevail.[200]

As a final alternative, the mediation procedure also terminates if at any time one party sends to the other party, the mediator, and the WIPO Center a written declaration.[201] While these termination alternatives equate to those of the ICPRCP procedure,[202] unlike the latter, however, the ICOM-WIPO Rules do not contain a provision explicitly allowing the parties to set a deadline for the mediation.[203]

Irrespective of how and why the mediation terminates, the mediator must promptly send to the WIPO Center a notice in writing that the mediation is terminated and indicate the date on which it ended, whether or not the mediation resulted in a settlement of the dispute and, if so, whether the settlement was full or partial.[204] A copy of this notice is also required to be sent to the parties involved in the now defunct mediation. The WIPO Center has to keep the notice of the mediator confidential subject to the well-known exceptions provided for in the rules.[205]

Finally, the ICOM-WIPO Mediation Rules contain, as the ICPRCP Rules, provisions on the financial aspects of the mediation. The notable difference here is that the regulations in the ICOM-WIPO Rules are much more detailed. While the ICPRCP Rules only include one article with two paragraphs pertaining to the costs,[206] the ICOM-WIPO Rules dedicate four articles with 12 paragraphs to the matter. In addition, the latter distinguishes between administration fees, fees of the mediator, deposits, and costs.

According to the ICOM-WIPO Rules, parties are required to pay a non-refundable administration fee to the WIPO Center.[207] Despite the declaration

---

[199] Article 22 (i) and (ii) of the ICOM-WIPO Mediation Rules.

[200] Article 16 (b) of the ICOM-WIPO Mediation Rules.

[201] Article 22 (iii) of the ICOM-WIPO Mediation Rules.

[202] Cf. Article 10 (1) of the ICPRCP Rules of Procedure for Mediation and Conciliation.

[203] Cf. Article 10 (1) (c) of the ICPRCP Rules of Procedure for Mediation and Conciliation.

[204] Article 23 (a) of the ICOM-WIPO Mediation Rules.

[205] Article 23 (b) of the ICOM-WIPO Mediation Rules.

[206] Article 11 of the ICPRCP Rules of Procedure for Mediation and Conciliation.

[207] Article 25 (a) and (b) of the ICOM-WIPO Mediation Rules.

of a not-for-profit basis of the mediation procedure,[208] no action will be taken by the WIPO Center until payment.[209] Moreover, if a party fails to pay within 7 days after a reminder in writing, it is deemed to have withdrawn its request for mediation.[210] The amount and currency of the fees of the mediator and the modalities and timing of their payment, on the other hand, are fixed by the WIPO Center after consultation with the mediator and the parties.[211]

Both the administration fee and the fees of the mediator are calculated on the basis of the Schedule of Fees provided by the ICOM-WIPO Mediation Rules.[212] However, regarding the fees of the mediator, they may be adjusted taking into account the amount in dispute, the complexity of the subject matter of the dispute, and any other relevant circumstances of the case.[213]

Taking the above into consideration, the WIPO Center may require each party to deposit an equal amount or supplementary deposits as an advance for the costs of the mediation, including particularly the estimated fees of the mediator and the other expenses of the mediation.[214] Again, if a party fails to pay the required deposit within 7 days after a reminder in writing, the mediation is deemed to be terminated.[215] Furthermore, after the termination of the mediation, the WIPO Center has to render an accounting to the parties of any deposits made and return any unexpended balance to the parties or require the payment of any amount owing from the parties.[216]

As a general rule, just as in the case of the ICPRCP procedure,[217] the administration fee, the fees of the mediator, and all other expenses of the mediation, including in particular the required travel expenses of the mediator and any expenses associated with obtaining expert advice, are borne in equal shares by the parties unless the parties agree otherwise.[218] This again is in light of a possible imbalance in the financial means of the parties involved in claims for return,[219] for instance, in the case of an indigenous community reclaiming an object from an industrialised country,[220] of the utmost importance, since it allows the party otherwise lacking the sufficient financial means to pursue its goal using the costs of the procedure as a bargaining chip. The requesting party may for instance accept

[208] http://www.wipo.int/amc/en/center/specific-sectors/art/icom/rules/.

[209] Article 25 (c) of the ICOM-WIPO Mediation Rules.

[210] Article 25 (d) of the ICOM-WIPO Mediation Rules.

[211] Article 26 (a) of the ICOM-WIPO Mediation Rules.

[212] For the Schedule of Fees cf. http://www.wipo.int/amc/en/center/specific-sectors/art/icom/fees/.

[213] Article 26 (b) of the ICOM-WIPO Mediation Rules.

[214] Article 27 (a) and (b) of the ICOM-WIPO Mediation Rules.

[215] Article 27 (c) of the ICOM-WIPO Mediation Rules.

[216] Article 27 (d) of the ICOM-WIPO Mediation Rules.

[217] Cf. Article 11 of the ICPRCP Rules of Procedure for Mediation and Conciliation.

[218] Article 28 of the ICOM-WIPO Mediation Rules.

[219] Urbinati (2014), p. 106.

[220] On indigenous peoples as claimants cf. Cornu and Renold (2010), pp. 5ff.

the cultural object in dispute as a permanent loan rather than having it returned with its title when in return the other party bears the costs of the procedure.

5.3.7 Final Remarks

The ICOM-WIPO Mediation Rules are the outcome of the cooperation of two international organisations which are experts in their respective fields of operation, the International Council of Museums and the World Intellectual Property Organization.[221] Hence, it is not surprising that these model clauses tailored for the special needs of disputes concerning cultural heritage[222] contain comprehensive regulations with regard to mediation. However, their scope goes far beyond disputes concerning the return and restitution of cultural material on which this chapter has focused. They are also applicable to disputes concerning loans, deposits, acquisitions, and intellectual property.[223]

The comprehensive character of the ICOM-WIPO Mediation Rules is also highlighted by the fact that the procedure is open to private parties rather than only to governments.[224] However, although the provisions of the ICOM-WIPO Mediation Rules are quite detailed and thorough, they are at the same time flexible enough to allow the parties to adjust them to their special needs. The appointment of the mediator, the conduct of the procedure, and its confidentiality are all subject to the configuration desired by the parties involved.[225]

Thus, the collaboration of WIPO and ICOM, which led to the adoption of the ICOM-WIPO Mediation Rules, has to be considered a particularly fruitful event. ICOM's expertise concerning cultural heritage paired with WIPO's experience with regard to alternative dispute resolution contributes to the juridification of the procedure concerning disputes over cultural artefacts. Furthermore, it is conducive to the solving of cultural material related disputes by bringing forth an adequate alternative dispute resolution mechanism to find comprehensive and amicable solutions to disputes concerning cultural property. It does so by establishing a formalised procedure in which parties to a cultural property related dispute can interact and fulfil their obligation to cooperate, an obligation set up particularly by the relevant soft law instruments, and by establishing general principles[226] in compliance with the spirit of the 1970 UNESCO and 1995 UNIDROIT

[221]Cf. Theurich (2010), pp. 580f.

[222]Cf. http://icom.museum/programmes/art-and-cultural-heritage-mediation/icom-wipo-mediation-rules/.

[223]Cf. Article 2 (a) of the ICOM-WIPO Mediation Rules.

[224]Cf. Article 2 (a) of the ICOM-WIPO Mediation Rules.

[225]Cf., for example, Article 7, 12 and 18 of the ICOM-WIPO Mediation Rules.

[226]Such as the requirement for the mediator to be impartial and independent provided for in Article 9 (a) of the ICOM-WIPO Mediation Rules.

Conventions, the ICPRPC, and the relevant soft law instruments, which are specifically designed to be employed in cultural heritage related disputes.

5.4 Alternative Dispute Resolution: Summary

Once, due to the two-pronged strategy, the focus of trying to find solutions to return shifted from using substantive law obligations to a more cooperative and procedural approach, the question of which form such a cooperative and procedural solution could take became in recent years the issue that needed elaboration. The answer came in the form of two bodies of rules of procedure; the ICPRCP Rules of Procedure for Mediation and Conciliation and the ICOM-WIPO Mediation Rules. Both instruments are products of a change in the mindset of the actors involved that has led to the idea of taking a path of cooperation rather than confrontation.

Even though their provisions are not mandatory, these two instruments establish a regulated framework to resolve cultural property related disputes incorporating principles of fairness, impartiality, and good faith as well as the idea that such disputes regularly involve complex legal, as well as sensitive non-legal issues of a cultural, economic, ethical, historical, moral, political, religious or spiritual nature and combine tangible as well as intangible matters in a single case and present challenges in terms of evidence and statutes of limitations. Both sets of rules of procedure create a comprehensive regulation with regard to mediation (and conciliation) following in the spirit of the 1970 UNESCO and 1995 UNIDROIT Conventions, the ICPRPC, and the soft law instruments.

Thus, in the end, jurisdification and formalisation has taken place in the context of cultural material related disputes. However, it has not occurred in the initially intended way, namely in the form of establishing legally binding substantive norms as was attempted with the 1970 UNESCO and 1995 UNIDROIT Conventions, but rather in the form of juridification of the procedural element of finding a solution. As this process gains further traction, it can be expected that this development will also be reflected in the material law dimension of the disputes. In both rules of procedure it is intended that the mediators and conciliators are to be elected from a list of independent experts on the return and restitution of cultural heritage. Thus, it is likely that based on their awareness and familiarity with the legal regime concerning the return of cultural material general principles, ideas and even rules of this regime will find their way into the solutions they will provide for the parties in dispute. Even though the solutions they present may not be legally binding in nature, this will further contribute to the juridification of cultural objects related disputes.

References

Bandle AL, Theurich S (2011) Alternative dispute resolution and art-law – a new research project of the Geneva Art-Law Centre. J Int Commer Law Technol 6:28–41

Barker I (2009) Thoughts of an alternative dispute resolution practitioner on an international ADR regime for repatriation of cultural property and works of art. In: Hoffman BT (ed) Art and cultural heritage: law, policy and practice. Cambridge University Press, Cambridge, pp 483–487

Beckmann NL (2008) Die internationale Kulturstiftung – Ein Beitrag zur Debatte über die Rückführung der nach dem Zweiten Weltkrieg kriegsbedingt verbrachten Kulturgüter. Verlag Dr. Kovac, Hamburg

Campfens E (2014) Alternative dispute resolution in restitution claims and the binding expert opinion procedure of the Dutch Restitutions Committee. In: Vadi V, Schneider HEGS (eds) Art, cultural heritage and the market: ethical and legal issues. Springer, Heidelberg, pp 61–91

Chechi A (2013) Plurality and coordination of dispute settlement methods in the field of cultural heritage. In: Francioni F, Gordley J (eds) Enforcing international cultural heritage law. Oxford University Press, Oxford, pp 177–205

Cornu M, Renold M-A (2010) New developments in the restitution of cultural property: alternative means of dispute resolution. Int J Cult Prop 17:1–31

Daly BW (2009) Arbitration of international cultural property disputes: the experience and initiatives of the permanent court of arbitration. In: Hoffman BT (ed) Art and cultural heritage: law, policy and practice. Cambridge University Press, Cambridge, pp 465–474

Francioni F (2013) Plurality and interaction of legal orders in the enforcement of cultural heritage law. In: Francioni F, Gordley J (eds) Enforcing international cultural heritage law. Oxford University Press, Oxford, pp 9–21

Groth S, Stoll PT, Sanmukri M (2015) Das zwischenstaatliche Komitee der WIPO zu geistigem Eigentum an traditionellem Wissen, traditionellen kulturellen Ausdrucksformen und genetischen Ressourcen. In: Groth S, Bendix RF, Spiller A (eds) Kultur als Eigentum: Instrumente, Querschnitte und Fallstudien. Universitätsverlag Göttingen, Göttingen, pp 17–29

Kuprecht K, Siehr K (2012) International trade in moveable tangible cultural heritage of indigenous peoples: a European perspective. In: Graber CB, Kuprecht K, Lai JC (eds) International trade in indigenous cultural heritage: legal and policy issues. Edward Elgar, Cheltenham, pp 246–271

Lyons CL (2014) Thinking about antiquities: museums and internationalism. Int J Cult Prop 21:251–265

Merrills JG (2011) International dispute settlement, 5th edn. Cambridge University Press, Cambridge

Nafziger JAR, Paterson RK, Renteln AD (2014) Cultural law: international, comparative, and indigenous. Cambridge University Press, Cambridge

Palmer N (2009) Alternative procedures – litigation: the best remedy? In: Prott LV (ed) Witness to history: a compendium of documents and writings on the return of cultural objects. UNESCO Publishing, Paris, pp 358–368

Palmer N (2013) Fetters and stumbling blocks: impediments to the recovery and return of unlawfully removed cultural objects: a common law perspective. In: Prott LV, Redmond-Cooper R, Urice S (eds) Realising cultural heritage law: Festschrift for Patrick Joseph O'Keefe. Institute of Art and Law, Builth Wells, pp 97–110

Renold MA (2015) Cultural co-ownership: preventing and solving cultural property claims. Int J Cult Prop 22:163–176

Shyllon F (2009) The recovery of cultural objects by African states through the UNESCO and UNIDROIT conventions and the role of arbitration. In: Prott LV (ed) Witness to history: a compendium of documents and writings on the return of cultural objects. UNESCO Publishing, Paris, pp 369–382

Shyllon F (2016) Cultural heritage and intellectual property: convergence, divergence, and interface. In: Logan W, Craith MN, Kockel U (eds) A companion to heritage studies. Wiley Blackwell, Chichester, pp 55–68

Stamatoudi IA (2009) Mediation and cultural diplomacy. Mus Int 61:116–120

Stamatoudi IA (2011) Cultural property law and restitution: a commentary to international conventions and European Union law. Edward Elgar, Cheltenham

Strother G (2014) Resolving cultural property disputes in the shadow of the law. Harv Negot Law Rev 19:335–376

Theurich S (2010) Alternative dispute resolution in art and cultural heritage – explored in the context of the World Intellectual Property Organization's work. In: Odendahl K, Weber PJ (eds) Kulturgüterschutz – Kunstrecht – Kulturrecht: Festschrift für Kurt Siehr zum 75. Geburtstag aus dem Kreis des Doktoranden- und Habilitandenseminars "Kunst und Recht". Nomos, Baden-Baden, pp 569–594

Urbinati S (2014) Alternative dispute resolution mechanisms in cultural property related disputes: UNESCO mediation and conciliation procedures. In: Vadi V, Schneider HEGS (eds) Art, cultural heritage and the market: ethical and legal issues. Springer, Heidelberg, pp 93–116

Varner E (2011–2012) Arbitrating cultural property disputes. Cardozo J Confl Resolution 13:477–526

von Schorlemer S (2007) UNESCO dispute settlement. In: Yusuf AA (ed) Standard-setting in UNESCO: normative action in education, science and culture, vol 1. UNESCO Publishing, Paris/Martinus Nijhoff Publishers, Leiden, pp 73–103

Vrdoljak AF (2008) International law, museums and the return of cultural objects. Cambridge University Press, Cambridge

Wichard JC, Wendland WB (2009) Mediation as an option for resolving disputes between indigenous/traditional communities and industry concerning traditional knowledge. In: Hoffman BT (ed) Art and cultural heritage: law, policy and practice. Cambridge University Press, Cambridge, pp 475–482

Chapter 6
Conclusion

Abstract In its endeavour to find a solution to disputes arising over the return of (illegally) transferred cultural artefacts, the international community has brought into being a number of instruments ranging from conventions to codes of ethics. These mechanisms and instruments can essentially be divided into two categories which reflect the different approaches to resolve the matter. On the one hand, there are the international treaties which represent the hard law method. This approach relies on legally binding obligations to guarantee the return of illegally transferred cultural heritage and establish mechanisms to prevent its illicit outflow to avoid disputes in the first place. On the other hand, there is the soft law approach which trusts in the good will of the parties involved and cooperation as the appropriate manner to address disputes concerning the return of transferred cultural objects. However, both methods simultaneously have merits and drawbacks. The conclusion of this text compares both approaches and highlights their respective advantages and disadvantages. More importantly, it points out how both approaches are intertwined, complement each other and how fruitful this linkage is.

The (illegal) outflow and return of their cultural heritage has been a concern to states for quite some time now. In the late nineteenth century they first tried to resolve this problem at the national level by enacting legislation prohibiting the export of certain cultural objects. However, they soon realised that due to the international dimension of the issue, national efforts alone were not sufficient to achieve their goal. Hence, they brought their concern to the attention of the international community.

In its endeavour to find a solution to disputes arising over the return of (illegally) transferred cultural artefacts, the international community has brought into being a number of instruments ranging from conventions to codes of ethics.[1] These mechanisms addressing the issue of the return of cultural material, particularly also by means of preventing the illegal outflow of such material to avoid cultural property related disputes in the first place, can be divided into two base categories which

[1]Cf. Sect. 2.1 for the first efforts of the international community to address the issue prior to the adoption of the 1970 UNESCO Convention, in particular the endeavours of the League of Nations and the Office International des Musées.

A. Taşdelen, *The Return of Cultural Artefacts*, DOI 10.1007/978-3-319-44060-6_6

reflect the different approaches to resolve the matter. On the one hand, there are the international treaties, the 1970 UNESCO (Sect. 2.2) and the 1995 UNIDROIT (Sect. 3.1) Conventions, which represent the hard law method. This approach relies on legally binding obligations to guarantee the return of illegally transferred cultural heritage and establish mechanisms to prevent its illicit outflow to avoid disputes in the first place.

On the other hand, there is the soft law approach which places its trust in the good will of the parties involved and a spirit of cooperation as the appropriate means to address disputes concerning the return of transferred cultural objects. This method is represented by the ICPRCP (Sect. 4.2), the ICOM (Sect. 4.3.2) and UNESCO (Sect. 4.3.3) Codes of Ethics, as well as the ILA Principles (Sect. 4.3.4).

However, both methods have their merits and drawbacks. International conventions have a higher level of legitimacy than soft law instruments adopted by private parties since they are adopted by states, the genuine legal subjects of international law. More importantly, however, the hard law approach clearly defines the relationship of the parties involved in a dispute over cultural heritage and their respective duties by means of legally binding provisions. Article 7 (b) (ii) of the 1970 UNESCO Convention, for instance, requires state parties, at the request of the state party of origin, to take appropriate steps to recover and return any cultural property which has been stolen from certain institutions in the requesting state party and which has been imported after the entry into force of the convention in both states concerned. According to the same provision, the requesting state, on the other hand, has to pay just compensation to an innocent purchaser or to a person who has valid title to that property and bear all expenses incident to the return and delivery of the cultural property.[2] This precise regulation of the relationship and duties of the parties involved creates legal certainty, in particular in context of the 1995 UNIDROIT Convention where both parties, the claimant and recipient, know that these obligations are legally enforceable in court.[3]

However, the tremendous advantage of hard law instruments comes at a price. Since states are aware that treaty obligations are legally enforceable, not only the negotiations and the adoption, but also the ratification of conventions prove difficult. This is particularly the case with regard to treaties covering emotionally charged issues such as disputes concerning cultural heritage. Thus, it is not surprising that this has been also true for both the 1970 UNESCO Convention and the 1995 UNIDROIT Convention.[4]

Despite the compromises source states were willing to accept in the negotiations for the 1970 UNESCO Convention, it was not until the mid-1990s that key market

[2]Cf. Sects. 2.2.5 and 2.2.6 for a detailed analysis of the legal provisions of the 1970 UNESCO Convention concerning the return of cultural property and those of its clauses setting up conditions supporting such return; cf. Sects. 3.1.5 and 3.1.6 for a detailed analysis of the respective provisions of the 1995 UNIDROIT Convention.

[3]Cf. Sect. 3.1.1 on the self-executing character of the 1995 UNIDROIT Convention.

[4]Cf. Sect. 2.2.2 for the negation and the adoption of the 1970 UNESCO Convention; cf. Sect. 3.1.2 for the respective processes in the context of the 1995 UNIDROIT Convention.

states began signing the treaty. Even now, when the number of state parties to the 1970 UNESCO Convention has reached 131 and it seems to be widely accepted, its acceptance remains more formalistic in nature; although many states have ratified the convention, many do not implement its norms into their national legislation—even source countries—rendering the agreement's regulations ineffective in practice. To address this problem, the state parties to the 1970 UNESCO Convention still see the need to work on draft guidelines and a fund for its implementation.[5]

This is all the more the case with the 1995 UNIDROIT Convention. For its tremendous regulatory achievements, such as establishing in Article 3 the unconditional duty of the possessor of a stolen cultural object to return it and providing in Article 4 (4) an international standard to assess whether or not a purchaser of cultural objects exercised due diligence, a high price has been paid with regard to its acceptance. To this day, only 37 states have ratified it—and that number fails to include even a single market state.

Moreover, the legally binding nature of the obligations states enter into when ratifying an international convention is the reason why both the 1970 UNESCO Convention and the 1995 UNIDROIT Convention have been adopted without a retroactive effect.[6]

Having a variance in nature though has proven to the advantage of the soft law instruments. They are negotiated and adopted much faster, they are granted retroactive effect,[7] and they receive much more acceptance since the parties involved are not in fear of entering into legally enforceable obligations. In fact, the obligations parties enter into in the context of soft law instruments are compared to those they undertake within the framework of conventions restricted in a number of key ways. Principle 2.2 of the ILA Principle, for example, requires the recipient of a request for return, regardless of whether it is a state or a private party, such as a museum, to respond in good faith and in writing to the request within a reasonable time, either agreeing with it or setting out reasons for disagreement with it and, in any event, proposing a timeframe for implementation or negotiations. Thus, as this example shows, in addition to not being legally binding, the obligation imposed by the soft law instruments on their respective addressees[8] is limited to one of cooperation rather than a strict duty to return—such as in the case of the hard law instruments. Besides, soft law instruments are formulated in a manner that allows parties to take

---

[5]Cf. Sect. 2.2.7 for the mechanism set up by the states party to the 1970 UNESCO Convention to improve its implementation and the achievements of this instrument.

[6]Cf. Sect. 2.2.4.3 on the dispute between the states negotiating the 1970 UNESCO Convention regarding whether or not to grant the convention retroactive effect and Sect. 3.1.4.4 for the same dispute in the context of the 1995 UNIDROIT Convention.

[7]Cf. Sect. 4.2.4 for the temporal scope of the ICPRCP, Sect. 4.3.2.3 for that of the ICOM Code of Ethics, Sect. 4.3.3.3 for that of the UNESCO Code and Sect. 4.3.4.2 for the temporal scope of the ILA Principles.

[8]Cf. Sect. 4.3.2.3 for the addressees of the ICOM Code of Ethics, Sect. 4.3.3.3 for those of the UNESCO Code and Sect. 4.3.4.2 for those of the ILA Principles.

the specific particularities of each case into account.[9] This more readily allows market states to accept the terms set forth by a soft law instrument.

Furthermore, soft law instruments involve private parties who are actually the ones on the ground and usually those facing claims for return, such as traders, museums, and private collectors of cultural material. This increases the likelihood of the soft law instruments to be both respected and employed by these groups which play such a key role in the fight against the illicit trafficking of cultural heritage and its return. The ICOM Code of Ethics, for instance, has been adopted by ICOM, a network of 20,000 museums, 35,000 experts, 119 national committees, 30 international committees, 5 regional alliances, and 21 affiliated organisations present in 136 countries and territories. Hence, in practice, ICOM's Code of Ethics self-imposes minimum standards of conduct on more key actors in the field of cultural heritage and creates more uniformity across territorial borders than, for instance, the 1995 UNIDROIT Convention which has only been ratified by 37 states thus far.[10]

However, despite its advantages, soft law is not a panacea. In fact, the very reason why soft law instruments, such as the ICOM and UNESCO Codes of Ethics as well as the ILA Principles, are so widely accepted by the respective actors is the fact that obligations imposed are not legally enforceable. This clearly is at the same time the greatest flaw of the soft law mechanism. Parties to the soft law instruments cannot be legally forced to obey their commitments and all the actors have to fear should they not live up to the standards that they have committed themselves to is reputational damage.[11]

Therefore, it is not surprising that despite the fact that more emphasis seems to have been given to soft law instruments in the last few years in comparison to conventions, due primarily to their ease of adoption and wider acceptance, and that the number of such soft law instruments has increased, the hard law approach of adopting and promoting legally binding conventions has not been abandoned. In fact, the hard law approach is still being pursued in addition to the soft law approach for a number of reasons. First of all, as mentioned above, for those cases which fall within their ambit, the 1970 UNESCO and the 1995 UNIDROIT Conventions provide clear regulations and legally binding duties of state parties to return cultural artefacts rather than just requiring cooperation. Furthermore, although it is much harder to negotiate and adopt an international convention, it remains easier to promote an already existing one than bringing into being a new soft law instrument. Most importantly, however, the 1970 UNESCO and the 1995 UNIDROIT Conventions on the one hand and the ICPRCP, the ILA Principles, the ICOM and UNESCO Codes of Ethics on the other hand mutually support each other.

[9] Cf. Sect. 4.3.4.3 for a detailed analysis of this provision; cf. in this context also the analyses on the return related regulations of the ICOM (Sect. 4.3.2.4) and the UNESCO (Sect. 4.3.3.4) Codes of Ethics.

[10] Cf. also Sect. 4.3.4.1 for more information on the ILA.

[11] Cf. Sect. 4.3.1 on the legal nature of soft law.

With the conventions and their legally binding obligations to return cultural artefacts putting pressure on market states, for such states, soft law instruments with their cooperational approach seem to be a much more attractive alternative. Soft law instruments, on the other hand, can be consulted for purposes of interpreting certain provisions of the 1970 UNESCO and 1995 UNIDROIT Conventions. At the same time, the soft law instruments bring the principles and the spirit of the 1970 UNESCO and 1995 UNIDROIT Conventions into states which are not party to the conventions. The ICOM Code of Ethics, for instance, dictates minimum standards of professional conduct carrying the spirit of the conventions to museums in 136 countries and territories, thus reaching more actors than the 1995 UNIDROIT Convention, which has only been ratified by 37 states.

Even further to this, by carrying the spirit and the principles of the 1970 UNESCO and 1995 UNIDROIT Conventions to states which are not party to them, the soft law instruments have and continue to contribute to the change in the mindset of actors in these countries hence paving the way for them to eventually accede to the conventions. This effect of soft law instruments can be seen as one of the factors—in addition to trying to avoid the ratification of the 1995 UNIDROIT Convention—why many market states have finally acceded to the 1970 UNESCO Convention despite their earlier reluctance.[12]

In recent years, however, another way in which both approaches mutually support each other has emerged. By combining the positive aspects of both methods—the formalistic legal framework of the hard law approach with the cooperative strategy making the soft law approach acceptable to market states—this new hybrid path leads to legalisation, but not legalisation as initially intended in the sense that the parties try anew to establish legally binding substantive norms providing for legal basis to reclaim cultural heritage, but rather the legalisation of the procedural element of finding a solution.

Although the seeds of this idea can be traced back to the 1970 UNESCO and the 1995 UNIDROIT Conventions, it has only been in recent years that in compliance with the idea of following the path of cooperation, which takes ever more form with each soft law instrument, the ICPRCP (Sect. 5.2) as well as ICOM in cooperation with WIPO (Sect. 5.3) have adopted rules of procedure for mediation (and conciliation). Even though these provisions are not mandatory, they establish a regulated framework to resolve cultural material related disputes incorporating principles of fairness, impartiality, and good faith as well as the idea that such disputes regularly involve complex legal as well as sensitive non-legal issues of a cultural, economic, ethical, historical, moral, political, religious or spiritual nature, combine tangible as well as intangible matters in a single case, and present challenges in terms of evidence and statutes of limitations. Both rules of procedure create a comprehensive regulation with regard to mediation (and conciliation) and thereby

[12]Cf. Sect. 4.3.1 on the legal relevance of soft law and its role in the development of binding law.

eventually lead to the formalisation and juridification of cultural property related disputes.[13]

The juridification of the procedural element, but also of the material law dimension of the disputes, will be further promoted by another factor which has to be taken into account: the actors or in this case the mediators. In both rules of procedure, it is intended that the mediators and conciliators are to be elected from a list of independent experts on the return and restitution of cultural heritage.[14] Such independent experts, however, are well aware of the legal regime concerning the return of cultural material and even if they do not issue legally binding decisions, it is highly likely that general principles, ideas, and even procedural and material rules of this regime will find their way into the solutions they provide for the parties in dispute. This will further contribute to the juridification of cultural heritage related disputes.

In this context it is interesting to note that there appears to be yet another development which would contribute to the solution and further juridification of cultural object related disputes. In contrast to cultural artefacts transferred in times of war, for which a rule of customary international law requiring their return has already been established,[15] market states have managed to avoid the enactment of any rule imposing a legally binding duty of general application to return cultural objects illicitly transferred in times of peace. However, to appease the source states and show their good will, market states had to be seen to offer something in return: cooperation. Not only do all of the instruments above emphasise the importance of cooperation, an increasing number of bilateral agreements among states as well as between states and museums also contains cooperation agreements or puts them into written form. In addition, courts increasingly give effect to laws of countries of origin of stolen or illicitly transferred cultural material. This development can be seen as the emergence of a state practice of cooperation in disputes concerning cultural property illicitly transferred in times of peace and a respective opinio juris—the two elements of customary international law.[16] Therefore, it can be argued that a rule of customary international law requiring states party to a dispute concerning cultural heritage illicitly transferred in times of peace to cooperate is in the process of formation.[17]

[13]Cf. Sects. 5.2.3–5.2.6 for the legal framework set up by the ICPRCP Rules to solve cultural heritage related disputes; cf. Sects. 5.3.3–5.3.6 for the respective regime of the ICOM-WIPO Rules.

[14]Cf. in this context Sects. 5.2.5 and 5.3.5.

[15]Stumpf (2003), p. 234.

[16]On the elements of customary international law see Scharf (2013), pp. 32ff.

[17]See further on this development Chechi (2012), pp. 362–368.

References

Chechi A (2012) Multi-level cooperation to safeguard the human dimension of cultural heritage and to secure the return of wrongfully removed cultural objects. In: Borelli S, Francioni F (eds) Cultural heritage, cultural rights, cultural diversity: New developments in international law. Martinus Nijhoff Publishers, Leiden, pp 347–368

Scharf MP (2013) Customary international law in times of fundamental change: recognizing Grotian moments. Cambridge University Press, Cambridge

Stumpf E (2003) Kulturgüterschutz im internationalen Recht unter besonderer Berücksichtigung der deutsch-russischen Beziehungen. Peter Lang, Frankfurt am Main

MIX
Papier aus verantwortungsvollen Quellen
Paper from responsible sources
FSC® C105338

If you have any concerns about our products,
you can contact us on
ProductSafety@springernature.com

In case Publisher is established outside the EU,
the EU authorized representative is:
Springer Nature Customer Service Center GmbH
Europaplatz 3, 69115 Heidelberg, Germany

Printed by Libri Plureos GmbH
in Hamburg, Germany